Network Security
Foundations

Network Security Foundations

Matthew Strebe

San Francisco ◆ London

Associate Publisher: Neil Edde
Acquisitions and Developmental Editor: Maureen Adams
Production Editor: Elizabeth Campbell
Technical Editor: Donald Fuller
Copyeditor: Judy Flynn
Compositor: Laurie Stewart, Happenstance Type-o-Rama
Proofreaders: Laurie O'Connell, Nancy Riddiough
Indexer: Nancy Guenther
Book Designer: Judy Fung
Cover Design: Ingalls + Associates
Cover Photo: Jerry Driendl, Taxi

An earlier version of this book was published under the title Network Security Jumpstart © 2002 SYBEX Inc.

Library of Congress Card Number: 2004109315

ISBN: 0-7821-4374-1

SYBEX and the SYBEX logo are either registered trademarks or trademarks of SYBEX Inc. in the United States and/or other countries.

Screen reproductions produced with FullShot 99. FullShot 99 © 1991-1999 Inbit Incorporated. All rights reserved.

FullShot is a trademark of Inbit Incorporated.

TRADEMARKS: SYBEX has attempted throughout this book to distinguish proprietary trademarks from descriptive terms by following the capitalization style used by the manufacturer.

The author and publisher have made their best efforts to prepare this book, and the content is based upon final release software whenever possible. Portions of the manuscript may be based upon pre-release versions supplied by software manufacturer(s). The author and the publisher make no representation or warranties of any kind with regard to the completeness or accuracy of the contents herein and accept no liability of any kind including but not limited to performance, merchantability, fitness for any particular purpose, or any losses or damages of any kind caused or alleged to be caused directly or indirectly from this book.

Manufactured in the United States of America

10 9 8 7 6 5 4 3 2 1

To Kira Rayleigh Strebe
Kira Lyra Loo,
I love you

Acknowledgments

My wife does an amazing job of handling our life, our house, and our kids so that I can run a business and write books. Without her, none of my books would have been written. I'd like to thank Seanna for prying off and losing the keycaps of the non-critical laptop, Nathan for only losing the ball out of the trackball twice during the production of this book, and Kira for not being able to walk yet and for not choking on the keycap she found under the couch.

I'd like to thank Maureen Adams, who is my friend more than my editor, for suggesting this title and steering it through the process. Elizabeth Campbell did an expert job managing the flurry of e-mail that constitutes the modern writing process, and did so with an infectious enthusiasm that made the process easy. Judy Flynn expanded the acronyms, excised the jargon (well, some of it, anyway), clarified the odd constructions, and corrected the capitalization (or standardized it, at least). Without her, this book would have been much harder to understand. Thanks also to the CD team of Dan Mummert and Kevin Ly for their work on the companion CD.

Contents

Introduction

When you're learning any new topic or technology, it's important to have all of the basics at your disposal. The Sybex Foundations series provides the building blocks of specific technologies that help you establish yourself in IT.

Recent major security vulnerabilities in Windows and Linux have caused problems for nearly every computer user in the world. The mysterious world of hackers, spies, and government agents has become the daily annoyance of spyware, spam, virus infection, and worm attacks. There was a time when you only needed to worry about security if you had something important to protect, but these days, if you don't understand computer security, the computers you are responsible for will be hacked.

My goal with *Network Security Foundations* is to introduce you to computer security concepts so that you'll come away with an intermediate understanding of security as it pertains to computers. This book isn't boringly technical; each topic is covered to sufficient depth, but not to an extreme.

As a former hacker, a military classified materials custodian, and network administrator, I have over twenty years experience working in the computer industry and on all sides of the computer security problem. Pulling from this experience, I've tried to present the relevant material in an interesting way, and I've included what I have found to be the most important concepts. The book includes several simple examples and diagrams in an effort to demystify computer security.

This book is neither operating system specific nor software specific. Concepts are presented so that you can gain an understanding of the topic without being tied to a particular platform.

NOTE

Who Should Read This Book?

Network Security Foundations is designed to teach the fundamentals of computer and network security to people who are fairly new to the topic:

- ◆ People interested in learning more about computer and network security
- ◆ Decision-makers who need to know the fundamentals in order to make valid, informed security choices
- ◆ Administrators who feel they are missing some of the foundational information about network security
- ◆ Small business owners interested in understanding the ramifications of their IT decisions

◆ Those interested in learning more about why computer security is a problem and what the solutions are

◆ Instructors teaching a network security fundamentals course

◆ Students enrolled in a network security fundamentals course

What This Book Covers

Working in computer security has been an interesting, exciting, and rewarding experience. No matter what sector of the computer industry you're employed in (or even if you're not employed in IT yet), it is absolutely essential that you understand computer security in order to secure the systems that you are responsible for against attack.

Network Security Foundations contains many drawings and charts that help create a comfortable learning environment. It provides many real-world analogies that you will be able to relate to and through which network security will become tangible. The analogies provide a simple way to understand the technical process of network security, and you will see that many of the security concepts are actually named after their real-world counterparts because the analogies are so apt.

This book continues to build your understanding about network security progressively, like climbing a ladder. Here's how the information is presented:

Chapters 1 and 2   These chapters introduce computer security and explain why the security problem exists and why hackers hack.

Chapter 3   This chapter explains encryption, a mathematical concept that is central to all computer security. Although encryption itself is mathematically complex, this chapter does not require a math background to understand and presents the major features of encryption and their uses without proving the theories behind them.

Chapter 4   This chapter describes security management—the human aspect of controlling the process of computer security. It covers such management aspects as computer security policy development, acceptable use policies, and how to automate policy enforcement.

Chapters 5 and 6   These chapters describe the major Internet security concepts of firewalling and virtual private networks, which are used to partition the Internet into separate networks with controlled borders and then connect the "islands of data" that are created back together again in a controlled, secure manner.

Chapter 7   This chapter discusses the special challenges of securing home users who may connect to your network. Home users create special problems. For example, you often have no control over their resources or you might have very little budget to solve their problems.

Chapters 8 and 9   These chapters discuss security issues outside the realm of direct attack by hackers: viruses, worms, Trojan horses, spyware, spam, and routine failure. Solutions to all of these problems are evaluated.

Chapters 10 through 12   These chapters detail the security features of Windows and Unix, which are the two most popular operating systems and used on 99 percent of all of the computers in the world.

Chapters 13 and 14   These chapters discuss the security ramifications of running public web and e-mail servers that must be made available on the Internet and are therefore especially vulnerable to hacking attacks.

Chapter 15   This chapter discusses intrusion detection and response: How to determine when someone is attempting to hack your systems, and what to do about it.

Making the Most of This Book

At the beginning of each chapter of *Network Security Foundations*, you'll find a list of the topics I'll cover within the chapter.

To help you absorb new material easily, I've highlighted new terms, such as *packet filter,* in italics and defined them in the page margins.

In addition, several special elements highlight important information:

Notes provide extra information and references to related information.

Tips are insights that help you perform tasks more easily and effectively.

Warnings let you know about things you should—or shouldn't—do as you learn more about security.

At the end of each chapter, you can test your knowledge of the chapter's relevant topics by answering the review questions. You'll find the answers to the review questions in Appendix A.

packet filter
A router that is capable of dropping packets that don't meet security requirements.

NOTE

TIP

WARNING

Chapter 1

Security Principles

In This Chapter

- Why computers aren't secure
- The history of computer security
- The theoretical underpinnings of network security

Security is the sum of all measures taken to prevent loss of any kind. Loss can occur because of user error, defects in code, malicious acts, hardware failure, and acts of nature. With holistic computer security, a number of methods are used to prevent these events, but it's primarily focused on preventing user error and malicious acts.

Security is the antithesis of convenience—generally, the more secure something is, the less convenient it is. Think about this in the context of your life: think of how easy it would be if you could just walk up and push a button to start your car without worrying about keys—or paying for car insurance. But the risk of theft and accidents makes these two security measures mandatory. Meanwhile, advanced technology like remote key fobs for cars is making automotive security easier, just as biometric scanners can make logging on to computers both more secure and less annoying at the same time.

Computer security is not complicated. It may seem that way, but the theory behind computer security is relatively simple. Hacking methods fall into just a few categories. And solutions to computer security problems are actually rather straightforward.

Why Computers Aren't Secure

Most people question why computers are so insecure—after all, people have been hacking for a long time. The vast majority of hacking incidents occur because of one of the following pervasive problems:

Security is an annoyance.   Administrators often fail to implement security features in operating systems because doing so causes problems for users. Users also circumvent security—by choosing easy-to-use (easy-to-guess) passwords like "123456," never changing those passwords, disclosing those passwords to co-workers, or sharing user accounts.

Vendors ship software so that it will install in the most feature-filled configuration with its security features disabled so that unskilled users won't run into roadblocks and don't have to understand and configure it correctly before they use it. This means that the vast majority of installations are never properly secured.

The fact that strong security is an annoyance that requires extra learning on the part of everyone involved is the most common reason for security failures.

Features are rushed to market.   Vendors concentrate their efforts on adding features that make their software more useful, with little thought to security. A perfect example of this is the addition of scripting language support to Microsoft Outlook and Outlook Express.

virus
Any program that automatically replicates itself.

When the Internet first took off, "e-mail *virus*" scares propagated around the Net via e-mail. Computer security experts ignored them, knowing that a virus required an execution environment like a computer language in order to actually propagate. They laughed at the possibility that anyone would actually tie a computer language to an e-mail system because anyone with any security consciousness at all would never let this happen. Despite the warnings, and even though the scripting language support built in to Microsoft Office had already been exploited to create "macro" viruses embedded in Word and Excel documents, Microsoft ignored the signs and the explicit warnings of its own employees and incorporated a scripting language into its e-mail software. Even worse, it was set up to automatically execute code contained in e-mail messages, configured to do so by default, and included features like "auto-preview" that even opened the messages upon arrival and executed the embedded code. To make matters even more egregious, Microsoft shipped this insecure software for free with every copy of their ubiquitous Windows operating system, thus ensuring that it would be widely deployed.

hacker
One who engages in hacking.

Thus, the plague that is e-mail viruses today arrived—well predicted, forewarned, and completely ignored by a vendor in order to implement a feature that less than 1 percent of legitimate users actually ever use. Microsoft simply didn't concern itself with even a cursory study of the security implications of adding this feature to its software. It couldn't have done a better job of implementing a new hacking exploit if it had been doing it on purpose.

Vendors who spend time on security are eclipsed by the competition.
Customers don't truly value security. If they did, they would use older, well-tested, security-proven software that doesn't have all the bells and whistles of the latest versions. Companies like Microsoft that retrofitted their existing products to work on the Internet decimated their competition. Had they waited to do it securely, they would have been beaten to market by someone who didn't. The end result? The least-secure products always get to market first and become standards.

Computers and software evolve very quickly. Computers and networking technology have been evolving far faster than companies can predict what might go wrong with them. Moore's law states that computer hardware will double in power every two years. His prediction has been eerily accurate for over three decades now.

Protocols that were not developed to be secure were adapted to purposes that they were never intended for and then grew in popularity to a far wider audience than the original creators could have imagined.

Programmers can't accurately predict flaws. Programmers rarely consider that the state of their functions might be externally changed to any possible value while the code is running, so they only check for values that they send to it themselves. Once the code passes its normal debugging checks, it's shipped without having been tested to pass a barrage of random data thrown at it. Even if they did attempt to predict flaws, the 10 programmers who created a project could never come up with the complete set of attacks that the million hackers who attempt to exploit it will.

There is little diversity in the software market. The duopoly of the *Windows* and *Unix* operating systems has narrowed the targets of hackers to minor variations on just two operating systems. In most applications, just one or two products make up the lion's share of the market, so hackers have to crack only one product to gain wide access to many people. Two web servers, Apache and IIS, compose more than 90 percent of the web service market. Two closely related families of operating systems, Windows and Unix, compose more than 90 percent of the operating system market for PCs.

Vendors are not motivated to reveal potential flaws. To avoid marketing fiascoes, vendors try to hide problems with their operating systems and thereby naturally discourage discussion of their flaws. Conversely, hackers publicize flaws they discover immediately to the entire world via the Internet. This dichotomy of discussion means that flaws are far more widely disseminated than the solutions to them are.

Windows
A family of single-user operating systems developed by Microsoft for small computers. The most recent version has incorporated enhancements to allow multiple users to run programs directly on the machine.

Unix
A family of multiuser operating systems that all conform completely to the Portable Operating System Interface for Unix (POSIX) specification and operate in very similar fashion; this includes Unix, BSD, Linux, and derivatives of these major versions.

firewall
A packet router that inspects the data flowing through it to decide which information to pass through based upon a set of programmed policies.

hacking
The act of attempting to gain access to computers without authorization.

protocol
An agreed-upon method of communicating between two computers.

Patches are not widely deployed and can cause problems when they are installed.   When security problems are found with a piece of software, the vendor will fix the problem, post a patch on the Internet, and send out an e-mail notice to registered customers. Unfortunately, not everyone gets the notice or installs the patch—in fact, the majority of users never install security patches for software unless they actually get hacked.

Even worse, vendors rush security patches to clients with unexposed bugs that can cause even more serious problems on their client's machines and even in the best cases require additional processing to find the flaws, thus slowing the systems. In some cases, the cure can be worse than the disease.

With these problems epidemic in the security market, you might wonder if the security problem will ever be solved. In fact, there will always be flaws in software. But there are many relatively easy things that can be done to fix these problems. Secure *protocols* can be layered on top of unsecured protocols or replace them outright. Border security with *firewalls* can prevent *hackers* from reaching most systems, thus making their security flaws unimportant. Compilers and computer languages can be modified to eliminate problems that programmers fail to check for. And vendors can find ways to make security more convenient, such as filtering easily guessed passwords using spell-checker technology. And, as hackers continue to exploit systems, customers will demand proactive security and reward vendors who emphasize security rather than those who ship feature-filled, but poorly thought-out, products.

NOTE

Why can't vendors make software secure out of the box? In truth, they can. In the OpenBSD operating system, there has been only one remotely exploitable flaw found in seven years. Its developers have accurately predicted and proactively closed *hacking* exploits before they could be exploited. But OpenBSD is not very popular because it doesn't have a lot of features—it's just a basic operating system, and your own software can still be exploited once you add it.

The History of Computer Security

When you understand the history of computer security, it becomes obvious why computers aren't secure.

worm
Any program that takes active measures to replicate itself onto other machines in a network. A network virus.

Stories of major, nearly catastrophic, hacking exploits happen all the time. 2001 was a particularly bad year for Internet security. The Code Red *worm* spread unchecked through the Internet—and once it was patched, the Nimbda virus did almost exactly the same thing; e-mail viruses spread with regularity, and Microsoft shipped its newest flagship operating system, Windows XP, with a security flaw so egregious that hackers could literally exploit any computer running it with no serious effort at all; the Linux standard FTP and DNS services were exploited, allowing hackers to enter websites and deface their contents at will. As of 2004, Nimda variants are still prowling the Internet, hitting newly installed machines while cousins like Sasser use the same old propagation code patched to attack new vulnerabilities. It seems like hacking is just getting worse, even as organizations spend more money on the problem. In fact, widespread hacking is getting more common.

In 1988, the year in which reporting began, the Computer Emergency Response Team (CERT) at Carnegie Mellon University, which tracks Internet security incidents, reported six hacking incidents. In 1999, they reported nearly 10,000. In 2000, they reported over 22,000. In 2001, they reported over 52,000 incidents. Numbers like these can sound scary, but when you factor in the growth of the Internet by counting incidents per computers attached to the Internet, security incidents are rising at a rate of 50 percent per year (rather than the 100 percent per year the raw numbers suggest) and have been since 1993, the first year for which reasonably reliable information is available about the overall size of the Internet. A slight decline in the percentage of incidents reported is evident since 2001, with 82,000 incidents in 2002 and 138,000 in 2003, so explosive growth trend appears to be slowing.

The following sections are a quick reprisal of computer security since the dawn of time. (See the graphic on the next page.)

–1945

Computers didn't exist in any real sense before 1945. The original need for security (beyond prevention of outright theft of equipment) sprang from the need for secure military and political communication. *Codes* and *ciphers* were originally studied because they could provide a way to secure messages if the messages were intercepted and could allow for distance communication like smoke, mirror, or pigeon signaling.

Before the advent of telegraphy, telephony, and radio communications, simply transmitting a message anywhere was extremely difficult. Wars were prosecuted slowly; intrigues were based on hunches, guesses, and paranoia because real information was difficult to come by. Messages transmitted by post or courier were highly likely to be intercepted, and when they were, the consequences were disastrous for the war or political effort.

For that reason, codes, which are far easier to implement than ciphers, formed the backbone of secure communications prior to the advent of automated computing. Codes are simple substitution ciphers—one word is used to transmit another word, concept, or phrase. Both parties encode and decode their messages using a codebook, and generally the codes were chosen so that they made reasonable sense when read in their coded form in an attempt to hide the fact that they were encoded—similar to the modern concept of steganography, or hiding encrypted data as noise inside other content like a digital picture or sound file. (Most militaries

code
An agreed-upon set of symbols that represent concepts. Both parties must be using the same code in order to communicate, and only predetermined concepts can be communicated.

cipher
A mathematical function used to transform a plain message into a form that cannot be read without decoding it. Ciphers can encode any message.

still use codes and codebooks for operational messages over unencrypted radio links as a holdover from earlier times, but as computing power becomes cheap, this practice is quickly fading into obscurity.) Unfortunately, both parties had to have the codebook, and the interception of a codebook meant that all encoded communication could be decoded.

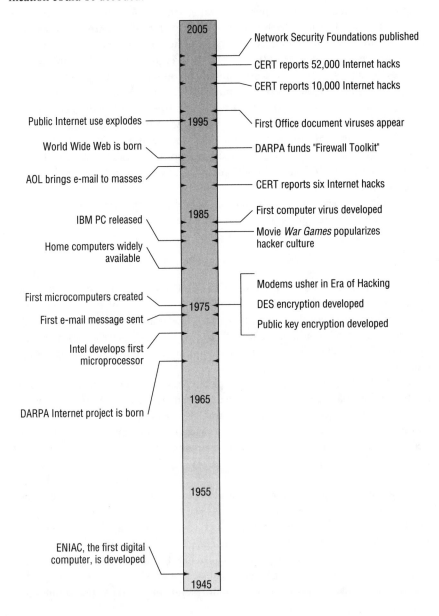

2005

Network Security Foundations published

CERT reports 52,000 Internet hacks

CERT reports 10,000 Internet hacks

Public Internet use explodes — 1995

First Office document viruses appear

World Wide Web is born

DARPA funds "Firewall Toolkit"

AOL brings e-mail to masses

CERT reports six Internet hacks

1985

First computer virus developed

IBM PC released

Movie *War Games* popularizes hacker culture

Home computers widely available

Modems usher in Era of Hacking

First microcomputers created — 1975

DES encryption developed

First e-mail message sent

Public key encryption developed

Intel develops first microprocessor

1965

DARPA Internet project is born

1955

ENIAC, the first digital computer, is developed

1945

1945–1955

A half-century ago, the first electronic computers were being developed. These gargantuan machines operated on vacuum tubes and had considerably less computing power than today's $50 calculator. They cost many millions of dollars to build and operate, and every compute cycle was precious. Wasting computing time on such luxuries as security was unheard of—but since you had to have both physical access and substantial training to operate these machines, security was not a problem. With so many other problems to solve, computer security wasn't even on the research horizon at this time.

1955–1965

As computers moved into the business world in the sixties, computer security was limited only to making sure that the occasional disgruntled employee couldn't cause harm and that the competition had no access to the computers. Both measures still relied upon physical security for the environment rather than security measures in software. Accounts and passwords, when implemented, were simple and used merely for tracking which users performed which actions in the system rather than for any form of true security. There's not a single verified instance of remote malicious hacking activity occurring during or before this era.

1965–1975

During the late sixties and early seventies, as *mainframes* grew more powerful and the number of users attached to them reached into the thousands, accountability became more important. To limit what typical users could do, the concept of limited user accounts and unlimited administrative accounts came into practice. Typical users could not perform actions that might corrupt data or disrupt other users, while administrators could do anything that was necessary on the system. User accounts protected by passwords were used to discriminate between the various types of users. Most mainframes shipped from the factory with a default password that the administrators were responsible for changing once they received the machine—a practice that is still common with simple network devices.

mainframe
A large and powerful (in context) computer that many users share via terminal displays.

Operating system research was beginning to take root in this period, and mainframe operating systems like Multics were beginning to be adapted to a much smaller breed of business-class machines, like minicomputers and the first single-user systems called workstations. The phone company was involved in a tremendous amount of operating research at the time, and developed a light version of Multics, called Unix. At the same time, Digital Equipment was developing a more portable version of its operating system, called VMS, while IBM worked on its various mainframe operating systems.

operating system
The program that controls the overall operation of a computer.

Hacking in this era consisted of mere rumors of rogue programmers performing illicit hacks—such as writing code that took the fractional remnants of rounded transactions and deposited them in their own bank accounts or writing back doors into their code so that they could always gain access to systems (as the original developers of Unix have insinuated that they did).

1975–1985

The lack of true security came to light in the seventies when companies started providing remote access to terminal users over modems that operated using the public telephone system. Modems allowed small offices to connect directly to central computers in the corporate headquarters. Companies also leased the newer digital phone circuits and began connecting remote offices directly to their systems over "leased lines" that did not require modems and could span the country—at great expense. And, since only direct connections could be made between mainframes and terminals, there was very little flexibility for routing information.

The military had been using computers for years at this point and had been chafing at the lack of flexibility in sending messages between mainframes. In 1969, the Defense Advanced Research Projects Agency (DARPA) initiated a project to explore the promise of packet-based networks, where individual tiny messages could be transmitted between two end systems and routed by intermediate systems connected in a loosely hierarchical method, thus allowing any participants on the network to communicate. These research efforts began to bear useful fruit in the late seventies.

The amount of computing power required to perform message (or packet) routing was impractical at the time, but it was clear that computers would quickly become powerful enough to make the problem trivial in the next few years. Because message routing required intermediate systems to perform work that didn't directly involve them, security was antithetical in the early packet-based research systems; intermediate systems could not waste the time to authenticate every packet that went through them, and requiring security would have kept the system from getting off the ground. But in the military, physical security and accountability more than made up for the lack of systems security, and since no untrusted users were attached to the system, security wasn't an issue.

Data Encryption Standard (DES)
A secret key encryption algorithm developed by IBM, under contract to the U.S. government, for public use.

But the government realized that security would become an issue and began funding major initiatives to improve computer security. IBM developed the *Data Encryption Standard (DES)* for the government in 1975. And at nearly the same time, Whitfield Diffie and Martin Hellman developed the concept of the *public key encryption (PKE)*, which solved the longstanding problem of secure key exchange. In 1977, Rivest, Shamir, and Adelman implemented PKE in the proprietary RSA encryption algorithm. These pioneering efforts in network encryption weren't widely deployed at the time, but they are the foundation of computer security today.

The development of the microprocessor by Intel in 1972 was beginning to bear fruit: four or five models were available to the public by 1975. Hobbyists could build their own computers from parts available through catalogs, and by 1978 complete computer systems could be purchased off the shelf by end users in any town in the U.S.

They could be purchased with modems that were capable of communicating directly with corporate computers as well, and the art and practice of hacking was born.

Hacking in those days consisted of "war-dialing" a range of phone numbers automatically by leaving hobby computers running overnight. Whenever a computer answered, the computer doing the war-dialing would typically print out the phone number. In any case, it would hang up immediately, causing numerous nuisance calls to people in the middle of the night. The hacker would then go through the list of found computers manually, looking for signs of computers that might be easy to break into, like mainframe computers whose default administrative *passwords* had never been changed.

After a few high-profile, apparently effortless cases of hackers breaking into computer systems occurred, the concept of *call-back security,* also known as dial-back security, was introduced. With call-back security, the answering computer (the system) accepts only a phone number from the calling computer (the client) and hangs up. The system then checks this phone number against an allowed list, and if it appears, the system calls back the client whose computer is set to listen for a call back. The fact that phone numbers can't easily be forged and that phone lines are somewhat difficult to tap made for all the security that was necessary in those days.

Hackers did have the ability to hack the telephone company's computers to reroute phone calls and manually direct where calls went, but hackers with these skills were extremely rare, and lacking any public discussion forum, every hacker pretty much had to learn these techniques on their own. By the mid-eighties, call-back security had solved the problem of computer security to the point that it was worth solving, and increased security by the public telephone companies made exploiting these systems very difficult.

1985–1995

In the mid-eighties, the popularity of PC computers exploded; PCs went from a novelty owned by geeks to an essential tool of nearly every desktop in the country in the span of 10 years. With the explosion in popularity grew the need to connect PC computers together directly, and so local area networks, pioneered in the previous decade, came out of the research closet and onto the desktop as well. These networks used business-grade versions of the military's packet-based networks that were optimized for small networks. By 1995, networked PCs were crucial to the business world.

At the same time, home computer enthusiasts with modems were creating online communities called *bulletin-board systems (BBS).* By using a single expensive PC with a lot of modems or an obsolete mainframe as a central server, home

public key encryption (PKE)
A method of encryption that solves the problem of exchanging secret keys by using different but related ciphers for encoding and decoding.

password
A secret known to both a system and a user that can be used to prove a user's identity.

call-back security
Security that is implemented by having the main system call the remote user back, thus ensuring that the user attempting to gain access is an authorized one (so long as the phone system remains secure).

bulletin-board system (BBS)
A single central computer to which many computers have intermittent access to shared information.

users could dial in to chat with friends, send text messages, and participate in online discussion groups and games. Without exception these services were text-based to make maximum use of the slow modem links and low processing power of the computers of the day.

Some of these BBSs became very large. CompuServe became the largest BBS at this time, linking millions of computer users by modem and allowing them to trade electronic mail and to "chat" or use text messages with one another in real time. Another company, America Online, took the BBS concept and put a graphical interface on it, making getting "on line" easy enough for computer novices.

BBSs allowed hackers to begin trading in information and to form distributed hacking cabals—usually targeting other BBSs because most business computers had become locked down with the advent of dial-up security. Hacking in this period worked largely the same way that it had in the seventies except that the targets were new phone companies, BBSs, and the occasional improperly secured corporate mainframe.

That is, unless you happened to be a student at a university. During these years, universities took over development of the military's original packet-routing protocols and developed them to solve real-world problems. Just like the military prototype, these systems relied on the fact that intermediate systems would route data without authentication in order to function. Security was a layer pasted on top, in the actual application that used the packet network, rather than at the network layer. This allowed clever students to watch data flowing through intermediate systems to gather passwords and then use those passwords to gain access to other systems. Because military installations and academic research companies were also connected to this "Internet," early hackers had the chance to cause real mischief—but rarely actually did.

During this period, e-mail grew out of simple messaging systems that allowed only interoffice communication into a messaging system that could span companies and allow anyone attached to the Internet to trade real, human information. Other research projects like FTP and Gopher allowed people to trade computer files and documents over the Internet. In 1990, Gopher was merged with a research concept called HyperText (previously seen by the public in Apple's HyperCard product) to produce "browsable documentation" that contained embedded links to other documents that could be automatically downloaded when the link was selected. This technology, called the World Wide Web, allowed scientists to publish their scientific papers immediately and was an immediate boon to the scientific and Internet computing communities.

The fact that hacking could occur on the nascent Internet didn't pass unnoticed, however. Every major entity attached to the Internet, including the military, universities, and mainframe computer companies like IBM and Digital, developed special intermediate systems that performed extra analysis of data flowing through them to determine if the data was legitimate and should be routed. These routers were called firewalls.

1995–2005

The Internet exploded on the public scene between late '94 and early '96 (we'll just call it '95). Borne largely by the twin utilities of universal e-mail and the World Wide Web, the Internet became so compelling that the owners of most BBSs began to connect their systems to the Internet and the government turned over management of it to a consortium of Internet service providers (ISPs). Universities frequently allowed wide access to their Internet connections early on, and soon, phone companies began installing pure "modem banks" to answer phone connections and put them directly on the Internet. The Universities, BBS operator, and phone companies all became Internet service providers, and within an amazingly short period of time, millions of people were connected directly to one another over the Internet. BBSs who didn't convert to ISPs, with the solitary exception of AOL (which provided a bridge to the Internet but maintained its proprietary BBS client software), became extinct almost overnight.

The Internet boom happened so fast that software vendors were caught completely off guard. Bill Gates, the chairman of Microsoft, said in 1994 that the Internet would blow over. His words merely echoed the typical response of most PC software developers. Some new companies, like Netscape, consisted of students who had been using the Internet at school and knew its potential, but these companies were few and far between.

By the next year, it was obvious that the Internet wasn't going to just blow over. In a telling incident, Mr. Gates called a meeting at his retreat and forced his entire staff to abandon their current developments and refocus their efforts on making every one of Microsoft's products "Internet Enabled." Other software companies couldn't react as quickly, and the Internet caused many of them to stumble, ship late, and become irrelevant. Only those who rushed to make their software and operating systems compatible with Internet protocols remained in the game. The very largest names in computer software at the time, like Borland, WordPerfect, Novell, IBM, and Lotus, were all simultaneously hobbled by the fact that Microsoft was able to make its products take advantage of this new technology in short order, while they chose to finish their current developments and wait for the next development cycle to make their products Internet-ready. By the time their next product revisions came out, nobody cared and Microsoft had completely eclipsed them all.

The rush to market, while a marketing coup for Microsoft, made security an afterthought. The folks at Microsoft actually believed their own hype about their flagship operating system, Windows NT, and felt that its office-grade security would make it the most secure operating system on the Internet. For their home use products like Windows 95, 98, and Me, security wasn't even attempted—you could gain access to the computer by clicking "cancel" at the log-in dialog, if one was even configured to appear. After all, if Microsoft had held up the development of these products to try to make them secure, end users would have just adopted somebody else's insecure products that were ready to go.

The Internet, with its totally nonsecure protocols, was the fertilizer that the hacking world needed after the sparse desert of the late eighties. Once phone companies had locked down their systems, hacking had frankly become rather boring and routine. Anybody you could hack wasn't going to be interesting anyway, so there was little point in trying. But suddenly, everyone was attached to the same insecure network, ripe for the plucking.

Microsoft's dominance of the PC software market meant that hackers could concentrate their efforts on understanding just two operating systems: Unix, the native OS of the Internet, and Windows, the operating system of the masses. By creating exploits to hack these two operating systems remotely over the Internet, hackers gained almost unlimited access to information on the Internet. Vendors scrambled to patch security problems as soon as they were discovered, but the lag between discovery and response left weeks during which hackers could broadcast their discoveries and cause widespread damage.

Businesses clamped down by installing firewalls, evolved from early military and commercial security research efforts, onto their leased lines at the point where they attached to their ISPs. Firewalls went a long way toward protecting interior systems from exploitation, but they still allowed users to circumvent security accidentally and did little to stop the exploitation of services that had to be allowed—like e-mail and web services. These two services now constitute the bulk of hacking targets because they can't be blocked while still operating correctly.

encryption
The process of encoding a message using a cipher.

Toward the close of this era, *encryption* gained wide use as the savior of the Internet. By implementing security protocols that could hide data and prove someone's identity while preserving the ease-of-use and ubiquity that made the Internet popular, encryption, along with firewalling, is basically saving the Internet from abandonment due to security concerns.

Hackers will continue to exploit insecure protocols, but as vendors learn to ship secure software or shore it up with integrated firewall code, and as implementers learn to secure their own systems, hacking is doomed to drift steadily toward the situation in the late eighties, when it was no longer that interesting because those remaining insecure users were trivial.

2005–

Hacking will drop off dramatically once Microsoft integrates strong firewalling software into all of its operating systems, which will occur late in 2004 when it realizes that the adoption of its new e-commerce .NET services depends upon security rather than features. The open-source community and their flagship Linux product had already integrated true firewalling years earlier, and Linux is seen as more secure than Windows—a situation that Microsoft will not tolerate for long. Apple will simply adapt the open-source firewalling services into Mac OS X, which is based upon BSD Unix, to prevent its exploitation, and every other commercial version of Unix will be completely eclipsed and made obsolete by the free, faster moving, and more secure Linux or BSD Unix operating systems by this time.

E-mail forgery and spamming will become more popular, until users begin to use the X.509 certificate-based encryption and digital signature capabilities already supported but rarely used. Someone (probably Microsoft, Yahoo, or AOL) will set up a free certificate authority for private users and make mail clients and web browsers automatically download certificates from it as part of an online digital identity that will be used to enable secure e-commerce services.

Once Microsoft and the open-source community tighten down the hatches on their operating systems and services, hacking exploits will become fewer and farther between. The government will catch up with hacking activity after it tapers off and begin making examples of people again. Hacking as a hobby will taper down to a trickle.

Until a researcher somewhere and somewhen discovers a fundamental mathematical flaw in the encryption software upon which all of these security measures are based...

Security Concepts

Computer security is based on the same concepts that physical security is: trust, knowledge of a secret to prove authenticity, possession of a key to open locks, and legal accountability. The metaphors are so apt that most computer security mechanisms even have the same names as their physical counterparts.

Trust

All computer security springs from the concept of inherent or original trust. Just as a child inherently trusts its parents, a secure computer system inherently trusts those who set it up. While this may seem rather obvious, it is an important concept because it is the origination of all subsequent security measures.

There's more inherent trust in computer security than simply the original establishment of a system. For example, you trust that there are no "back doors" in the software you use that could be exploited by a knowledgeable person to gain access. You trust that the login screen that you are looking at is actually the system's true login screen and not a mimic designed to collect your password and then pass it to a remote system. Finally, you trust that the designers of the system have not made any serious mistakes that could obviate your security measures.

Authentication

Authentication is the process of determining the identity of a user. Forcing the user to prove that they know a secret that should be known only to them proves that they are who they say they are.

authentication
The process of determining the identification of a user.

user account
A record containing information that identifies a user, including a secret password.

User accounts are associated with some form of secret, such as a password, PIN, biometric hash, or a device like a *smart card* that contains a larger, more secure password than a human could remember. To the system, there is no concept of a human; there is only a secret, information tied to that secret, and information to which that secret has access.

Authentication is only useful in so far as it is accurate. Passwords are probably the least reliable form of authentication in common use today, but they're also the most easily implemented—they require no special hardware and no sophisticated algorithms for basic use. However, they are easily guessed, and even when they're carefully chosen it's still possible to simply guess the entire range of possible passwords on many systems in short order.

smart card
An electronic device containing a simple calculator preprogrammed with a code that cannot be retrieved. When given a challenge, it can calculate a response that proves it knows the code without revealing what the code is.

A less common but more secure method of authentication is to physically possess a unique key. This is analogous to most physical locks. In computer security systems, "keys" are actually large numbers generated by special algorithms that incorporate information about the user and are stored on removable media like smart cards. The problem with keys is that, like physical keys, they can be lost or stolen. However, when combined with a password, they are very secure and difficult to thwart.

Another form of authentication provides inherent identification by using a physical property of the user. This is called biometric authentication, and it relies upon unique and unchangeable physical properties of a human, such as handwriting characteristics, fingerprints, facial characteristics, and so forth. Biometric authentication has the potential to be the most reliable form of authentication because it's easy to use, nearly impossible to fake when correctly implemented, and can't be circumvented for the sake of convenience. Some forms of biometric authentication are easier to "forge" than others, and naïve implementations can sometimes be easily faked. But when well implemented, biometric authentication is the most secure form of authentication and the only form that can be truly said to uniquely and unmistakably identify a user.

Chain of Authority

trust provider
A trusted third party that certifies the identity of all parties in a secure transaction. Trust providers do this by verifying the identity of each party and generating digital certificates that can be used to determine that identity. Trust providers perform a function analogous to a notary public.

During the installation of a security system, the original administrator will create the root account. From the root account (called the "administrator" account in Windows and the "Supervisor" account in NetWare), all other accounts, keys, and certificates spring. Every account on a system, even massive systems containing millions of accounts, spring from this chain of authority. The concept of chains of authority isn't often discussed because it is inherent in a secure system.

Certificate systems are also based on a chain of authority. Consider the case of separate businesses that do a lot of work together. It would be convenient if users from Business Alpha could automatically log on to computers at Business Beta. But because these two systems have two different chains of authority, there's no way for Business Alpha to trust that users who say they are from Business Beta actually are. This problem is solved by having both businesses trust a third-party *trust provider,* or a company that specializes in verifying identity and creating secure certificates that can be used to prove identity to foreign systems. As long as both businesses trust the same trust provider, they are rooted in the same chain of authority and can trust certificates that are generated by that trust provider. Trust providers are the digital equivalent of a notary public. Examples of trust providers are VeriSign and Thawte.

Accountability

Accountability is where the secret meets the user. Users don't try to circumvent security because their identity would be known and they would be held legally accountable for their actions. It is accountability, rather than access controls, that prevents illegal behavior.

In pure accountability-based systems, no access control mechanisms are present. Users simply know that their every action is being logged, and since their identity is known and their activities are tracked, they won't do things that could jeopardize their position (unless something happens to make them no longer care).

The problem with accountability-based systems is twofold—they only work if identity can't be faked, and there are rare occasions where users lose their inhibitions. Without access control, these users can destroy the entire system. For these reasons, accountability-based security is normally used to augment access control systems rather than to replace them.

Access Control

Access control is the security methodology that allows access to information based on identity. Users who have been given permission or keys to information can access it—otherwise, access is denied.

Permissions-Based Access Control

Once the system knows the identity of an individual because they've been authenticated, the system can selectively allow or deny access to resources like stored files based on that identity. This is called permissions-based security because users are either granted or denied permission to access a *file* or other resource.

file
A sequence of related information referenced by a filename in a directory.

The question of who has access to which files is typically either defined by administrators when the system is implemented or created according to some set of default rules programmed into the system; for instance, the original creator (owner) of a file is the only user who can change it.

Access controls are typically implemented either as directory permissions that apply to all files within the directory or by an access control list, which is a component of a file that explicitly lists which users can access it. Typically, when a file is created, an ACL is automatically copied from the parent directory's ACL, so it is said to "inherit" permissions from the containing directory.

Unfortunately, none of these security controls works if the operating system can be circumvented. By shutting off the system and mounting its storage in another computer, a foreign system can read off all the files without interference because it's not asking for permission from the operating system. Essentially, permissions can be circumvented the same way kids can disobey their parents—by simply not asking for permission in the first place.

Encryption-Based Access Control (Privacy)

private key
The key used to decode public key messages that must be kept private.

A totally different way to control access is to simply encrypt data using public key encryption. Access to the encrypted data is given to those who want it, but it's worthless to them unless they have the *private key* required to decode it. Using PKE to secure data works very well, but it requires considerably more processing power to encode and decode data.

TIP

Encryption is such an important topic in computer security that it requires its own chapter to be covered properly. If you don't understand the terms used in this section, just reread it after you read Chapter 3.

Encryption-based access control is also dangerous because data can be irrevocably lost if the private key required to decrypt it is lost. For this reason, most practical systems store a copy of a resource's private key in a key repository that can be accessed by an administrator, and the copy itself is encrypted using another key. The problem of potential loss of information doesn't go away, but the system includes more participants and therefore permanent loss is less likely to happen.

Practical systems also don't encrypt files with a unique public key for each file or user—in fact, they encrypt files using a secret key registered to an entire group and then encrypt the list of secret keys for the group using a private key. The private key is given to each member of the group (possession of the private key makes one a member of the group). Thus, members of the group have the key to decrypt the store that contains the secret key required to decrypt the file. This way, when an account is deleted, no keys are irrevocably lost because other members still have the key.

In pure encryption-based access control systems, the keys for a group are stored in a file that is encrypted using a user's smart card. By possessing the smart card, a user can decrypt the store that contains the keys for the groups they are members of, and those keys in turn can be used to decrypt the store that contains the keys that are used to decrypt individual files. This is how a chain of authority is created using encryption, and systems that work this way are called Public Key Infrastructure (PKI) systems.

No common systems work this way yet, but support for PKI is being retrofitted into both Windows and Unix. Shortly, most systems will work this way.

Encryption-based access control solves the problem of requiring the operating system to arbitrate access to secure data. Even if the operating system has been circumvented, stored data is still encrypted. Encrypted data can be transmitted over public media like the Internet without concern for its privacy.

Terms to Know

authentication	operating system
bulletin-board systems (BBS)	passwords
call-back security	private key
ciphers	protocols
codes	public key encryption (PKE)
Data Encryption Standard (DES)	smart card
encryption	trust provider
file	Unix
firewalls	user accounts
hackers	virus
hacking	Windows
mainframes	worm

Review Questions

1. What is security?

2. What is the most common reason security measures fail?

3. Why would vendors release a product even when they suspected that there could be security problems with the software?

4. How many operating systems make up 90 percent of the operating system market?

5. Factoring in the growth of the Internet, at what rate is the number of computer security incidents increasing?

6. Why weren't computers designed with security in mind from the beginning?

7. During what era did "hacking" begin to occur en masse?

8. In what year was public key encryption developed?

9. Prior to the Internet, how did most hackers share information?

10. Why is it likely that applications (other than those designed to implement security) that concentrate on security will fail in the marketplace?

11. What is the process of determining the identity of a user called?

12. When a new computer is first set up, how does the system know that the person setting up the computer is authorized to do so?

13. What is the most secure form of authentication?

14. How can a hacker circumvent permissions-based access control?

15. How can a hacker circumvent correctly implemented encryption-based access control?

Chapter 2

Understanding Hacking

Know thy enemy. Hackers are the reason you need to implement computer security, and an in-depth defense against any adversary requires an in-depth understanding of that adversary. This chapter describes hackers, their motivations, and their methods.

By knowing a hacker's motivations, you can predict your own risk level and adapt your specific defenses to ward off the type of hackers you expect to attack your network while retaining as much usability as possible for your legitimate users.

What Is Hacking?

Hacking is quite simply the attempt to gain access to a computer system without authorization. Originally, the term *hacker* simply referred to an adept computer user, and gurus still use the term to refer to themselves in that original sense. But when breaking into computer systems (technically known as *cracking*) became popular, the media used the *hacker* to refer only to computer criminals, thus popularizing only the negative connotation. In this book, we refer only to that negative connotation as well.

Hacking is illegal. Title 18, United States Code, Section 1030, first enacted by Congress in 1984, criminalized hacking. Technically, the code requires that the perpetrator actually "do" something other than simply obtain access and read information—but then, if that's all they did, you probably wouldn't know you'd been hacked anyway. The law specifically states that the perpetrator must "knowingly" commit the crime—thereby requiring that at least some sort of notification that unauthorized access is illegal be posted or that some authentication hurdle be established in order to make the activity prosecutable.

According to the FBI, for a computer-related crime to become a federal crime, the attacker must be shown to have caused at least $5,000 worth of damage. This is why spammers who access open relay mail servers get away with transmitting their floods of e-mail through other people's mail servers without being prosecuted—they're not doing enough financial damage to any one victim to really be prosecutable, and the SMTP servers are not performing authentication so there's no reasonable expectation of security. But, because spam has become such a plague lately, the 2004 CANSPAM Act specifically criminalizes the transmission of unsolicited commercial e-mail without an existing business relationship.

Types of Hackers

Learning to hack takes an enormous amount of time, as does perpetrating actual acts of hacking. Because of the time it takes, there are only two serious types of hackers: the underemployed and those hackers being paid by someone to hack. The word *hacker* conjures up images of skinny teenage boys aglow in the phosphor of their monitors. Indeed, this group makes up the largest portion of the teeming millions of hackers, but they are far from the most serious threat.

Hackers fall quite specifically into these categories, in order of increasing threat:

- Security experts
- Script kiddies
- Underemployed adults
- Ideological hackers
- Criminal hackers
- Corporate spies
- Disgruntled employees

Security Experts

Most security experts are capable of hacking but decline to do so for moral or economic reasons. Computer security experts have found that there's more money in preventing hacking than in perpetrating it, so they spend their time keeping up with the hacking community and current techniques in order to make themselves more effective in the fight against it. A number of larger Internet service companies employ ethical hackers to test their security systems and those of their large customers, and hundreds of former hackers now consult independently as security experts to medium-sized businesses. These experts often are the first to find new hacking exploits, and they often write software to test or exacerbate a condition. Practicing hackers can exploit this software just as they can exploit any other software.

Script Kiddies

Script kiddies are students who hack and are currently enrolled in some scholastic endeavor—junior high, high school, or college. Their parents support them, and if they have a job, it's only part-time. They are usually enrolled in whatever computer-related courses are available, if only to have access to the computer lab. These hackers may use their own computers, or (especially at colleges) they may use the more powerful resources of the school to perpetrate their hacks.

script kiddie
A novice hacker.

Script kiddies joyride through cyberspace looking for targets of opportunity and are concerned mostly with impressing their peers and not getting caught. They usually are not motivated to harm you, and in most instances, you'll never know they were there unless you have software that detects unusual activity and notifies you or a firewall that logs attacks—or unless they make a mistake. These hackers constitute about 90 percent of the total manual hacking activity on the Internet.

If you consider the hacking community as an economic endeavor, these hackers are the consumers. They use the tools produced by others, stand in awe of the hacking feats of others, and generally produce a fan base to whom more serious script kiddies and underemployed adult hackers play. Any serious attempt at security will keep these hackers at bay.

In addition to the desire to impress their peers, script kiddies hack primarily to get free stuff: software and music, mostly. They share pirated software amongst themselves, make MP3 compressed audio tracks from CDs of their favorite music, and trade the serial numbers needed to unlock the full functionality of demo software that can be downloaded from the Internet.

Underemployed Adult Hackers

Underemployed adults are former script kiddies who have either dropped out of school or failed to achieve full-time employment and family commitments for some other reason. They usually hold "pay the rent" jobs (often as computer support professionals). Their first love is probably hacking, and they are quite good at it. Many of the tools script kiddies use are created by these adult hackers.

Adult hackers are not intentional criminals in that they do not intend to harm others. However, the same disrespect for law that makes them hackers makes nearly all of them software and content pirates. Adult hackers often create the "crackz" applied by other hackers to unlock commercial software. This group also writes the majority of the software viruses. These are the hackers who form the notorious hacking cabals.

Adult hackers hack for notoriety in the hacking community—they want to impress their peers with exploits, gain information, and make a statement of defiance against the government or business. These hackers hack for the technical challenge. This group constitutes only about a tenth of the hacking community if that much, but they are the source for the vast majority of the software written specifically for hackers.

The global nature of the Internet means that literally anyone anywhere has access to your Internet-connected machines. In the old days, it cost money or talent to reach out and hack someone. These days, there's no difference between hacking a computer in your neighborhood and hacking one on the other side of the world. The problem is that in many countries, hacking is not a crime because intellectual property isn't strongly protected by law. If you're being hacked from outside your country, you wouldn't be able to bring the perpetrator to justice (even if you found out who it was) unless they also committed some major crime, like grand theft of something besides intellectual property. Underemployed adult hackers are a risk if your company has any sort of intellectual property to protect.

Ideological Hackers

Ideological hackers are those who hack to further some political purpose. Since the year 2000, ideological hacking has gone from just a few verified cases to a full-blown information war. Ideological hacking is most common in hot political arenas like environmentalism and nationalism.

denial of service (DoS) attack
A hacking attack in which the only intended purpose is to crash a computer or otherwise prevent a service from operating.

In an attempt to defend their cause, these hackers (usually) deface websites or perpetrate *denial of service (DoS) attacks* against their ideological enemies. They're usually looking for mass media coverage of their exploits, and because they nearly always come from foreign countries and often have the implicit support of their home government, they are impervious to prosecution and local law.

Although they almost never direct their attacks against targets that aren't their enemies, innocent bystanders frequently get caught in the crossfire. Examples of ideological hacking are the defacement of newspaper and government sites by Palestinian and Israeli hackers (both promulgating their specific agendas to the world) or the exploitation of hundreds of thousands of Internet Information Server (IIS) web servers by the Code Red worm originating in China (which defaced websites with a message denigrating the U.S. government).

This sort of hacking comes in waves whenever major events occur in political arenas. While it's merely a nuisance at this time, in the future these sorts of attacks will consume so much bandwidth that they will cause chaotic "weather-like" packet storms. Ideological hackers are of little risk because they are really only spraying the computer version of graffiti as far and wide as possible.

Criminal Hackers

Criminal hackers hack for revenge, to perpetrate theft, or for the sheer satisfaction of causing damage. This category doesn't bespeak a level of skill so much as an ethical standard. Criminal hackers are the ones you hear about in the paper—those who have compromised Internet servers to steal credit card numbers, performed wire transfers from banks, or hacked the Internet banking mechanism of a bank to steal money.

These hackers are as socially deformed as any real criminal—they are out to get what they can from whomever they can regardless of the cost to the victim. Criminal hackers are exceedingly rare because the intelligence required to hack usually also provides ample opportunity for the individual to find some socially acceptable means of support. Criminal hackers are of little risk to institutions that do not deal in large volumes of computer-based financial transactions.

That said, it is becoming somewhat common for organized crime (from any country foreign to the victim's home country) to use easily perpetrated denial of service attacks to extort protection money from companies whose revenue is based on a public website. Because denial of service attacks cannot be prevented (they could appear to be a large number of legitimate requests), victims often feel that they have no choice but to pay.

Corporate Spies

Actual corporate spies are very rare because it's extremely costly and legally very risky to employ illegal hacking tactics against competing companies. Who does have the time, money, and interest to use these tactics? Believe it or not, these tactics are usually employed against high-technology businesses by foreign governments. Many high technology businesses are young and naïve about security, making them ripe for the picking by the experienced intelligence agencies of foreign governments. These agencies already have budgets for spying, and taking on a few medium-sized businesses to extract technology that would give their own national corporations an edge is commonplace.

Nearly all high-level military spy cases involve individuals who have incredible access to information but as public servants don't make much money. This is a recipe for disaster. Low pay and wide access is probably the worst security breach you could have.

Disgruntled Employees

Disgruntled employees are the most dangerous—and most likely—security problem of all. An employee with an axe to grind has both the means and the motive to do serious damage to your network. Attacks by disgruntled employees are difficult to detect before they happen, but some sort of behavioral warning generally precipitates them.

Unfortunately, there's very little you can do about a disgruntled employee's ability to damage your network. Attacks range from the complex (a network administrator who spends time reading other people's e-mail) to the simple (a frustrated clerk who takes a fire axe to your database server).

It's most effective to let all employees know that the IT department audits all user activity for the purpose of security. This prevents problems from starting because hacking attempts would be a dead giveaway and because you know the identity of all the users.

Vectors That Hackers Exploit

There are only four ways for a hacker to access your network:

- By connecting over the Internet
- By using a computer on your network directly
- By dialing in via a Remote Access Service (RAS) server
- By connecting via a nonsecure wireless network

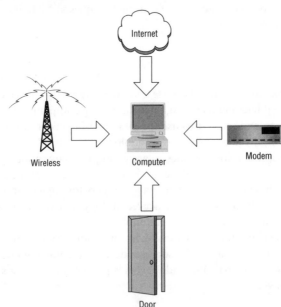

There are no other possible vectors. This small number of possible vectors defines the boundaries of the security problem quite well and, as the following sections show, makes it possible to contain them even further. The preceding graphic shows all the vectors that a hacker could potentially use to gain access to a computer.

Direct Intrusion

Hackers are notoriously nonchalant and have, on numerous occasions, simply walked into businesses, sat down at a local terminal or network client, and begun setting the stage for further remote penetration.

In large companies, there's no way to know everyone by sight, so an unfamiliar worker in the IT department isn't uncommon or suspicious at all. In companies that don't have ID badges or security guards, it isn't anybody's job to check credentials, so penetration is relatively easy. And even in small companies, it's easy to put on a pair of coveralls and pretend to be with a telephone or network wiring company or even pose as the spouse of a fictitious employee. With a simple excuse like telephone problems in the area, access to the server room is granted (oddly, these are nearly always colocated with telephone equipment). If left unattended, a hacker can simply create a new administrative user account. In less than a minute, a small external modem or wireless access point can be attached without even rebooting your server.

Solving the direct intrusion problem is easy: Employ strong physical security at your premises and treat any cable or connection that leaves the building as a security concern. This means putting firewalls between your WAN links and your internal network or behind wireless links. By employing your firewalls to monitor any connections that leave the building, you are able to eliminate direct intrusion as a vector.

Dial-Up

Dial-up hacking, via modems, used to be the only sort of hacking that existed, but it has quickly fallen to second place after Internet intrusions. (Hacking over the Internet is simply easier and more interesting for hackers.)

This doesn't mean that the dial-up vector has gone away—hackers with a specific target will employ any available means to gain access.

Although the dial-up problem usually means exploiting a modem attached to a Remote Access Service (RAS) server, it also includes the problem of dialing into individual computers. Any modem that has been set to answer for the purpose of allowing remote access or remote control for the employee who uses the computer presents a security concern. Many organizations allow employees to remotely access their computers from home using this method.

Containing the dial-up problem is conceptually easy: Put your RAS servers outside your firewall in the public security zone, and force legitimate users to authenticate with your firewall first to gain access to private network resources. Allow no device to answer a telephone line behind your firewall. This eliminates dial-up as a vector by forcing it to work like any other Internet connection.

Internet

Internet intrusion is the most available, most easily exploited, and most problematic vector of intrusion into your network. This vector is the primary topic of this book. If you follow the advice in this section, the Internet will be the only true vector into your network.

You already know that the Internet vector is solved by using firewalls, so there's no point in belaboring the topic here. The remainder of this book is about solving the Internet intrusion vector.

Wireless

Wireless, especially the extremely popular *802.11b* protocol that operates at 11Mbs and is nearly as cheap as standard Ethernet adapters and hubs, has taken root in the corporate world and grown like a weed. Based on the earlier and much less popular 802.11 standard, 802.11b allows administrators to attach *Wireless Access Points (WAPs)* to their network and allow wireless users (usually attached to laptops) to roam the premises without restriction. In another mode, two WAPs can be pointed at one another to form a wireless bridge between buildings, which can save companies tens of thousands of dollars in construction or circuit costs.

802.11b came with a much-touted built-in encryption scheme called the *Wired-Equivalent Privacy (WEP)* that promised to allow secure networking with the same security as wired networks have. It sounded great. Too bad it took less than 11 hours for security experts to hack it. Nobody paid attention at first, so these same researchers released software that automatically hacked it. WEP is so thoroughly compromised at this point that it should be treated as an insecure connection from the Internet. All wireless devices should be placed on the public side of your Internet, and users should have to authenticate with your firewall. The newer 128-bit WEP service is more secure, but it should still not be considered actually equivalent to wired security.

This leaves just one remaining problem: theft of service. You can take a laptop down the sidewalks of San Francisco at this very moment and authenticate with any one of over 800 (by a recent count published on Slashdot) 802.11b networks. While you might be outside the corporate firewall, if you're just looking to browse the Web, you're in luck. It's especially lucky if you're a hacker looking to hide your trail behind someone else's IP address.

802.11b
A very popular wireless networking standard that operates at 11Mbps and allows roaming computers to connect to a local area network.

Wireless Access Point (WAP)
An 802.11b wireless network hub.

Wired-Equivalent Privacy (WEP)
A flawed encryption protocol used by the 802.11b wireless networking protocol.

There are faster wireless protocols now, including the 54Mb 802.11g and 802.11a protocols, but (perhaps because there are two) it is unlikely that either will supplant 802.11b any time soon. 802.11b is cheap, ubiquitous, and faster than whatever circuit is being used to connect to the Internet, so the higher speed protocols that sacrifice distance won't replace it.

The forthcoming 802.11i protocol will solve many of the security problems inherent in wireless networking, but until it is released in its final form, it won't be possible to talk about theoretical or actual weaknesses. Irrespective, it will be a lot stronger than the current wireless implementations, but it remains to be seen whether people will replace their existing equipment to support it.

Hacking Techniques

Hacking attacks progress in a series of stages, using various tools and techniques. A hacking session consists of the following stages:

◆ Target selection

◆ Information gathering

◆ Attack

The hacker will attempt to find out more about your network through each successive attack, so these stages actually feed back into the process as more information is gathered from failed attacks.

Target Selection

Target selection is the stage where a hacker identifies a specific computer to attack. To pass this stage, some vector of attack must be available, so the machine must have either advertised its presence or have been found through some search activity.

DNS Lookup

Hackers who are looking for a specific target use the same method that Internet browsers use to find a host: they look up the domain name using the *Domain Name System (DNS)*. Although it's simple, and technically not qualified as an attack, you can actually defend against this target selection technique by simply not registering public domain names for any hosts except your mail and web servers. Then you've limited your major defense problem to just those servers.

Domain Name System (DNS)
The hostname-to-IP address directory service of the Internet.

For the interior of your network, use internal DNS servers that are not available to the Internet and that do not perform DNS zone transfers with public DNS servers. This is easily accomplished by registering your ".com" names with your ISP and using Windows Active Directory or Bind in Unix on an interior server that is not reachable from the Internet to manage your interior names.

Network Address Scanning

Hackers looking for targets of opportunity use a technique called network address *scanning* to find them. The hacker will specify beginning and ending addresses to scan, and then the hacker's computer program will send an ICMP echo message to each of those network addresses in turn. If a computer answers from any one of those addresses, then the hacker has found another target.

Address scans are being performed constantly on the Internet. If you have a computer connected to the public Internet, it's probably being address-scanned at least once per hour.

The best way to foil this kind of attack is to configure machines not to reply to ICMP echos. This prevents hackers from easily determining that your machine exists.

Port Scanning

Once a hacker has selected a target computer, they will attempt to determine which operating system it's running and which services it's providing to network clients. On a TCP/IP-based network (such as the Internet), services are provided on numbered connections called *ports*. The ports that a computer responds to often identify the operating system and supported services of the target computer.

There are a number of tools available on the Internet that a hacker can use to determine which ports are responding to network connection requests. These tools try each port in turn and report to the hacker which ports refuse connections and which do not. The hacker can then concentrate on ports corresponding to services that are often left unsecured or that have security problems.

Port scanning can reveal which operating system your computer is running because each OS has a different set of default services. For example, by scanning the TCP ports between 0 and 150, a hacker can discern Windows hosts (by the presence of port 139 in the scan list), NT hosts (by the presence of port 135 in the list), and various Unix hosts (by the presence of simple TCP/IP services like port 23 [Telnet], which NT and Windows do not install by default). This information tells the hacker which tools to use to further compromise your network.

Port scans are direct evidence that an individual hacker is specifically targeting your network. As such, port scans should be responded to and investigated seriously.

Service Scanning

Internet worms, which are automated hacking attacks that are perpetrated by programs running on exploited computers rather than by humans, operate by implementing a single attack and then searching for computers that are vulnerable to it. Invariably, this search takes the form of a port scan against just the one port that the attack exploits. Because the worm scans just a single port, it won't show up as either an address scan (because it's not ICMP) or a port scan (because it only hits a single port). In fact, there's no way to tell whether a single service scan is a legitimate connection attempt or a malicious service scan.

Typically, the service scan is followed up either by an architecture probe (if the worm is sophisticated) or simply by an attempted service-specific attack like a *buffer overrun*.

buffer overrun
A hacking exploit that sends specifically malformed information to a listening service in order to execute code of the hacker's choice on the target computer, thus paving the way for further exploitation.

Information Gathering

Information gathering is the stage where the hacker determines the characteristics of the target before actually engaging it. This may be through publicly available information published about the target or by probing the target using non-attack methods to glean information from it.

SNMP Data Gathering

The *Simple Network Management Protocol (SNMP)* is an essential tool for managing large TCP/IP networks. SNMP allows the administrator to remotely query the status of and control the operation of network devices that support it. Unfortunately, hackers can also use SNMP to gather data about a network or interfere with its operation.

Simple Network Management Protocol (SNMP)
A protocol with no inherent security used to query equipment status and modify the configuration of network devices.

Simple Network Management Protocol was designed to automatically provide the configuration details of network devices. As such, "leaky" devices on the public side of your network can provide a wealth of information about the interior of your network.

Nearly every type of network device, from hubs to switches to routers to servers, can be configured to provide SNMP configuration and management information. Interfaces like DSL adapters and cable modems are frequently SNMP configurable, as are many firewalls. Because of the ubiquitous nature of SNMP, it is frequently overlooked on devices that exist outside the public firewall, providing a source of information about your network and the possibility that a device could be remotely managed by a hacker.

Architecture Probes

Architecture *probes* work by "fingerprinting" the sorts of error messages that computers reply with when problems occur. Rather than attempting to perpetrate an attack, probes merely attempt to coax a response out of a system in order to examine that response; hackers may be able to determine the operating system running on the target machine based on the exact nature of the error message because each type of operating system responds slightly differently.

probe
An attempt to elicit a response from a host in order to glean information from the host.

Hackers examine the responses to bad packet transmissions from a target host using an automated tool that contains a database of known response types. Because no standard response definition exists, each operating system responds in a unique manner. By comparing unique responses to a database of known responses, hackers can often determine which operating system the target host is running.

Assume hackers can determine which operating system your public host is running. Plan your defenses such that you do not rely upon security through obscurity. For example, you shouldn't assume a hacker couldn't tell you're running Windows NT Server on your machine because you've blocked identifying ports. You should still take all security measures to secure an operating system, even if you don't think a hacker knows which operating system it is.

Directory Service Lookups

Lightweight Directory Access Protocol (LDAP)
A protocol that is used to read, modify, or write information about users, computers, and other resources on a network to a directory service.

The *Lightweight Directory Access Protocol (LDAP)* is yet another information-leaking service. By providing LDAP information to the public, you provide a wealth of information that might include valuable clues into the nature of your network and its users to hackers. Hackers use the LDAP, as well as older directory services like Finger and Whois, to glean information about the systems inside your network and their users.

Sniffing

sniffing
The process of wiretapping and recording information that flows over a network for analytical purposes.

Sniffing, or collecting all the packets that flow over a network and examining their contents, can be used to determine nearly anything about a network. Sniffing is the computer form of wiretapping. Although encrypted packets can be collected through sniffing, they are useless unless the collector has some means of decrypting them.

Sniffing is technically an information-gathering attack, but it cannot be performed without either gaining physical access to the network or having already successfully compromised a computer inside the network. It's not possible to remotely wiretap a connection except by performing a successful man-in-the-middle attack against it. As such, these exploits are extremely rare.

Attacks

Hackers use a wide variety of attacks against various systems; most of the attacks are custom-tailored to exploit a specific network service. This section profiles the most common and most broadly applicable types of hacking attacks. The remainder of this book explains how to defend against them.

These attacks are profiled in the order of how difficult they are to perpetrate.

Denial of Service

Networked computers implement a specific protocol for transmitting data, and they expect that protocol to transmit meaningful information. When the protocol is implemented incorrectly and sufficient error checking to detect the error isn't performed, a denial of service attack is likely to occur. In some cases, the attacked computer will crash or hang. In other cases, the service being attacked will fail without causing the computer to crash.

Perhaps the most ominous sounding network layer attack is the aptly named Ping of Death. A specially constructed ICMP packet that violates the rules for constructing ICMP packets can cause the recipient computer to crash if that computer's networking software does not check for invalid ICMP packets. Most operating systems perform this check, so this specific exploit is no longer effective, but many other service-specific denial of service attacks exist, and more are being discovered all the time.

Many implementations of DNS, RPC, and WINS are particularly vulnerable to random information being sent to their ports. Some implementations of DNS also crash if they receive a DNS response without having first sent a DNS request.

The more complex a service is, the more likely it is to be subject to a denial of service attack. Denial of service attacks are the easiest and least useful form of attack, and as such, most hackers eschew their use.

Floods

Floods are simple denial of service attacks that work by using up scarce resources like network bandwidth or computer processing power.

For example, SYN floods exploit the connection mechanism of TCP. When a TCP/IP session is opened, the requesting client transmits a SYN message to the host's requesting service and the receiving server responds with a SYN-ACK message accepting the connection. The client then responds with an ACK message, after which traffic can flow over the established bidirectional TCP connection.

When a server receives the initial SYN message, it typically creates a new process thread to handle the client connection requests. This process thread creation requires CPU compute time and allocates a certain amount of memory. By flooding a public server with SYN packets that are never followed by an ACK, hackers can cause public servers to allocate memory and processor time to handle them, thus denying legitimate users those same resources. The practical effect of a SYN flood is that the attacked server becomes very sluggish and legitimate users' connections time out rather than be correctly serviced.

There's a scary future for SYN flood attacks. Since the SYN flood source machine isn't looking for a response, there's no reason why the SYN flood attack software can't simply use randomly generated IP addresses in the source field. This sort of SYN flood could not be discerned from the simple high volume of traffic and would be able to get past SYN flood filters. Some large ISPs have recently begun filtering out packets that claim to come from computers outside the ISP's own network range (which would not be possible for legitimate traffic), which goes a long way toward preventing this sort of attack.

Another type of flood attack, more aptly called an avalanche attack, preys on the direct broadcast addressing features of Network layer protocols like IP and UDP. This causes an avalanche of responses to broadcast queries that are redirected to a host other than the hacker.

flood
A hacking attack that attempts to overwhelm a resource by transmitting large volumes of traffic.

A simple avalanche attack proceeds by flooding a victim's host with ICMP echo request (ping) packets that have the reply address set to the broadcast address of the victim's network. This causes all the hosts in the network to reply to the ICMP echo request, thereby generating even more traffic—typically one to two orders of magnitude more traffic than the initial ping flood.

A more complex avalanche attack proceeds as described but with the source IP address of the echo request changed to the address of a third-party victim, which receives all the echo responses generated by the targeted subnet of hosts. This attack is useful to hackers because they can use a relatively slow link, like a modem, to cause an avalanche of ping traffic to be sent to any location on the Internet. In this way, a hacker with a slower link to the Internet than his ultimate victim can still flood the ultimate victim's pipe by avalanching a higher speed network.

Forged E-mail

Hackers can create e-mail that appears to be coming from anyone they want. In a variation of this attack, they can spoof the reply-to address as well, making the forgery undetectable.

Trojan horse
A program that is surreptitiously installed on a computer for the purpose of providing access to a hacker.

Using a technique as simple as configuring an e-mail client with incorrect information, hackers can forge an e-mail address to an internal client. By claiming to be from someone the client knows and trusts, this e-mail is a form of psychological attack that induces the reader to return useful information, including an installable *Trojan horse* or a link to a malicious website. This is the easiest way to gain access to a specific targeted network.

Internet e-mail does not authenticate the identity of a sender, and many versions of e-mail programs do not log enough information to properly track the source of an e-mail message. By simply signing up for a hosted e-mail account with a false identity, a hacker can deftly hide their identity, even if the e-mail can be traced to its source.

The only feasible defense against e-mail forgery (getting everyone in the world to use public key encryption for all e-mail is infeasible) is user awareness; make sure your users understand that e-mail forgery is possible and constitutes a likely attack mechanism in well-defended networks.

Most popular e-mail clients allow the installation of personal encryption certificate keys to sign e-mail from all internal users. All unsigned e-mail should be considered potentially suspect. Filter executable attachments, such as files with .exe, .cmd, and .bat files, out of e-mail at the firewall or e-mail server.

Automated Password Guessing

NetBIOS
Network Basic Input Output System. An older network file- and print-sharing service developed by IBM and adopted by Microsoft for use in Windows.

Once a hacker has identified a host and found an exploitable user account or services like *NetBIOS*, Telnet, and *Network File System (NFS)*, a successful password guess will provide control of the machine.

Most services are protected with an account name and password combination as their last line of defense. When a hacker finds an exploitable service running on a target machine, the hacker must still provide a valid account name and password in order to log in.

Automated password guessing software uses lists of common passwords, names, and words from the dictionary to attempt to guess high-profile or important account names, such as the root user password on Unix systems or the Administrator account in NT systems. The software typically takes a list of account names and a list of possible passwords and simply tries each account name with each password.

Hackers are using new "common password" lists to make these attacks faster. These lists are derived from the statistical analysis of account information stolen from exploited servers. By combining lists of stolen passwords and analyzing the lists for password frequency, hackers have created lists of passwords sorted by how commonly they are used. This means that if any accounts on your network have relatively common passwords, hackers will get in, and quickly. Hackers use these lists to gain administrative access to servers in as little as a few seconds over the Internet.

Phishing

Phishing refers to the process of "fishing" for accounts and passwords by setting up a fake user interface such as a website that appears to be real and sending an e-mail message to trigger people to log on. (Hackers frequently change the initial *f* in a word to *ph* and the plural *s* to *z* in their jargon.)

For example, you may receive an e-mail message stating that your eBay account needs to be updated for some reason. You click the embedded link in the message and what appears to be the eBay logon page appears. You enter your account name and password and receive an error message that you typed your password incorrectly. When you click the link to try again, you get in and update the information as requested.

What really happened is that a hacker sent you an e-mail containing a link to a web page that they created to mimic exactly the appearance of the eBay site. When you typed in your user account and password, they were recorded and then you were redirected to the legitimate web page, so the second time you entered your password, it worked.

A good phishing expedition can net thousands of legitimate account and password combinations for online banking sites, stock trading sites, or any type of site where financial gain could be made from exploiting someone's credentials.

Furthermore, because people generally use the same password on websites that they use at work, hackers could easily break into work systems (where you work is often indicated by your e-mail address) using phished passwords.

Always confirm the address of any website you clicked from a link that asks for account information of any sort.

Network File System (NFS)
A widely supported Unix file system.

phish
To troll for account credentials by creating a website that mimics the look of a legitimate website and inducing legitimate account holders to log on, usually by sending a link in an e-mail message that appears to be legitimate.

Trojan Horses

Trojan horses are programs that are surreptitiously installed on a target system directly by a hacker, by a computer virus or worm, or by an unsuspecting user. Once installed, the Trojan horse either returns information to the hacker or provides direct access to the computer.

The most useful sorts of Trojan horses are called backdoors. These programs provide a mechanism whereby the hacker can control the machine directly. Examples include maliciously designed programs like NetBus, Back Orifice, and BO2K, as well as benign programs that can be exploited to give control of a system, like netcat, VNC, and pcAnywhere. Ideal backdoors are small and quickly installable, and they run transparently.

Trojan horses are usually carried by e-mail–borne viruses or sent as attachments to e-mail.

Buffer Overruns

Buffer overruns are a class of attacks that exploit a specific weakness common in software. Buffer overruns exploit the fact that most software allocates blocks of memory in fixed-size chunks to create a scratchpad area called a *buffer,* within which it processes inbound network information. Often these buffers are programmed to a fixed maximum size, or they are programmed to trust the message to correctly indicate its size.

Buffer overruns are caused when a message lies about its size or is deliberately longer than the allowed maximum length. For example, if a message says it's 240 bytes long but it's actually 256 bytes long, the receiving service may allocate a buffer only 240 bytes long but then copy 256 bytes of information into that buffer. The 16 bytes of memory beyond the end of the buffer will be overwritten with whatever the last 16 bytes of the message contains. Hackers exploit these problems by including machine language code in the section of the message that is past the buffer end. Even more disturbing is the fact that software is often written in such a way that code execution begins after the end of the buffer location, thus allowing hackers to execute code in the security context of the running service.

By writing a short exploit to open a security hole further and postfixing that code to the buffer payload, hackers can gain control of the system.

New buffer overrun attacks are found all the time. IIS has been hit with so many new buffer overrun attacks that many corporations are moving away from it as a service platform. Automated worms that exploit common IIS buffer overruns have swamped the Net with scanning and copying activity as they search for victims and propagate.

Buffer overrun attacks are the most serious hacking threat at the moment and are likely to remain so for quite some time. Defend against them on public servers by staying up-to-date on the latest security bulletins for your operating system or by using security proxies that can drop suspicious or malformed connections before they reach your server.

Source Routing

The TCP/IP protocol suite includes a little-used option for specifying the exact route a packet should take as it crosses a TCP/IP-based network (such as the Internet). This option is called *source routing,* and it allows a hacker to send data from one computer and make it look like it came from another (usually more trusted) computer. Source routing is a useful tool for diagnosing network failures and circumventing network problems, but it is too easily exploited by hackers and so you should not use it in your TCP/IP network. Configure your firewalls to drop all source-routed TCP/IP packets from the Internet.

    The hacker can use source routing to impersonate a user who is already connected and inject additional information into an otherwise benign communication between a server and the authorized client computer. For example, a hacker might detect that an administrator has logged on to a server from a client computer. If that administrator is at a command prompt, the hacker could inject into the communications stream a packet that appears to come from the administrator and tells the server to execute the change password command, locking out the administrator account and letting the hacker in.

    The hacker also might use source routing to impersonate a trusted computer and write DNS updates to your DNS server. This allows the redirecting of the network clients that rely on the DNS server to translate Internet names into IP addresses so that the client computers go instead to a hostile server under the control of the hacker. The hacker could then use the hostile server to capture passwords.

source routing
A test mechanism allowed by the IP protocol that allows the sender to specify the route that a packet should take through a network rather than rely upon the routing tables built into intermediate routers.

Session Hijacking

Hackers can sometimes *hijack* an already established and authenticated networking connection.

    In order to hijack an existing TCP connection, a hacker must be able to predict TCP sequence numbers, which the two communicating computers use to keep IP packets in order and to ensure that they all arrive at the destination. This isn't necessarily as difficult as it might seem because most current TCP/IP implementations use flawed pseudorandom number generators (explained in Chapter 3, "Encryption and Authentication") that generate somewhat predictable sequence numbers.

    The hacker must also be able to redirect the TCP/IP connection to the hacker computer and launch a denial of service attack against the client computer so that the client computer does not indicate to the server computer that something is wrong. In order to hijack an Server Message Block (SMB) session (such as a drive mapping to a NetBIOS share), the hacker must also be able to predict the correct NetBIOS Frame ID, the correct Tree ID, and the correct user ID at the server level of an existing NetBIOS communications link.

    While an exploit of this nature is theoretically possible, tools for hijacking SMB connections are not readily available to the garden-variety hacker (as

hijack
A complex attack that subsumes an existing authenticated connection between two hosts, thereby allowing a hacker to assume the credentials of the account used to establish the connection.

opposed to TCP hijacking tools, which can be downloaded from the Internet). A properly secured Internet site will not expose NetBIOS to the Internet anyway, however.

TCP/IP isn't the only protocol susceptible to session hijacking—most protocols, including wireless 802.11b and digital cellular phone protocols, are also potentially susceptible to session hijacking.

Man-in-the-Middle Attacks

man-in-the-middle
Any of a broad range of attacks in which an attacking computer redirects connections from a client through itself and then to the ultimate server, acting transparently to monitor and change the communication between the destinations.

Man-in-the-middle attacks are rare and difficult to perpetrate, but they are extraordinarily effective when they work. In a man-in-the-middle attack, the hacker operates between one computer and another on your network or between a client computer on the Internet or other WAN network and your server computer in your secure LAN. When the client computer opens a connection to the server computer, the hacker's computer intercepts it through some means, perhaps via a DNS or DHCP impersonation attack, by rerouting the IP traffic from the client to a compromised computer, or perhaps by using Address Resolution Protocol (ARP) to redirect an Ethernet switch. The hacker computer opens a connection to the server computer on behalf of the client computer. Ideally (from the hacker's point of view), the client will think it is communicating with the server, and the server will think it is communicating with the client, and the hacker computer in the middle will be able to observe all of the communications between the client and the server and make changes to the communicated data.

Depending on the nature of the communications, the hacker computer may be able to use a man-in-the-middle attack to gain greater access to your network. For example, if the connection is an Administrator-level telnet into a server from a client computer, the hacker computer in the middle could (after passing through the logon credentials to gain entry to the server) download the password file from the server to the hacker's computer. On an insecure network such as the Internet, it is difficult to defend against a man-in-the-middle attack. Fortunately, it is also difficult to construct a successful man-in-the-middle attack. The measures you take to protect your network against data gathering, denial of service, and impersonation will help protect you from a man-in-the-middle attack. Nevertheless, you should never connect to your network using an administrative account over an insecure network.

You can use encryption to create secure communications links over a TCP/IP network and you can use third-party authentication packages to ensure that your client computers are communicating directly with a trusted host computer (and vice versa).

Terms to Know

802.11b	ports
buffer overrun	probes
denial of service (DoS) attacks	scanning
Domain Name Service (DNS)	script kiddies
floods	Simple Network Management Protocol (SNMP)
hijack	sniffing
Lightweight Directory Access Protocol (LDAP)	source routing
man-in-the-middle	Trojan horse
NetBIOS	Wired-Equivalent Privacy (WEP)
Network File System (NFS)	Wireless Access Points (WAPs)

Review Questions

1. What is the most common type of hacker?

2. Which type of hacker represents the most likely risk to your network?

3. What is the most damaging type of hacker?

4. What four methods can hackers use to connect to a network?

5. What is the most common vector used by hackers to connect to networks?

6. What are the three phases of a hacking session?

7. What method would a hacker use to find random targets?

8. What type of target selection indicates that a hacker has specifically targeted your systems for attack?

9. Which method of target selection attack is employed by worms to find targets?

10. What activity does sniffing refer to?

11. What is the simplest type of attack a hacker can perpetrate?

12. What security mechanisms are implemented by e-mail to prevent forgery?

13. What would a hacker use a Trojan horse for?

14. Currently, what is the most serious hacking threat?

Chapter 3

Encryption and Authentication

Nearly all modern security mechanisms are based on keeping secrets private to certain individuals. Security systems use encryption to keep secrets, and they use authentication to prove the identity of individuals. These two basic security mechanisms are the foundation upon which nearly all security mechanisms are based.

Encryption

encryption

The process of encoding a plain-text message so that it cannot be understood by intermediate parties who do not know the key to decrypt it.

The primary purpose of *encryption* is to keep secrets. It has other uses, but encryption was first used to protect messages so that only the person that knew the trick to decoding a message could read it. Today, encryption allows computers to keep secrets by transforming data to an unintelligible form using a mathematical function.

Just like simple arithmetic, encryption functions combine the message and the encryption key to produce an encrypted result. Without knowing the *secret key*, the result makes no sense.

For example, let's say I need to hide the combination to a lock. In this case, the combination (also called the *message*) is 9-19-69. To keep things simple, I'm going to add (adding is the *algorithm*) 25 (which is the key) to each of the numbers to produce the encrypted value: 34-44-94. I can post this value right on the combination lock so I won't forget it because that number won't do anyone who doesn't know how to use it any good. I just need to remember the algorithm, subtract, and the key, 25. The encrypted text is worthless without the key. I can also simply tell my friends what the key and the algorithm are, and they can combine that knowledge with the encrypted data to decode the original combination.

secret key

A key that must be kept secret by all parties because it can be used to both encrypt and decrypt messages.

You may have noticed that in this example I used the opposite mathematical operation to decode the encrypted text; I added 25 to encode and subtracted 25 to decode. Simple arithmetic algorithms are called *symmetrical algorithms* because the algorithm used to encode can be reversed in order to decode the data. Since most mathematical operations can be easily reversed, symmetrical algorithms are common.

algorithm

A method expressed in a mathematical form (such as computer code) for performing a specific function or operation.

Although this example may seem simplistic, it is exactly what happens with modern secret-key *cryptosystems*. The only differences are in the complexity of the algorithm and the length of the key. This example, despite its simplicity, shows exactly how all symmetric encryption systems work. Here is another example, using a slightly more complex key. Notice how the key is repeated as many times as necessary to encode the entire message.

symmetrical algorithm

An algorithm that uses the same secret key for encryption and for decryption.

ENCRYPT

D	E	A	R		D	I	A	R	Y	,		I	T	'	S		B	E	E

+

S	E	C	R	E	T	C	O	D	E	S	E	C	R	E	T	C	O	D	E

W	J	D	J	E	X	M	P	V	D	S	E	L	W	E	M	C	Q	I	J

DECRYPT

W	J	D	J	E	X	M	P	V	D	S	E	L	W	E	M	C	Q	I	J

−

S	E	C	R	E	T	C	O	D	E	S	E	C	R	E	T	C	O	D	E

D	E	A	R		D	I	A	R	Y	,		I	T	'	S		B	E	E

The most common use for encryption with computers is to protect communications between users and communications devices. This use of encryption is an extension of the role codes and *ciphers* have played throughout history. The only difference is that, instead of a human being laboriously converting messages to and from an encoded form, the computer does all the hard work.

Encryption isn't just for communication. It can also be used to protect data in storage, such as data on a hard drive. Most modern operating systems like Unix or Windows are configured to allow only authorized users to access files while the operating system is running, but when you turn your computer off, all those security features go away and your data is left defenseless. An intruder could load another operating system on the computer or even remove the hard drive and place it in another computer that does not respect the security settings of the original computer, and your data would be accessible. Encryption solves this problem by ensuring that the data is unintelligible if the correct key isn't provided, irrespective of whether the computer is still running in order to protect the data.

Secret Key Encryption

Our example in the last section was an example of *secret key encryption*. In secret key encryption, the same key is used to both encode and decode the message, so it is said to be symmetrical—because both keys are the same. Secret key encryption requires that both parties know the algorithm and the key in order to decode the message. Until the development of *public key encryption* by cryptographers in the 1970s, secret key encryption was the only type of encryption available.

Secret key encryption works well for keeping secrets, but both parties have to know the same secret key in order to decode the message. There's no secure way to transfer the key from one party to the other without going to extraordinary lengths, like having both parties meet in the same secluded area to exchange keys. There's certainly no way to exchange keys over an electronic medium without the possibility of a wiretap intercepting the key.

One-Way Functions (Hashes)

Hashes are used to verify the correctness of information and are based on mathematical algorithms called one-way functions. Some mathematical functions cannot be reversed to retrieve the original number. For example, let's say that we're going to divide 46,835,345 by 26,585. This results in 1,761 with a remainder of 19,160. So let's say that we have an algorithm that simply returns the remainder (19,160) and discards the quotient (1,761). Now, if we have just the remainder (called a modulus) and one of the original numbers, there's no way to reconstruct the other operand because the quotient has been discarded. The remainder alone does not retain enough information to reconstruct the original number.

cryptosystem
A computing system that implements one or more specific encryption algorithms.

cipher
An algorithm specifically used for encryption.

secret key encryption
Encryption by means of a secret key.

public key encryption
Encryption by means of a public key; an encryption methodology that allows the distribution of an encryption key that does not compromise the secrecy of the decrypting private key due to the utilization of a related pair of one-way functions.

plaintext
An unencrypted text, either before it has been encrypted or after it has been decrypted. The encrypted version is referred to as a ciphertext.

The following illustration shows an extremely simple hash. In this algorithm, two numbers are added, and if the result is even, a binary 1 is the result. If the result is odd, a 0 is the result. The combination of binary digits forms the hash. Because the actual numbers are lost, the hash cannot be reconstructed, but it can be used to determine with reasonable certainty whether or not two plaintexts match. Simple hashes are often called *checksums*. This hashing algorithm is not appropriate for security because there are many other plaintexts that will produce the same result, so the probability of an accidental match is too risky.

HASH

D	E	A	R		D	I	A	R	Y	,		I	T	'	S		B	E	E
? S | E | C | R | E | T | C | O | D | E | S | E | C | R | E | T | C | O | D | E |

| 0 | 1 | 1 | 1 | 0 | 1 | 0 | 1 | 1 | 1 | 0 | 0 | 1 | 0 | 0 | 0 | 0 | 0 | 0 | 1 | = 482433

DECODE

0	1	1	1	0	1	0	1	1	1	0	0	1	0	0	0	0	0	0	1
¿ S | E | C | R | E | T | C | O | D | E | S | E | C | R | E | T | C | O | D | E |

| A | B | B | B | A | B | A | B | B | B | A | A | B | A | A | A | A | A | A | B |

one-way function
An algorithm that has no reciprocal function and cannot therefore be reversed in order to discover the data originally encoded.

Of course, since we can't reconstruct the original number, we can't use *one-way functions* to encode and decode information. But we can use them to be certain that two people know the same number without revealing what that number is. If two people were aware of the original dividend (46,835,345) in the previous scenario and you told them to divide the number they knew by 26,585, discard the whole product, and tell you the remainder, they would both report 19,160—thus proving that they knew the same original number or that they were amazingly lucky, because there is only a 1 in 26,585 chance that they could have guessed the correct remainder. By simply making the number large enough that the odds of guessing the correct remainder are impossibly high, you can use this one-way nonreversible function to prove that two parties know a number without ever revealing what that number actually is to anyone who might overhear you.

For example, let's say a system requires logon authentication in the form of a user providing their name and password. They could simply enter their name and password and the computer could check that against a list of stored passwords. If the passwords matched, the user would be allowed in. But let's say that hackers gained access to the computer. They could steal the list and then have everyone's password. Once other people know a user's password, you can no longer hold that user accountable for their actions because you can't guarantee that they actually performed those actions on a system.

We can't use secret key encryption to encrypt the password file because the secret key would need to be stored on the system in order for the system to decode the password file. Because we've already stipulated that hackers have access to the system, they would also have access to the secret key and could use that to decrypt the password file.

This is a situation in which one-way functions work well. Rather than storing the user's *password,* we can store a *hash,* or the result of a one-way function, instead. Then, when they enter their password, we perform the one-way function on the data they entered and compare it to the hash that's stored on disk. Because only the hash is stored and the hashing algorithm can't be reversed to find the original password, hackers can't compromise the authentication system by stealing this list of password hashes.

Hashes allow a user to prove that they know the password without the system having to know what the password actually is. Protecting passwords is the most common use for using hashing algorithms in computer security.

password
A secret key that is remembered by humans.

hash
The result of applying a one-way function to a value.

Public Key Encryption

Whereas symmetric ciphers like secret key algorithms use the same key to encrypt and decrypt messages, public key encryption uses one key to encrypt a message and a different key to decrypt it, so they are called *asymmetric algorithms*. In a public key encryption system, the encryption key is called the public key because it can be made public. The decryption key is called the *private key* because it must be kept private in order to remain secure.

The problem with secret key encryption is this: Both the sender and the recipient must have the same key in order to exchange encrypted messages over an nonsecure medium. If two parties decide to exchange private messages, or if two computers' network devices or programs must establish a secure channel, the two parties must decide on a common key. Either party may simply decide on a key, but that party will have no way to send it to the other without the risk of it being intercepted on its way. It's a chicken-and-egg problem: Without a secure channel, there is no way to establish a secure channel.

With public key encryption, the receiver can send a public encryption key to the sender. There is no need to keep the *public key* a secret because it can be used only to encode messages, not decode them. You can publish your public key to the world for anyone to use for encoding message they send to you.

When the receiver gets a message that has been encoded with their public key, they can use their private key to decode the message. Revealing their public key to the world for encoding does not allow anyone else to decode their private messages.

asymmetrical algorithm
A mathematical function that has no reciprocal function.

private key
A secretly held key for an asymmetrical encryption algorithm that can be used only to decode messages or encode digital signatures.

public key
A publicly distributed key for an asymmetrical encryption algorithm; a public key can be used only to encode messages or decode digital signatures.

cryptography
The study of codes, ciphers, and encryption.

Public key cryptography is a relatively new development in *cryptography*, one that solves many long-standing problems with cryptographic systems—especially the chicken-and-egg conundrum of how to exchange secret keys. In 1976, Witfield Diffie and Martin Hellman figured out a way out of the secure channel dilemma. They found that some one-way functions could be undone by using a different key for decryption than was used for encryption. Their solution (called public key cryptography) takes advantage of a characteristic of prime and almost prime numbers, specifically, how hard it is to find the two factors of a large number that has only two factors, both of which are prime. Since Diffie and Hellman developed their system, some other public key ciphers have been introduced using even more difficult one-way functions.

One problem that plagues secure public key ciphers is that they are slow—much slower than symmetric ciphers. You can expect a good public key cipher to take 1,000 times as long to encrypt the same amount of data as a good symmetric cipher would take. This can be quite a drag on your computer's performance if you have a lot of data to transmit or receive.

Hybrid Cryptosystems

Although it is much slower than symmetric systems, the public key/private key system neatly solves the problem that bedevils symmetric cryptosystems—exchanging secret keys.

hybrid cryptosystem
A cryptosystem that exchanges secret keys using public key encryption to secure the key exchange and then using the higher speed allowed by secret key encryption to transmit subsequent data.

But there's no need to give up the speed of secret key cryptosystems just because secret keys can't be exchanged securely. *Hybrid cryptosystems* use public key encryption to exchange secret keys and then use the secret keys to establish a communication channel. Nearly all modern cryptosystems work this way.

When two people (or devices) need to establish a secure channel for communication, one of them can generate a random secret key and then encrypt that secret key using the receiver's public key. The encrypted key is then sent to the receiver. Even if the key is intercepted, only the intended recipient, by using their private key, can decrypt the message containing the secret key.

Once both parties have the secret key, they can begin using a much faster secret key cryptosystem to exchange secret messages.

Authentication

authentication
The process of determining a user's identity in order to allow access.

Authentication is used to verify the identity of users to control access to resources, to prevent unauthorized users from gaining access to the system, and to record the activities of users in order to hold them accountable for their activities.

Authentication is used to verify the identity of users logging on to computers, it's used to ensure that software you download from the Internet comes from a reputable source, and it's used to ensure that the person who sends a message is really who they say they are.

Password Authentication

Passwords are the oldest and simplest form of authentication—they've been used since time immemorial to prove that an individual should be given access to some resource. Technically, passwords are secret keys.

Password authentication is simple: By knowing a secret key, you could prove that the individual who invented the secret trusted you with that secret key and that the trust should be bestowed upon you. This sort of password authentication proves only that access to a resource should be allowed—it does not prove identity.

To prove identity, a password must be unique to a specific person. In secure computer systems, this is accomplished by creating user accounts, which are assigned to individuals. The account contains information about who the owner is and includes a unique account name and password.

When a user logs on to the system, they simply type in their account name to assert their identity, and then they provide the password associated with that user account to prove that they are allowed to use that account. If the entered password matches the stored password, the user is allowed access to the system.

Password authentication can fail in a number of ways:

- ◆ There's no way to control password distribution. If the account holder loses control of the password, it can be distributed to anyone. Once a password has been compromised, password authentication can no longer be used to prove identity.

- ◆ Passwords are often simple and easy to guess, and many systems limit passwords to lengths that lend themselves to *brute-force* guessing—that is, simply trying all possible combinations. This can lead to password compromise and is one of the most common ways that hackers gain access to systems.

- ◆ Naïve implementations may not protect the password in transit or may be compromised through simple techniques like *replay*.

Despite the common failure of password-based systems to actually prove identity and restrict access, they are by a wide margin the most common way to secure computers.

brute-force attack
An attack in which every possible combination of values is tried in sequence against a password system. Given an unlimited amount of time, these attacks will always succeed, but they are impractical against long passwords, which could require more time than the age of the universe to crack.

replay attack
An attack in which a secret value like a hash is captured and then reused at a later time to gain access to a system without ever decrypting or decoding the hash. Replay attacks only work against systems that don't uniquely encrypt hashes for each session.

Password Hashing

To prevent hackers from capturing your password from your computer's hard disk or while it transits the network, passwords can be encrypted using a one-way function or hashing algorithm to keep them from being revealed.

In most modern operating systems, the operating system does not compare your password to a stored password. Instead, it encrypts your password using a one-way cryptographic function and then compares the result to the original result that was stored when you created your password. Because the hashing function is one way, it cannot be reversed to decrypt your password.

However, password hashing is susceptible to brute-force indexed decryption. Using this technique, hackers create a "dictionary" of all possible passwords by encrypting every possible password (i.e., AAAAAA through ZZZZZZ in a system limited to six letters) using the same hashing function as the password system and storing the results in a database along with the original text. Then, by capturing your hash, they can look up the matching value in their database of hashed values and find the original password. Although compiling this sort of dictionary can take a long time for a single computer, it is the sort of problem that could be easily distributed over a network of computers (like the Internet) to speed up completion. Once finished, the hashing algorithm would be all but worthless for encrypting passwords and a new algorithm would be required to maintain password security.

Challenge/Response Authentication

One-way hashes are great for preventing password lists from being exploited, but they can't be used securely over a network. The problem is that a hacker might be wiretapping or "sniffing" the network connection between the two computers and could intercept the hashed password and "replay" it later to gain access. This is actually a very common problem that can occur whether or not the password has been hashed. A large number of older TCP/IP protocols like FTP and Telnet are susceptible to sniffing and replay attacks.

Challenge/response authentication defeats replay by encrypting the hashed password using secret key encryption. A challenge and response authentication session works like this:

challenge/response
A method used to prove that a party knows a password without transmitting the password in any recoverable form over a network.

1. The client requests a connection.

2. The server sends a random secret key to the client.

3. The client encrypts the random secret key using a hashed password and transmits the result to the server.

4. The server decrypts the secret using the stored hashed password and compares it to the original secret key to decide whether to accept the logon.

This system works because the password is never transmitted over the network, even in hashed form; only a random number and an encrypted random number are sent, and no amount of cryptographic work can be used to decrypt the encrypted random number because all possible results are equally likely.

Challenge and response authentication can also be used to defeat a brute-force indexed hash decryption as well—as long as the hacker's computer isn't the one you're trying to gain access to. If it is, the hacker can decrypt your hash because they sent you the secret key that you encrypted. By decrypting the secret key, they have your hash and can then compare it to their database of encrypted hashes. For this reason, it's imperative that you never log on to a hacker's system using your system's encrypted hash.

Internet Explorer will automatically hand over an encrypted hash of your Windows logon account name and password to any website that asks for it—behind the scenes and without asking for your permission. This means that by attracting you to a website, hackers could steal your account name and password for your local system. This is one of the many esoteric security flaws that Microsoft has committed in the name of ease of use.

WARNING

Session Authentication

Sessions are used to ensure that, once authentication has occurred, further communications between the parties can be trusted—in other words, that others cannot hijack the connection by forging packets. The authentication that occurs at the beginning of the session can be reliably carried forward throughout the remainder of the packet stream until both parties agree to end the session.

As you know, all modern networking systems are packet based. Packets transmitted from one computer to the next are reconstructed into a communication stream by being put back in their original order using a special number called a sequence number embedded in each packet.

Sequence numbers are exactly that—a number that indicates which packet in the stream a specific packet represents. Sequence numbers could be simple serial numbers, like 1, 2, 3, 4, and so on. Unfortunately, that would be too easy to predict, and a hacker could insert the fifth packet in a stream by simply inserting it into the communication with a sequence number of 5.

To prevent sequence number prediction, sequence numbers are not sequentially generated; they're generated using a special function called a *pseudorandom number generator (PRNG)*, which can reliably create the same sequence of random numbers given a known *seed* number.

session
An authenticated stream of related packets.

pseudorandom number
A member of a set of numbers that has all the same properties as a similarly sized set of truly random numbers, such as even distribution in a set, no predictable reoccurrences, and incompressibility, but that occur in a predictable order from a given starting point (seed).

pseudorandom number generator (PRNG)
An algorithm that generates pseudo random numbers.

NOTE

Computers are very good at performing the same calculations reliably every time. But the property of reliability makes them terrible at generating random numbers. To generate truly random numbers, computers require some real-world external input. But computers can generate numbers that seem to be random—*pseudorandom numbers.*

seed
The starting point for a specific set of pseudorandom numbers for a specific PRNG.

Pseudorandom numbers have all of the same properties as random numbers, such as even distribution in a set, no predictable recurrences, and so forth. They're not, however, truly random because they use the same PRNG algorithm to generate numbers from the same starting number (or seed), hence the exact same series of pseudorandom numbers will be generated every time.

For example, consider the number pi. As we all know, it starts with 3.1415926 and goes on ad infinitum. There is no known sequence to the numbers in pi, and the numbers in the series seem to be completely random one to the next. So, if an algorithm can calculate a specific digit in pi—let's call the function pi, so that pi(473) would give you the 473rd number in pi—the number pi($n+1$) is completely random compared to pi(n). We can generate seemingly random numbers by simply starting at pi(1) and sequencing through the algorithm. This is exactly how pseudorandom number generators work. In fact, a number of them are based on calculating pi or the square root of 2 or other such irrational numbers. In this example, n, or the location in the series, is the seed.

NOTE

PRNGs are terrible for games because games would play the exact same way each time given the same user input and the same starting number, but they're great for the specific purpose of generating session sequence numbers.

If a hacker does not know the seed number for a PRNG, the pseudorandom numbers in a sequence are, for all intents and purposes, completely random and unpredictable. But if a remote computer does know the seed, then the series of pseudorandom numbers is as predictable a sequence as 1, 2, 3. This is how sessions pass authentication from one packet to the next. When the sequence starts with a known encrypted seed number, every packet following in the session with the correct sequence number is known to have a chain of authentication back to the securely transmitted and authenticated seed number.

Public Key Authentication

key
A secret value used to encrypt information.

To use public *key* cryptography for authentication, the system administrator can install a user's public key on the system. For a user to gain access, the system sends a random number to the user, who then encrypts the number using their private key. This number is then sent to the remote system. If the system can decrypt the number using the stored public key and the result is the same random number that was originally provided, then the user has proven that they have the private key.

This proves that the administrator installed the corresponding public key and that the user should therefore be granted access to the system.

Public key authentication is often used when authentication should be performed automatically without user intervention. The systems involved can trade public keys and authentication information without the user interacting with the system. For this reason, public key–based authentication and its derivatives like *certificate*-based authentication are frequently used for machine authentication and for establishing anonymous encrypted sessions such as Secure Sockets Layer (SSL).

public key authentication
Authentication by means of a digital signature.

Certificate-Based Authentication

Certificates are simply *digital signatures* that have themselves been "signed" using the digital signature of some trusted authority, thus creating a "chain" of authentication.

certificate
A digital signature that has been digitally signed by one or more trusted authorities.

Digital signatures are used to prove that a specific piece of information came from a certain individual or other legal entity. Digital signatures do this by performing public key encryption in reverse—that is, the document is encrypted using the private key (which cannot be encrypted by any other key) and decrypted by anyone using the sender's public key.

Because everyone can have the sender's public key, the encrypted information cannot be considered secure or secret, but it can be trusted as authentic because only the person holding the original private key could possibly have created the digital signature.

digital signature
Any identity information encrypted with a private key and therefore decryptable—with a public key. Digital signatures are used to prove the validity of publicly available documents by proving that they were encrypted with a specific secretly held private key.

Typically, a digital signature contains identity information that is easily recognizable, such as the signer's name, physical address, and other easily verifiable information, along with a hash of the entire document that can be used to prove that the signed document has not been modified. If a document has been modified, the hash inside the encrypted signature (which cannot be modified) would not match a new hashing of the document during the authentication process.

The signature is usually appended to the end of the document and appears as a series of hexadecimal or ASCII text. When a document has been hashed and has a digital signature attached to it, it is said to have been "digitally signed."

Certificates are useful when you want to allow wide access to a system by means of distributed authenticators. For example, the government could set up a system whereby public notaries are given digital certificates created by the government. Then, when a member of the public at large wants a certificate that could be used to prove their identity, they could go to a notary public, prove their identity, and have the notary generate a certificate for them. Because that certificate contains a digital signature that can be proven to have come from a notary, which in turn contains a digital signature that can be proven to have come from a government body, anyone who trusts the government body to verify identity can trust that the person using the certificate is who they say they are.

Root Certifying Authority
An organization that exists simply to be trusted by participants in order to provide transitive trust. Root CAs certify the identities of all members so that members who trust the Root CA can trust anyone that they've certified. A Root CA is analogous to a notary public.

In a certificate hierarchy, the ultimate authority is called the *Root Certifying Authority (Root CA)*. Users of the system simply have to trust that the Root CA is a legitimate body. Currently, the vast majority of "rooted" certificates come from a single company, VeriSign, or its subsidiary, Thawte. Entrust is another large Root CA.

Certificates can be used for authentication in the same way that digital signatures can, but authentication systems can be configured to allow access based on higher-level certificates. For example, if your company received a single certificate from a Root CA, the system administrator could use it to generate unique certificates for each department. The department administrators could then generate unique certificates for each user. Then, when you needed to access a resource, the resource server could use the certificate to verify your identity (or the identity of the department that signed your certificate or the company that you work for). If the resource server only cared that you worked for the company, the company signature in your certificate would be the only data that it checked.

Biometric Authentication

biometric authentication
Authentication by means of invariant and unique biological characteristics such as fingerprints or DNA.

Biometric authentication uses physical sensors to detect patterns that uniquely identify a person, such as facial features, fingerprints, handprints, vocal characteristics, blood vessels in the eye, or DNA. These patterns are applied through a hashing algorithm to come up with a hash value that is invariant (in other words, a secret key) and can be matched to a stored value on a server.

Biometric scanning devices can range from simple to complex:

- Microphone (vocal characteristics)
- Optical scanner (fingerprint, handprint)
- Electrostatic grid (fingerprint, handprint)
- Digital video camera (facial features, retinal pattern)
- Deoxyribonucleic Acid Sequencer (DNA)

Currently, low-cost (<$150) fingerprint scanners are popular choices for biometric authentication, but I think they will probably be supplanted by voiceprint recognition because most computers already contain the hardware necessary to perform voiceprint authentication. Voiceprint sensors can also be sensitive enough to fail when stress is detected in the user's voice (such as when they're being coerced into providing access to a system).

Usually, biometric authentication devices use a challenge/response mechanism to ensure that the hashed value never leaves the sensor because it could be captured in transit and "replayed" to foil the authentication system. Because biometric "scans" are never exactly the same twice and must be hashed to generate the key, the system can store a copy of each authentication (or a separate type of hash that is unique) to record a "history" of logins, which can be compared to new attempts to ensure that they are unique and not replays (for example, a recording of a user's voice).

An example of a replay attack against a biometric algorithm would be the recording and playback of a person's *pass phrase*. Without replay detection, there would be no way for the sensing algorithm to determine that a recording (and not the authorized user's actual voice) was being used to gain access to the system. Biometric sensors usually must include additional hardware to ensure that they are not being faked by a replay attack. This usually includes sensors to verify that other requirements of the system are actually in place. For example, a fingerprint scanner doesn't allow access for a person, it allows access for a fingerprint. They can be fooled by something as simple as a color photograph of a valid fingerprint.

What the system designers really want to do is prove that the person with the fingerprint is the one accessing the system, so they must include "live finger detection" in addition to fingerprint detection. Therefore, the system could include other simple biometric sensors such as temperature, pulse, and even blood oxygen sensors that would be extraordinarily difficult to fake.

pass phrase
A very long password consisting of multiple words.

Terms to Know

algorithm	pass phrase
asymmetric algorithms	password
Authentication	private key
biometric authentication	pseudorandom number generator (PRNG)
brute-force	pseudorandom numbers
certificate	public key
challenge/response	public key authentication
ciphers	public key encryption
cryptography	replay attack
cryptosystems	Root Certifying Authority (Root CA)
digital signatures	secret key
encryption	secret key encryption
hash	seed
hybrid cryptosystems	sessions
key	symmetrical algorithms
one-way functions	

Review Questions

1. What is the primary purpose of encryption?

2. Secret key encryption is said to be symmetrical. Why?

3. What is a hash?

4. What is the most common use for hashing algorithms?

5. What is the difference between public key encryption and secret key encryption?

6. What long-standing security problem does public key encryption solve?

7. What is the major problem with public key encryption when compared to secret key encryption?

8. What is a hybrid cryptosystem?

9. What is authentication used for?

10. What hacking attack is challenge/response authentication used to prevent?

11. How are sessions kept secure against hijacking?

12. What is the difference between a random number and a pseudorandom number?

13. What is a digital signature?

14. What is the difference between a certificate and a digital signature?

15. What sort of characteristics are typically used for biometric authentication?

Chapter 4

Managing Security

In This Chapter

- Developing a security policy
- Implementing the security policy
- Updating the security policy in response to new threats

Managing computer and network security is easier than it may seem, especially if you establish a process of continual improvement—to keep the various requirements in perspective and to avoid forgetting about aspects of security.

Security management centers on the concept of a security policy, which is a document containing a set of rules that describes how security should be configured for all systems to defend against a complete set of known threats. The security policy creates a balance between security and usability. The executive management team of your organization should determine where to draw the line between security concerns and ease of use. Just think of a security policy as the security rules for your organization along with policies for continual enforcement and improvement.

Developing a Security Policy

policy
A collection of rules.

The first step in developing a security *policy* is to establish your network usability *requirements* by examining what things users must be able to do with the network. For example, the ability to send e-mail may be a requirement. Once you know what you are required to allow, you have a basis to determine which security measures need to be taken.

TIP

Physically, a security policy document is just a document, not software or software settings. Consider creating your security policy document as a web page that can be stored on your organization's intranet. This makes it easy to update and ensures that whenever someone reads it, they're reading the most recent version.

requirements
A list of functions that are necessary in a system.

After you've got your requirements, make a list of features that users may want but that are not expressly required. Add these to the list of requirements, but be sure to indicate that they can be eliminated if they conflict with a security requirement.

Finally, create a list of security requirements—things users should not be able to perform, protections that should be taken against anonymous access, and so forth.

The list of all of these requirements should simply be a series of sweeping statements like those in the following list:

◆ Users must be able to send and receive e-mail on the Internet. (use requirement)

◆ Users must be able to store documents on internal servers. (use requirement)

◆ Hackers should have no access to the interior of the network. (security requirement)

◆ There should be no way that users can accidentally circumvent file system permissions. (security requirement)

◆ Passwords should be impossible to guess and take at least a year to discover using an automated attack with currently available technology. (security requirement)

◆ Users should be able to determine exactly who should have access to the files they create. (security requirement)

Creating a Policy Requirements Outline

Once you have a list of sweeping statements about requirements and restrictions, examine each statement to determine how it can be implemented. For example, preventing hacker access could be implemented by not having an Internet connection, or more practically, a strong firewall could help ensure that hackers will have no access to your network.

Create an outline, with the requirements as the major headings, and then break them down into methods that could be used to implement them. Include all possible ways that each requirement could be met. For example, to prevent public access, you could implement a firewall or you could simply not have an Internet connection. Don't eliminate possibilities at this point, even if you know that some of them will conflict with other requirements. The idea at this point is to get a complete set of options that will be reduced later.

Continue to analyze the methods that you write down, replacing each with newer and more specific methods in turn, until you are left with a set of policies that can be implemented in outline format. Here is an example:

I. Hackers should have no access to the interior of the network.

   A. Allow no Internet connection.

   B. Implement a firewall for Internet connections.

      1. Block all inbound access at the firewall.

      2. Block dangerous outbound requests:

        (a) Strip e-mail attachments.

        (b) Block downloads via HTTP and FTP.

   C. Allow no dial-up access.

   D. Require call-back security for dial-up access.

When you create this outline, be sure to include every possible method of implementing the security requirement. This will allow you to eliminate those methods that mutually exclude some other requirement, leaving you with the set that can be implemented.

Eliminate Conflicting Requirements

Once you have the complete set of use and security requirements and you've broken them down to specific steps that can be implemented, analyze the document and eliminate those security steps that conflict with network requirements.

It's likely that you will find irreconcilable differences between use requirements and security requirements. When this happens, you need to determine whether the specific use requirement is more important than the conflicting security requirement. The more often you eliminate the security requirement, the less secure the resulting system will be.

Distilling the Security Policy

Once you've pared down the security requirements outline to include only those policies that will work in your organization, it's time to extract the individual rules into a simple list. Then, take that list and group the rules by the *system* that will implement them. For example, in the outline earlier, "Strip e-mail attachments" is one of the individual policy rules and it would be grouped with other

system
A collection of processing entities, such as computers, firewalls, domain controllers, network devices, e-mail systems, and humans.

rules that pertain to e-mail handling. By extracting the individual rules out of the outline and then regrouping them by the systems in which they are implemented, you can create a coherent policy that you can easily deploy. This reorganization changes the security requirements outline, which is organized by requirements, into a final security policy document that should be organized by systems.

Selecting Enforceable Policy Rules

firewall
A device that filters communications between a private network and a public network based on a company's security policy.

Relying on humans to implement security policies rather than establishing automatic security limitations is analogous to painting lines on the road instead of building median barricades. A center double yellow line doesn't actually prevent people from driving on the wrong side of the road; it just makes it a violation if they do. A central barricade between opposing lanes absolutely prevents anyone from driving on the wrong side, so further enforcement is not necessary. When you determine how to implement policy rules, remember to construct barricades (like file system permissions and firewall port blocking) rather than paint lines (like saying, "Users may not check personal e-mail on work computers" or "Users should not send documents as e-mail attachments")—that way, you don't have to enforce the policy and your users won't be tempted to cheat.

group policies
In Windows, a collection of security options that are managed as a set and that can be applied to various collections of user accounts or computer systems.

Security configurations for computers are the barricades that you will set up. These configurations, when documented, are the security policies for the individual devices. *Firewalls* have a rule base that describes their configuration. Windows servers allow you to control use by using *group policies* and *permissions*. Unix network services are individually configured for security based on files that are usually stored in the /etc directory. No matter how automated policies are managed by specific systems, they should be derived from your human-readable security policy so that when new applications are added to the network, the way that they should be configured will be obvious. Most of the remainder of this book details how to implement these automated security policies.

Creating an Appropriate Use Policy

permissions
A security mechanism that controls access to individual resources, like files, based on user identity.

An *appropriate use policy* is the portion of your security policy that users will be required to enforce because the system does not have the capability to enforce it automatically. An appropriate use policy is simply a document for users stating how computers may be used in your organization. It is the part of the security policy that remains after you've automated enforcement as much as you possibly can—it's the painted lines that you couldn't avoid using because systems could not be configured to implement the barrier automatically.

appropriate use policy
A policy that explains how humans are allowed to use a system.

The computer appropriate use policy is a document for users that explains what rules have been placed into effect for the network automatically and what behaviors they should avoid.

NOTE

Your automated policy for firewall configuration, server security settings, backup tape rotation, and other such administrative rules need not be explained to end users because they won't be responsible for implementing them.

The computer appropriate use policy can vary widely from one organization to the next depending on each company's security requirements and management edicts. For example, in some organizations, Web browsing is encouraged, whereas in others, Web use is forbidden altogether.

Users are the least reliable component of a security strategy, so you should rely on them only when there is no way to automate a particular component of a security policy. In the beginning, you may find that your entire security policy has to be implemented through rules for users because you haven't had time to configure devices for security. This is the natural starting point. Ultimately, the best computer appropriate use policy has no entries because all security rules have been automated. This is your goal as a security administrator: to take all the rules that humans have to enforce manually and make them automatic (and therefore uncircumventable) over time.

The following section is a simple example of a single computer use rule.

Policy: Users shall not e-mail document attachments.

Let's look at this policy more closely:

> **Justification:** E-mailed documents represent a threat for numerous reasons. First, e-mail requests for a document can be forged. A hacker may forge an e-mail requesting a document, coercing a user to e-mail the document outside the company. Users may accidentally e-mail documents outside the organization in a mass reply or thinking that a specific user is internal to the company. Second, e-mailing a document nullifies the file system permissions for a document, making it highly likely that a document may be e-mailed to a user who should not have permission to see it. Once a document has been e-mailed, its security can no longer be managed by the system. Last, attachments are a serious storage burden on the e-mail system and cause numerous document versioning problems. They increase the likelihood of malfunction of office and e-mail applications.

> **Remedy:** Users shall e-mail links to documents stored on servers. This way, border firewalls will prevent documents from leaking outside the company and the server can enforce permissions.

> **Enforcement:** Currently, users are asked to not send document attachments. In the future, enforcement will be automatic and attachments will be stripped on the e-mail server and will not be forwarded from our e-mail system.

This example is straightforward and shows the structure you may want to use for individual rules. It's important to include a justification for rules; people are far more likely to agree and abide by a rule if they understand why it exists. Unjustified rules will seem like heavy-handed control-mongering on the part of the security staff. Once the software to implement this rule automatically has been activated, it can be removed from the acceptable use policy because humans will no longer be relied upon to enforce it.

NOTE This is also a good example of why a computer use policy must be tailored to your organization. Although this rule is effective and appropriate for most businesses, it would have been difficult to produce this book without e-mailing attachments. The book production process is largely managed using e-mail attachments.

Security Policy Best Practices

So far, this chapter has introduced a lot of theory but very little practical policy information. This section shares some security best practices to get you started with your policy document.

Password Policies

password
A secret key or word that is used to prove someone's or something's identity.

It's difficult to talk about a security policy without bringing up *passwords*. Passwords are used to secure almost all security systems in one way or another, and because of their ubiquity, they form a fundamental part of a security policy. Hopefully, this won't be the case for much longer—password security is very flawed because the theory is strong but the implementation is weak. In theory, a 14-character password could take so long to crack that the universe would end before a hacker would gain access by automated guessing. But in practice, hackers crack passwords on servers over the Internet in mere seconds because end users choose easily guessed passwords.

Problems with Passwords

Using passwords is the easiest way to gain unauthorized access to a system. Why? Because your network is protected by passwords that average only 6 characters in length and most are combinations of just 26 letters—this yields a mere 320 million possibilities. That may sound like a large number, but cracking software exists that can run through a 100 million passwords per day over the Internet. Since most passwords are common English words or names, they are limited to a field of about 50,000 possibilities. Any modern computer can check that number of passwords against a password file in a few minutes. Try typing your personal password into a word processor. If it passes the spell checker unchallenged, change it.

WARNING A flaw in Windows 2000 allows hackers to use a freely downloadable tool to check passwords over the Internet at a rate of over 72,000 passwords *per minute* by exploiting the new (and rarely blocked) SMB over TCP/IP service on port 445. Never use Windows servers on the public Internet without blocking ports 135, 139, and 445 at a bare minimum.

Though most of your network users may have strong passwords, it only takes one user with a poorly chosen password for a hacker to gain access to your network.

When guessing passwords, most hackers don't bother checking a large number of passwords against a single account—they check a large number of accounts against a few passwords. The more accounts you have on your system, the more likely it is that a hacker will find a valid account name/password combination.

Passwords are generally chosen out of the information people already have to remember anyway. This means that anyone familiar with a network account holder stands a reasonable chance of guessing their password. Also consider that most people don't change their password unless they are forced to, and then they typically rotate among two or three favorite passwords. This is a natural consequence of the fact that people simply can't be expected to frequently devise and remember a strong, unique new password.

Here are some common sources of passwords:

◆ Names of pets or close relatives

◆ Slang swear words (these are the easiest to guess)

◆ Birthdays or anniversaries

◆ Phone numbers and social security numbers

◆ Permutations, such as the name of the account, the name of the account holder, the company name, the word *password,* or any of these spelled backward.

◆ Simple sequences, such as 1234, 123456, 9876, and asdf.

Most people also tend to use the same account names and passwords on all systems. For instance, a person may choose to use their network account name and password on an online service or on a membership website. That way they don't have to remember a different account name and password for every different service they use. This means that a security breach on a system you don't control can quite plausibly yield account names and passwords that work on your system.

Random passwords tend to be difficult for people to remember. Writing passwords down is the natural way for users to solve that problem—thus making their Day-Timer or palm device a codebook for network access.

One major hole in many network systems is the initial password problem: how does a network administrator create a number of new accounts and assign passwords that people can use immediately to all users? Usually, they do so by assigning a default password like "password" or the user account name itself as the password and then requiring that the user change the password the first time they log in. The problem with this approach is that out of 100 employees, typically only 98 of them actually log on and change it. For whatever reason, two of the users don't actually need accounts—because they don't have computers, or they're the janitor, or whatever. This leaves two percent of your accounts with easily hacked passwords just waiting for the right hacker to come along. The best way to handle initial passwords is for the administrator to assign a long and cryptic random password and have the user report to the administrator in person to receive it.

Many membership-based websites don't take measures to encrypt the transmission of user account names and passwords while they are in transit over the Internet, so if people reuse network information on these sites, an interception can also provide valid account names and passwords that can be used to attack your network.

Last, there exists the slight possibility that a membership website may be set up with the covert purpose of gleaning account names and passwords from the public at large to provide targets of opportunity for hackers. The e-mail address you provide generally indicates another network on which that account name and password will work.

Effective Password Management

There are a variety of steps you can take to make passwords more effective. First, set the network password policy to force users to create long passwords. Eight characters is the bare minimum required to significantly lessen the odds of a brute-force password attack using currently available computing power.

Don't force frequent periodic password changes. This recommendation runs counter to traditional IT practice, but the policy of requiring users to change passwords often causes them to select very easily guessed passwords or to modify their simple passwords only slightly so they can keep reusing them. Rather than enforcing frequent password changes, require each user to memorize a highly cryptic password and only change it when they suspect that it may have been compromised.

Mandate that all systems lock users out after no more than five incorrect password logon attempts and remain locked out until an administrator resets the account. This is the most effective way to thwart automated password guessing attacks.

WARNING

The built-in Windows Administrator account cannot be locked out. For this reason, this is the account that hackers will always attempt to exploit. Rename the Administrator account to prevent this problem, and create a disabled account named Administrator to foil attacks against it. You can then monitor access to the decoy account using a Windows 2000 audit policy, knowing that any attempt to use it is fraudulent.

Ask users to select and remember at least three passwords at the same time: a simple password for use on Web-based subscription services, a stronger password for their own personal and financial use outside the company, and a highly cryptic password randomly created by the security manager and memorized by the user for use on the LAN. Tell users that any use of their LAN password outside the company is a violation of the computer acceptable use policy.

Consider disallowing users from changing their own passwords unless you can automatically enforce strong passwords. Have users include punctuation in their passwords to keep them from being exposed to brute-force dictionary hacks or password guessing.

Watch out for users with international keyboards—some keyboards cannot create all the punctuation characters an administrator might include in an assigned password.

————————— *TIP* —————————

Set up e-mail accounts using the employee's real name instead of their account name. Never use network account names on anything that goes outside your organization.

Set up a security/recycling policy that requires printouts to be thrown away in special security/recycling containers, or set up a document shredding policy.

Make sure everyone knows that no one should ever ask for a user's password. If an administrator needs to log on as a user, the administrator can change the user's password, complete the administrative work, and then sit down with the user to change the password back to the user's chosen password. This way a user will know if an administrator has logged into their accounts.

Implement a secure method to assign initial passwords, such as, for example, by having employees report directly to the network administrator to have their password set.

Application Security

Some *applications* are a lot more dangerous to a system's security than others. In particular, any application that contains an *execution environment,* like *Java,* a web browser, or a *macro*-enabled office program, represents special security challenges and should be specifically addressed in your security policy.

What is an execution environment? Quite simply, it's any system that interprets codes and carries out actions on the computer host outside the scope of the interpreting program. What makes that different than, say, codes in a word processing document is that word processing codes affect only the activity of the word processor—they merely indicate how text should be displayed according to a very limited set of possibilities. When the set of possibilities is as wide as a programming language, then you have an execution environment to be feared.

Office Documents

Viruses require an execution environment in order to propagate. A word processor document alone cannot spread viruses. But if you add a programming language to the word processing program (Visual Basic, for example), you create an execution environment that can spread viruses.

application
Software that allows users to perform their work, as opposed to software used to manage systems, entertain, or perform other utility functions. Applications are the reason that systems are implemented.

execution environment
A portion of an application that interprets codes and carries out actions on the computer host irrespective of the scope or security context of the application.

Java
A cross-platform execution environment developed by Sun Microsystems that allows the same program to be executed across many different operating systems. Java applets can be delivered automatically from web servers to browsers and executed within the web browser's security context.

macro
A script for an execution environment that is embedded within an application.

Microsoft has virus-enabled all of their Office applications; Excel, Word, PowerPoint, Outlook, Access, Project, and Visio all contain Visual Basic and can all act as hosts for viruses. Outlook (and its feature-disabled cousin Outlook Express) is especially dangerous because it can automatically e-mail viruses to everyone you know.

Disable macro execution in all Office programs. Unless your company's work is the processing of documents (if your company is a publishing company, for example), there's little reason you should rely on macros in Office. If you really think you need macros, you probably need an office automation system way beyond what Microsoft Office is really going to do for you anyway.

E-mail Security and Policy

E-mail is not secure. The best e-mail policy is simply to make certain that everyone knows that. If a user receives a strange request from someone, instruct them to phone the sender to verify the request and to make sure that it's not a forged e-mail.

attachment
A file inserted into to an e-mail.

E-mailing *attachments* is extremely dangerous. E-mail viruses and Trojan horses are spread primarily through e-mail attachments. Without attachments or executable environments embedded in mail programs, e-mail would not be a significant security threat.

NOTE

E-mailing attachments within the boundaries of a single facility is always the wrong way to work, anyway. It creates uncontrolled versions of documents, eliminates document permissions, and creates an extreme load on e-mail servers, local e-mail storage, and the network. Teach users to e-mail links to documents rather than the documents themselves to solve all of these problems.

ActiveX
An execution environment for the Microsoft Internet Explorer web browser and applications that allow code to be delivered over the Internet and executed on the local machine.

Get rid of Microsoft Outlook and Outlook Express, if possible. These two programs are the platform for every automatic e-mail virus to date. No other e-mail software is written with as little security in mind as these two, and their ease of use translates to ease of misuse for most users. If you can't get rid of Outlook, set your servers up to strip inbound and outbound attachments. Attachments of particular concern are executables, such as files with `.exe`, `.cmd`, `.com`, `.bat`, `.scr`, `.js`, `.vb`, and `.pif` extensions.

Web Browsing Security and Policy

There are four major web browser security problems:

1. Executable programs that are actually Trojan horses, viruses, or *spyware* are often downloaded.

2. Users connect to executable content like *ActiveX* or Java controls that can exploit the local system (this is actually a subset of problem #1).

3. Bugs in web browsers can sometimes be exploited to gain access to a computer.

4. Web browsers may automate the transmission of your network password to a web server.

In theory, Java is supposed to be limited to a security *sandbox* environment that cannot reach the executing host. Unfortunately, this limitation is an artificial boundary that has been punched through many times by various exploits, all of which have been patched by Sun as they were found. But because the limitation is not inherent, more vulnerabilities will certainly be found.

ActiveX is like Java minus any serious attempt to implement security. ActiveX controls are native computer programs designed to be plugged into the web browser and executed on demand—they are web browser plug-ins (modules) that download and execute automatically. There are no restrictions on the actions that an ActiveX control can take.

Microsoft's attempt at security for ActiveX controls is called *content signing,* which means that digital signatures affirm that the code hasn't been modified between the provider and you. It does not indicate that the code is secure or that the writers aren't modifying your computer settings or uploading information from your computer. The theory goes like this: If the ActiveX control is signed, if you trust the signing authority, if you trust the motivation of the code provider, and you trust that they don't have any bugs in their code, go ahead and download. That's far too extenuated to make any sense in the real world, and most people have no idea what it means anyway or how they would validate the signing authority even if they did know what it meant.

These problems are relatively easy to mitigate with a content-inspecting firewall or proxy server. Configure your firewall or proxy to strip ActiveX, Java, and executable attachments (including those embedded in compressed files). This will prevent users from accidentally downloading dangerous content. Avoid using services that rely on these inherently unsafe practices in order to operate.

The automatic password problem is a lot more sinister. Microsoft Internet Explorer will automatically transmit your network account name and a hash of your password to any server that is configured to require Windows Challenge/Response as its authentication method. This hash can be decrypted to reveal your actual network password. Be sure to configure Internet Explorer's security settings to prevent this or use Netscape Navigator instead of Internet Explorer to decouple the web browser from the operating system.

Implementing Security Policy

Once you've completed your security policy document, it's time to translate it from human-readable form into the various configurations that will actually implement the policy.

Implementation varies from one system to the next. A policy of "Strip e-mail attachments on all mail servers" is implemented far differently in Unix Sendmail, Microsoft Exchange, or Lotus Notes. Your policies should not be written specifically to certain systems; they should be general statements that apply to any system that performs the specified function.

sandbox
An execution environment that does not allow accesses outside itself and so cannot be exploited to cause problems on the host system.

NOTE

content signing
The process of embedding a hash in a document or executable code to prove that the content has not been modified and to identify with certainty the author of the content.

Implementation occurs when a security policy is applied to a specific system. But nothing in your policy will help you select which systems to use to implement the policy. A policy that states that "Permissions can be used to block access to certain documents" does not stipulate Windows 2000, Unix, or the Mac OS X systems—they can all perform this function. It does eliminate the choice of Windows 98, MS-DOS, or the original Mac OS because they have no true permissions infrastructure. In order to select systems that match your security policy requirements, make a complete list of possible systems and eliminate those systems that cannot implement your security requirements. Select the systems that can implement your security requirements most easily from the remaining candidates.

Of course, this only works in the theoretical world where security requirements are defined before systems are built rather than after hackers exploit systems in a major way and reveal the lack of security. When you are retrofitting security policy, be prepared for the fact that some of your systems and software may have to be replaced in order to achieve real security.

Applying Automated Policy

The method you'll use to apply automated policy differs for each system in your network. On firewalls, you'll use a web browser or an "enterprise manager" application. In Windows 2000, you'll modify Group Policy objects in the Active Directory. In Linux, you'll directly edit text files in the /etc directory. You may change the startup type of a service or remove operating system components that provide unnecessary services. You may block certain port ranges on your firewall or allow only approved outbound connections.

There is no standardized way to apply an automated policy. A few attempts have been made at automating policy by various vendors, but the lack of consensus and protocol keeps that from happening.

So what is a security administrator to do? That's the hard part. You have to learn and understand the security interface for each type of system in your network. Typically, this will mean understanding the interface for every operating system in use in your network and each security-related device. This is the major reason why consolidating on a single operating system is a good idea.

Most modern operating systems have graphical user interfaces that combine security configuration management into some sort of unified view. In Windows 2000, this is called the Group Policy Management Console. In most firewalls, it's either a web-based user interface or a program that runs on an administrator's computer. The remainder of this book contains details for applying automated policy, but for the most part, the technical manuals for your various systems will teach you how to apply their specific security policies.

Human Security

After everything that can be automated has been automated, humans must implement any parts of the security policy that are left over. They are therefore an integral and necessary component of computer security.

People are the most likely breach in any security environment, including secure networks. Most breaches are completely accidental; few people actually set out to sabotage network security. In fact, most people never find out that they've compromised the network's security. Hackers routinely exploit weaknesses in network security caused by this lack of awareness among users.

For example, humans select memorable passwords by nature and then write them down on Post-it notes so they don't forget them. Employees are sometimes enticed to provide information for favors, money, or higher-paying jobs. Traveling salespeople can leave your office and head for the office of your competition with interesting tidbits of information to trade.

Of course, it is not the intent of this chapter to leave you feeling that your co-workers and business associates cannot be trusted. The vast majority of them can, but it takes only one individual in your entire organization with access to your network to compromise its security. Unfortunately, this means that security restrictions must be applied to everyone because you don't know who is going to slip up in the future.

There are several reasons people cause security problems:

They don't understand security.   Security is not an instinct—it must be taught. You cannot simply tell people to choose strong passwords and expect to have an impenetrable fortress. You must teach security to every person who participates in a secure environment.

They underestimate the threat.   Many people simply don't believe that much of a problem really exists. They've never met or known anyone affected by a hacker, and they've never seen a disgruntled worker cause serious problems. For them, security is an abstraction that simply isn't all that important. As a security manager, your job is to explain the threat clearly. This is getting easier because most people have been affected by a computer virus at least once.

They fail to make security a work habit.   Many people simply don't change easily. They have old habits—and old passwords. Habitual security is hard to force, so make it as simple for users as possible by implementing automated policies that don't rely on people; have policies that are enforced by the network and by the work environment.

They forget about security outside the work environment.   Many people leave their work at work—and their security habits too. They may take an employee list home and throw it in their trash. They may brag to a recent acquaintance about the importance of their job. They may write down their password on a sticky note and leave it in their Day-Timer. These sorts of problems can only be dealt with by reminding people to leave work completely at work—don't talk about it except in vague references and don't transfer company materials between work and home. Remind them never to reuse their work password or account name on other systems, like membership websites.

They passively resist security measures.   Many people see security as an abridgement of their personal liberty and freedoms or as an indication that they are not trusted. Remind them that they are free to live their lives as they please when they are not at work, but that as an employee they have a responsibility to safeguard the company's proprietary information. Explain that security policies by nature must deal with the lowest common denominator of trust and that security should not be viewed as an insult to any single individual.

Human security is problematic because it is the only aspect of total network security not directly controlled by the information system staff. Unlike computers, your co-workers cannot simply be programmed with a strong security policy and let run. They must be taught, reminded, and encouraged.

Security managers are often given the responsibility to enforce security policy without being given the authority to enforce security on end users. You probably won't be able to fire anyone for a major security breach, you can't dock their pay, and you may not even be able to write an administrative letter of reprimand. Without some form of force, the concept of enforcement is meaningless.

lessons learned
A documented failure analysis that is disseminated to system users in order to prevent the a failure from recurring.

Fortunately, humans are gregarious creatures and respond well to group opinion. This means that for serious security breaches, you can use publicity both to embarrass the people at fault and to teach everyone else what not to do. Publicize security failures within the company as part of a *lessons learned* document, usually in the form of an e-mail message to everyone in the company. Whether or not you identify people by name is up to you and probably depends largely on company policy and the severity of the breach (and even if you don't name them, the buzz around the water cooler will). Each lesson learned should be appended to your security policy for further analysis so these breaches can be prevented in the future.

Teaching Security Principles

The best way to avoid security lapses due to human activity is to teach proactive security and to get every user to commit to taking security seriously.

Teaching security is not that difficult. Set up security seminars for groups of employees that are small enough to be interactive—up to about 25 at a time in my experience—and simply go through the computer acceptable use policy item by item. Let's face it: e-mailing (a link to) `caup.doc` to every user in your system will encourage exactly nobody to actually read it. By holding a seminar, you will simply be reading it to them, with a darkened room, a projector, and donuts to mesmerize them into listening.

But you'll also have the opportunity to explain why the policies are important and which threats the company is worried about. You can provide anecdotes about hacker break-ins, what happened at companies that didn't implement policy, and so forth.

Understanding policy is the key to gaining the all-important "buy-in," or the acceptance of a personal responsibility to implement security policy. Without buy-in, users are likely to at best ignore and at worst circumvent an acceptable use policy.

At the end of the security training, present each user with a certificate of completion/contract that lets them agree in writing to abide by the company's acceptable use policy. By requiring their signature on a security contract, you will let users know exactly how serious security is to the organization.

Users should go through the security training seminar when they are hired and once per year thereafter so they can learn about new threats, ask questions about restrictions they've run into, and otherwise stay in the security loop.

Updating the Security Policy

So, you've outlined your security requirements, derived a security policy, refined elements of policy, separated them into human security and automated policy, created an acceptable use policy, read it to the end users, and applied the security settings required by policy for all of your systems.

Now you're done, right?

Wrong. Now you start over.

Security administration is a perpetual cycle because new threats appear all the time. Every time you integrate a new device into your network, you need to consider its security ramifications and update your security policy. In short, you're never done.

The Security Cycle

Security administration is work that must be continually performed to keep a system as free from the loss or compromise of company data as is practicable. As a security administrator, it is your job to determine which security measures need to be taken and whether those security measures have been properly executed. Although the task is daunting, it can be broken down into discreet steps that can be methodically executed. The cycle of security administration is as follows:

- ◆ Identify potential vulnerabilities.
- ◆ Evaluate vulnerabilities to determine how they can be effectively nullified.
- ◆ Determine which of the identified countermeasures you can effectively employ against the vulnerabilities.

- Employ countermeasures.
- Test countermeasures for effectiveness by simulating an attack.
- Monitor server logs and firewalls for evidence of security breaches.
- Investigate any indications of a breach to determine the breach progression and identify new potential vulnerabilities.
- Study public security sources for news of newly discovered security vulnerabilities.
- Repeat the cycle of security administration.

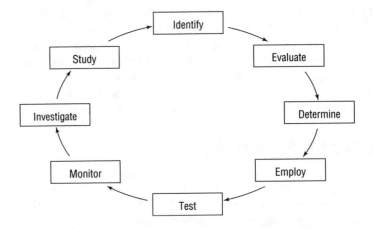

The cyclical nature of security cannot be stressed enough. Unlike a vault, which is static through time and suffers from only a few well-known vulnerabilities, computer networks are not static—they change constantly. Every new addition, be it software or hardware, must be evaluated in the context of security to determine if it will add a new vulnerability to the system. The methods used by hackers to gain access to a system must be continually researched, and system software must be updated as new security fixes are released. Network security is like walking against a treadmill—you have to keep moving just to stay in place because as time goes by, new vectors of attack will be discovered and your network will become less secure without any changes at all on your part.

Terms to Know

ActiveX	lessons learned
application	macro
appropriate use policy	passwords
attachments	permissions
content signing	policy
execution environment	requirements
firewalls	sandbox
group policies	spyware
Java	system

Review Questions

1. What is the purpose of a security policy?

2. What is the first step in developing a security policy?

3. Why is it important to automate security policies as much as possible?

4. Why is an appropriate use policy important?

5. How often should users be required to change their passwords?

6. What is the minimum length of a password that could be considered to be "strong" in the context of today's computing power?

7. Why is the inconvenient policy of enforcing a password lockout after a few incorrect attempts important?

8. Why are execution environments dangerous?

9. Which is more secure: ActiveX or Java?

10. Why doesn't a digital signature mean that an ActiveX control is secure?

Chapter 5

Border Security

Where does your network stop and the Internet begin? That's like asking where one country stops and another starts. The line between them is merely a subjective boundary where one set of rules start and another set of rules stop. But like the border between China and Russia, where one country is built out and densely populated right to the edge while the other is nothing but forest for hundreds of miles, the place where the force of these two sets of networking rules meet delineates a dramatic change in character of the networking landscape.

Firewalls, also called border gateways, are routers whose purpose is to give administrators fine-grain control over which traffic is passed to and from the Internet and which is rejected. Modern firewalls also perform on-the-fly modification of streams, authentication, and tunneling in order to further eliminate threats from the Internet.

Firewalls are the foundation of border security. The strength of your border security is equal to the strength of your firewalls and their proper configuration. Firewall security is by far the most important aspect of Internet security.

In This Chapter

- The principles of border security
- Understanding firewalls
- Fundamental firewall functions, such as packet filtering, Network Address Translation (NAT), and proxy services
- Selecting a firewall that's right for your network

Principles of Border Security

Your network and the Internet both utilize TCP/IP as a connection methodology, and since you have at least some valid Internet addresses, your network is technically just part of the larger Internet. From a security standpoint, "your" network is actually defined as that place where you begin to enforce rules about how the network will be used. Outside those borders, it's no-man's land.

Like nations, you could simply have open borders and enforce security within every city. This would be analogous to having servers and clients placed directly on the Internet and requiring them to each handle their own security. This is exactly how the Internet worked originally. Prior to 1990, there were so few hacking attempts (CERT listed only six for 1988) that serious attempts at security would have been an unnecessary distraction.

TIP

This chapter serves as an introduction to border security. Border security is a vast topic that would easily fill a book. I recommend mine: *Firewalls 24seven, 2nd Ed.* (Sybex, 2002).

But today, enforcing security at every machine within your network would put a serious burden on your users and staff, and you would have no control over the use of bandwidth within your network—hacking attempts could reach inside your network and propagate there. (Universities began having this problem in the early nineties as students began setting up their own web servers, which suddenly became popular and begin consuming tremendous bandwidth.)

Border security theory requires these measures:

demilitarized zone
A security zone with a separate, more relaxed security policy that is used to partition public servers like e-mail and web servers away from the internal network while providing them firewall protection.

Control every crossing.   You can control all the data flowing between your network and the Internet by placing firewalls at every connection to your network. In this case, "every crossing" literally means every connection. Controlling every possible connection to the Internet is the most important measure you can take to control security on your network. A single connection into your network that isn't monitored by firewalls could allow an intrusion. Like a leaking dam, your security policy means nothing if it is not universally enforced. This means that wireless network access points, modems, and any other method of transmitting data must be taken into account (eliminated or firewalled) in order to truly secure your network.

Apply the same policy universally.   If you want to control a specific type of traffic, you have to control it the same way at every crossing because the net effect of your security policy is equal to the loosest policy on any single firewall; if you allow a protocol to pass on one firewall, you're allowing that protocol in, so blocking it on another firewall is essentially pointless.

If you need two different levels of security for different purposes, put a firewall behind the machines that require expanded Internet access so that if they are breached, the remainder of your network is still firewalled. This

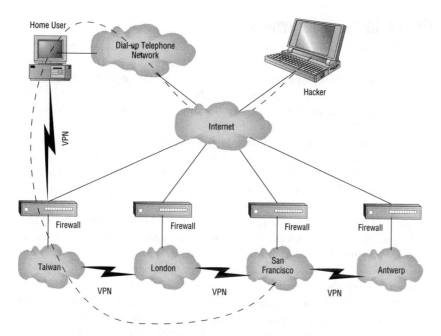

configuration is called a *demilitarized zone* (DMZ). A DMZ is simply a separate interface to which you can apply a separate and more relaxed firewall policy.

Enterprise-level firewalls, like Check Point FireWall-1, allow you to create a single policy and then apply it to all firewalls. Most other firewalls require vigilance on the part of security administrators to ensure that their policies are uniform across their pool of firewalls.

Deny by default. Early firewalls allowed all Internet traffic except that which was specifically blocked. This didn't work for long. To be secure, you must deny all traffic except that which you specifically want to allow. This is important for both incoming and outgoing data. The effect of accidentally downloading a Trojan horse is mitigated if the Trojan horse can't open an outgoing connection through your firewall.

Hide as much information as possible. Firewalls should not reveal anything about the nature of the interior of the network—in fact, they shouldn't reveal their own existence, if possible. When hackers scan for networks using Ping scanners, they rely upon the victim to respond. No response means no victim, so your firewalls should be configured to hide their presence by not responding to these sorts of scans. This also means that technologies like Simple Network Management Protocol (SNMP) should not be used to manage firewalls from the public side and that the administrator should be able to reach the firewall only from the private interface.

Understanding Firewalls

firewall
A gateway that connects a private network to a public network and enforces a security policy by allowing only those connections that match the device's security settings.

border gateway
A firewall.

Firewalls keep your Internet connection as secure as possible by inspecting and then approving or rejecting each connection attempt made between your internal network and external networks like the Internet. Strong firewalls protect your network at all software layers—from the Data link (such as Ethernet) layer up through the Network layer (such as TCP/IP) and up to the Application layer (such as HTTP).

Firewalls sit on the borders of your network, connected directly to the circuits that provide access to other networks. For that reason, firewalls are frequently referred to as border security. The concept of border security is important—without it, every host on your network would have to perform the functions of a firewall itself, needlessly consuming computing resources and increasing the amount of time required to connect, authenticate, and encrypt data in local area, high-speed networks. Firewalls allow you to centralize all network security services in machines that are optimized for and dedicated to the task. Inspecting traffic at the *border gateways* also has the benefit of preventing hacking traffic from consuming the bandwidth on your internal network.

By their nature, firewalls create bottlenecks between the internal and external networks because all traffic transiting between the internal network and the external must pass through a single point of control. This is a small price to pay for security. Since external leased-line connections are relatively slow compared to the speed of modern computers, the latency caused by firewalls can be completely transparent. For most users, relatively inexpensive firewall devices are more than sufficient to keep up with a standard T1 connection to the Internet. For businesses and ISPs whose Internet traffic is far higher, a new breed of extremely high-speed (and high-cost) firewalls has been developed that can keep up with even the most demanding private networks. Some countries actually censor the entire Internet using high-speed firewalls.

Fundamental Firewall Functions

There are three basic functions that modern firewalls perform:

- Packet filtering
- Network Address Translation
- Proxy service

Nearly all firewalls use these basic methods to provide a security service. There are literally hundreds of firewall products on the market now, all vying for your security dollar. Most are very strong products that vary only in superficial details.

You could use devices or servers that perform only one of these functions; for instance, you could have a router that performs packet filtering and then have a *proxy server* in a separate machine. That way, either the packet filter must pass traffic through to the proxy server or the proxy server must sit outside your network without the protection of packet filtering. Both scenarios are more dangerous than using a single firewall product that performs all the security functions in one place.

Many strong firewalls do not actually perform proxy services, but the strongest firewalls do. Proxy services strengthen the security of a firewall by inspecting information at the Application layer—however, very few firewalls actually proxy any protocols other than HTTP and SMTP.

Packet Filtering

Packet filters implemented inside firewalls prevent suspicious traffic from reaching the destination network. Filtered routers protect all the machines on the destination network from suspicious traffic. Filters typically follow these rules:

- ◆ Dropping inbound connection attempts but allowing outbound connection attempts to pass.

- ◆ Eliminating TCP packets bound for ports that shouldn't be available to the Internet (such as the NetBIOS session port) but allowing packets that are required (such as SMTP) to pass. Most filters can specify exactly which server a specific sort of traffic should go to—for instance, SMTP traffic on port 25 should only go to the IP address of a mail server.

- ◆ Restricting inbound access to internal IP ranges.

Sophisticated filters examine the states of all connections that flow through them, looking for the telltale signs of hacking, such as *source routing*, ICMP redirection, and IP spoofing. Connections that exhibit these characteristics are dropped.

Internal clients are generally allowed to create connections to outside hosts, and external hosts are usually prevented from initiating connection attempts. When an internal host decides to initiate a TCP connection, it sends a TCP message to the IP address and port number of the public server (for example, www.microsoft.com:80 to connect to Microsoft's website). In the connection initiation message, it tells the remote server what its IP address is and on which port it is listening for a response (for example, 192.168.212.35:2050).

proxy server
A server that hosts application proxies.

packet filter
A router that is capable of dropping packets that don't meet security requirements.

source routing
An often-abused TCP/IP troubleshooting mechanism that allows the sender of a packet to define a list of routers through which the packet must flow.

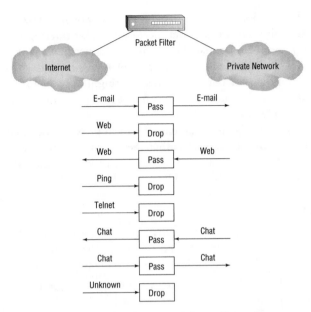

There are three primary types of Network layer firewalls:

◆ *Stateless packet filters,* which do not maintain the state of connections and make pass/drop decisions based purely upon information contained within each individual packet. Stateless packet filters are obsolete unless used along with NAT or proxy services, because they cannot block the complete range of threatening data.

◆ *Stateful inspection* packet filters, which maintain tables of information about the connections flowing through them. They can pass or drop packets based on information contained in earlier packets in a connection stream.

◆ *Circuit-layer switches* (also called TCP proxy servers) terminate a TCP connection on one interface and regenerate it on the other. This allows the interior network to be hidden from the external network (similar to the way a network address translator works) and also completely regenerates the TCP/IP packets, so malformed packets are not passed through. Circuit-layer switches break the routed connection between networks, but they are not specific to higher-level protocols the way application proxies are.

All modern firewalls are either stateful inspectors or circuit-layer switches. Since your firewall inspects all the traffic exchanged between both hosts, it knows that the connection was initiated by an internal host attached to its internal interface, what that host's IP address is, and which port that host expects to receive return traffic on. The firewall then remembers to allow the host addressed in the connection message to return traffic to the internal host's IP address only at the port specified.

When the hosts involved in the connection close down the TCP connection, the firewall removes the entry in its state table (its connection memory) that allows the remote host to return traffic to the internal host. If the internal host stops responding before closing the TCP connection (because, for example, it has crashed) or if the protocol in question does not support sessions (for example, UDP), then the firewall will remove the entry in its state table after a programmed time-out of usually a few minutes.

Filtering does not completely solve the Internet security problem. First, the IP addresses of computers inside the filter are present in outbound traffic, which makes it somewhat easy to determine the type and number of Internet hosts inside a filter and to target attacks against those addresses. Filtering does not hide the identity of hosts behind the filter (but circuit layer switches do).

Filters cannot check all the fragments of an IP message based on higher-level protocols like TCP headers because the header exists only in the first fragment. Subsequent fragments have no TCP header information and can only be compared to IP level rules, which are usually relaxed to allow some traffic through the filter. This allows bugs in the destination IP stacks of computers on the network to be exploited and could allow communications with a Trojan horse installed inside the network.

Finally, filters are not complex enough to check the legitimacy of the protocols inside the Network-layer packets. For example, filters don't inspect the HTTP data contained in TCP packets to determine if it contains data that exploits the web browser or web server on your end of the connection. Most modern hacking attempts are based upon exploiting higher-level services because firewalls have nearly eliminated successful Network-layer hacking (beyond the nuisance of denial of service attacks).

Network Address Translation (NAT)

Network Address Translation allows you to multiplex a single public IP address across an entire network. Many small companies rely upon the services of an upstream Internet service provider that may be reluctant to provide large blocks of addresses because their own range is relatively restricted. You may want to share a single dial-up or cable modem address without telling your ISP. These options are all possible using Network Address Translation.

The difference between NAT and circuit layer switching is somewhat esoteric: They both achieve nearly the same effect. The difference is that NAT merely rewrites the addresses of packets that otherwise flow through the device without changing the rest of the header, whereas circuit layer switches terminate the external TCP connection and generate an entirely new TCP (or UDP) connection on the private side, passing the data inside the TCP/IP packets from the external to the internal interface. The difference is in the complete regeneration of the TCP/IP packets. However, because circuit layer switches take

Network Address Translation (NAT)
The process of rewriting the IP addresses of a packet stream as it flows through a router for the purpose of multiplexing a single IP address across a network of interior computers and for hiding internal hosts.

considerably more resources to perform what is nearly the same function, NAT devices have become more popular. Circuit layer switches remain more secure, however, because they block malformed packet attacks that might flow through a NAT and they are immune to source routed attacks that can flow right through NATs that do not check for them specifically.

NAT was originally developed because it was difficult to get large blocks of public IP addresses and networks frequently ran out of their assigned pool before they could request more addresses from InterNIC. InterNIC began conserving addresses when the Internet boom began because the pool of available addresses was quickly running out. By multiplexing a single public address to numerous interior hosts in a private IP range, a company could get by with as little as one single public IP address.

Fortuitously, Network Address Translation also solves the problem of hiding internal hosts. NAT is actually a Network-layer proxy: On the Internet, it appears as if a single host makes requests on behalf of all internal hosts, thus hiding their identity from the public network.

NAT hides internal IP addresses by converting all internal host addresses to the public address of the firewall. The firewall then translates the address of the internal host from its own address, using the TCP port number to keep track of which connections on the public side map to which hosts on the private side. To the Internet, all the traffic on your network appears to be coming from one extremely busy computer.

NAT effectively hides all TCP/IP-level information about your internal hosts from prying eyes on the Internet. Address translation also allows you to use any IP address range you want on your internal network, even if those addresses are already in use elsewhere on the Internet. This means you don't have to register a large block of addresses from InterNIC or reassign network numbers you were using before you connected your network to the Internet.

On the down side, NAT is implemented only at the TCP/IP level. This means that information hidden in the data payload of TCP/IP traffic could be transmitted to a higher-level service and used to exploit weaknesses in higher-level traffic or to communicate with a Trojan horse. You'll still have to use a higher-level service like a proxy to prevent higher-level service security breaches.

Finally, many protocols also include the host's IP address in the data payload, so when the address is rewritten while passing through NAT, the address in the payload becomes invalid. This occurs with active-mode FTP, H.323, IPSec, and nearly every other protocol that relies upon establishing a secondary communication stream between the client and the server. It is also not possible to connect to a host inside the private network because there is no way to address hosts directly from the Internet. Most NAT implementations work around this problem for these protocols by "holding open the door" for the return path of protocols that they know will be coming back, like FTP. Because the host connection went out through the translator, it knows to expect a return connection attempt from these protocols and it knows which interior computer to translate the return channel for. So as long as a NAT device is "aware" of these problem protocols, it can handle them. New protocols or applications can often be problematic to implement through NAT devices for this reason.

Using an obsolete troubleshooting feature of TCP/IP called "source routing," where a list of IP addresses that determines the route it should take are provided with a packet, it's possible to connect directly through many early NAT implementations. If you are using NAT for security, make sure that the NAT device drops source-routed packets.

WARNING

NAT is also a problem for network administrators who may want to connect to clients behind the NAT server for administrative purposes. Because the NAT server has only one IP address, there's no way to specify which internal client you want to reach. This keeps hackers from connecting to internal clients, but it also keeps legitimate users at bay as well. Fortunately, most modern NAT implementations allow you to create port-forwarding rules that allow internal hosts to be reached.

Windows 2000 and XP, Linux, and many modern Unix operating systems provide this function as part of the operating system distribution. Windows NT does not.

NOTE

Proxy Services

NAT solves many of the problems associated with direct Internet connections, but it still doesn't completely restrict the flow of packets through your firewall. It's possible for someone with a network monitor to watch traffic coming out of your firewall and determine that the firewall is translating addresses for other machines. It is then possible for a hacker to hijack TCP connections or to spoof connections back through the firewall.

Application-layer proxies prevent this. Application-layer proxies allow you to completely disconnect the flow of Network-layer protocols through your firewall and restrict traffic only to higher-level protocols like HTTP (for web service), FTP (for downloads), and SMTP (for e-mail). When a connection is made through a proxy server, the proxy server receives the connection, extracts the high-level protocol (like HTTP), examines it, and makes decisions on its content based on its security policy. The proxy server then creates a new TCP connection on the public interface to the ultimate destination and sends the high-level protocol out through the new connection. Because both the Application-layer and Network-layer protocols are completely regenerated, attacks that rely upon malformed TCP/IP packets or malformed web or e-mail messages are eliminated.

Proxies straddle two networks that are not connected by routers. When a client on the protected network makes a connection to a server on the public side, the proxy receives the connection request and then makes the connection on behalf of the protected client. The proxy then forwards the response from the public server on to the internal network. The following graphic shows this process in detail.

Application-layer proxy
A service for a specific application-layer protocol like HTTP or SMTP that makes connections to the public Internet on behalf of internal private clients. Because application-layer proxies understand the specific protocol for which they proxy, they are able to detect and block malformed or maliciously modified streams.

NOTE Proxies are a good example of how an intermediate system between you and another end system could potentially perform any sort of processing—with or without your permission. A rogue proxy hidden between a client and a server would be performing a man-in-the-middle attack.

Application proxies (like Microsoft Internet Security and Acceleration Server) are unlike network address translators and filters in that the Internet client application is (usually) set up to talk to the proxy. For instance, you tell Internet Explorer the address of your web proxy and Internet Explorer sends all web requests to that server rather than resolving the IP address and establishing a connection directly. Most modern firewalls support transparent proxying, where they appear to be routers but actually perform Application-layer protocol proxying rather than forwarding packets.

Application proxies don't have to run on firewalls; any server can perform the role of a proxy, either inside or outside of your network. Without a firewall, you still don't have any real security, so you need both. At least some sort of packet filter must be in place to protect the proxy server from Network-layer denial of service attacks (like the infamous Ping of Death). And, if the proxy doesn't run on the firewall, you'll have to open a channel through your firewall in one way or another. Ideally, your firewall should perform the proxy function. This keeps packets from the public side from being forwarded through your firewall.

Some firewall proxies are more sophisticated than others. Because they have the functionality of an IP filter and network address translator, they can simply block outbound connection attempts (on port 80 in the case of HTTP) to remote hosts rather than having the client software configured to address the proxy service specifically. The firewall proxy then connects to the remote server and requests data on behalf of the blocked client. The retrieved data is returned to the requesting client using the firewall's NAT functionality, appearing as if no filtering had occurred. Proxies that operate in this manner are said to be *transparent*.

transparent
A proxy server that is capable of automatically proxying a protocol without the client's awareness.

Security proxies are even capable of performing Application-level filtering for specific content. For instance, some firewall HTTP proxies look for tags in HTML pages that refer to Java or ActiveX embedded applets and then strip them out. This prevents the applet from executing on your client computers and eliminates the risk that a user will accidentally download a Trojan horse. This sort of filtering is extremely important because filtering, proxying, and masquerading can't prevent your network from being compromised if your users are lured into downloading a Trojan horse embedded in an ActiveX applet.

You may have noticed that as we've climbed through the networking layers, the security services have gotten more specific. For instance, filtering is specific to IP and then to TCP and UDP. Applications that use IP with other unusual protocols like Banyan Vines must use special high-cost or unusually robust firewalls.

Proxies are extremely specific because they can only work for a specific application. For instance, you must have a proxy software module for HTTP, another proxy module for FTP, and another module for Telnet. As these protocols evolve (HTTP is particularly fast moving), the proxy modules will have to be updated.

Many protocols exist that are either proprietary or rare enough that no security proxies exist. Proxies don't exist for proprietary application protocols like Lotus Notes, so those protocols must either be sent through a Network-layer filter or proxied by a generic TCP proxy that regenerates the packet and simply transfers the payload. SOCKS is a specific form of generic proxy that is sometimes called a circuit-level gateway. Although generic proxying cannot prevent attacks from the content of a protocol, it is still more secure than filtered routing because the Network-layer packets are completely regenerated and thus scrubbed of malformations that might not be detected by the firewall.

Whenever possible, use proxy servers for all application protocols. Consider disallowing application protocols for which you do not have proxy servers. Use high-level proxies capable of stripping executable content like ActiveX and Java from web pages.

Firewall Privacy Services

Firewall Privacy Services are used to allow appropriate connections through the firewall, either from remote users or from firewalls at other sites belonging to the same company. These services are as follows:

- Encrypted authentication
- Virtual private networking

With many firewalls, these services are extra-cost options that must be enabled, but some manufacturers include them at no additional cost. As with basic firewalling functions, these services could be performed by other devices on your network, but they are more secure when combined into a border router.

You don't have to incorporate these functions on your firewall—you could use a VPN device and a firewall in parallel, each performing its separate function. But then you have a situation in which the VPN device itself is not firewalled and could be exploited (this was a serious problem with a widely deployed brand of VPN device) and extra routers are required to properly route outbound traffic through either the VPN or the firewall. By combining VPN and firewall functions on a single device, these problems are eliminated.

Authentication

Authentication allows users on the public network to prove their identity to the firewall in order to gain access to the private network.

Essentially, authentication allows users to "log in" to the firewall itself, which will then allow the sessions from their computer to pass through it. For example, you might use this feature to allow remote salespeople to log into their e-mail accounts. Rather than leaving the IMAP, POP3, or MAPI ports open to the public, the firewall will only open these ports to those IP addresses that have successfully passed an authentication challenge. This keeps hackers from trying to run attacks against those ports, and you're not relying solely on the often-insecure login features of the application itself.

Often, authentication is combined with a VPN, but there's nothing that inherently restricts encrypted authentication from working alone.

Virtual Private Networks

Virtual private networking (also called secure *tunneling*) establishes a secure connection between two private networks over a public medium like the Internet. This allows physically separated networks to use the Internet rather than leased-line connections to communicate as though they were directly connected. VPNs are also called encrypted tunnels.

VPNs are extremely important to TCP/IP security and are the exclusive topic of Chapter 6.

Other Border Services

While not specifically related to TCP/IP security, the following security-related services are easily performed on border firewalls:

♦ Virus scanning

♦ Content filtering

There's no limit to the number of services that could be performed on a border firewall—but increasing the amount of software on any computing device increases the odds that a bug will make the software vulnerable to attack. For that reason, firewalls should only run software that is required to enact your security policy.

Virus Scanning

Virus scanning means searching inbound data streams for the signatures of viruses. Keeping up with current virus signatures requires a subscription to the virus update service provided by the firewall vendor.

Chapter 8 discusses virus scanning options in detail.

Content Blocking

Content blocking allows you to block internal users from accessing certain types of content by category, such as pornography, websites relating to hate groups, pornography, hacking sites, and pornography. Keeping up with the current list of blocked sites for a specific category also requires a subscription.

In my experience, content blocking doesn't work. There are so many new sites of these types cropping up that blocking vendors can't keep track of them. Users often feel as if any site that isn't blocked is fair game, so content filtering frequently turns into a childish game of escalation between users and the IT staff. For example, you can't keep legitimate web users from using Google, but its Google Images search feature could easily be used to browse for unblocked pornography. Filters often "over block" by simply blocking on keywords, which leads to the blocking of legitimate sites that mention, for example, breast cancer or the holocaust.

virtual private network
An encrypted tunnel.

virus scanning
Searching a file or communication stream for the identifying signature of a virus. A virus signature is simply a series of bytes that is deemed to be unique to the virus.

NOTE
---

tunneling
The process of encapsulating packets within IP packets for the purpose of transporting the interior packets through many public intermediate systems. When reassembled at the remote end, the interior packets will appear to have transited only one router on the private networks.

content blocking
A security measure that blocks access to websites based on keywords contained in the content.

A more realistic and manageable approach is to simply tell users that their website visits are logged on the firewall and that they will be asked to justify browsing any suspicious sites. This will keep them from doing anything that violates your policy, allow broad access to legitimate sites, and won't require content-blocking subscriptions. You can often set up logs to include the amount of time a user spent on a specific website, so you can watch for inordinately long periods of random surfing and eliminate "false hits," when a pop-up window in a justifiable site opens up a web page on the seedy side of the Internet.

Selecting a Firewall

There are hundreds of firewalls on the market, running on numerous different platforms. Selecting a firewall that matches your security requirements could take quite a bit of time.

Fortunately for you, the firewall market has shaken out a lot of competitors lately. Among the remaining firewalls, you need only seriously consider the following, which are among the strongest in the field and remain reasonably inexpensive. They are listed here in order of ease of use (easiest to hardest) and security (increasingly strong) order:

SonicWALL Firewalls   The easiest to use and least expensive device-based firewalls. They do not include proxy-level filtering, but they can forward traffic to a proxy. Very similar to Firewall-1 in security and configuration, with a web interface.

WatchGuard Firebox Series   Strong security in a low-priced device-based firewall. These are the only true devices (no hard disk drive) that actually proxy the protocols. Based on Linux and the original open-source Firewall Toolkit (FWTK) underneath, with an administrative application that runs only in Windows.

Symantec VelociRaptor Security Device   A device (with hard disks) version of the strong Raptor security proxy. These are Sun RaQ computers preconfigured with Raptor Firewall.

Fortinet Fortigate Antivirus Firewalls   Fortigate firewalls are very comparible to Sonicwall devices in their overall feature set, but they excel at high-speed antivirus, content blocking, and intrusion detection and blocking. These firewalls feature a custom application-specific microprocessor that uses signature-based detection of Application layer content that provides most of the features of a proxy server at the speed of a packet filter.

Cisco PIX Firewall   A firewall developed entirely from its own original sources by Cisco, PIX is the leader in high-speed firewalling and should be considered any time firewalling circuits faster than 10 Mb/s are required. While other firewalls may have 100Mb/s ports, they don't really firewall at 100Mb/s. High-end PIX firewalls can, and are used by ISPs and larger dot-coms to handle their high-speed firewalling requirements.

There's no reason to select a firewall just because it runs on the same operating system as the rest of your network. Most firewalls that run on operating systems are significantly less secure than device-based firewalls because they rely on the operating system to withstand denial of service attacks at the lower layers and because other insecure services may be running on the operating system.

The majority of firewalls are configured by creating a specific policy called a rule base, which typically lists pass/fail rules for specific protocols and ports. Usually, these rules are searched in top-down order, and the final order in the rule base is a "deny all" rule.

NOTE

Once you've selected a firewall, configuration depends entirely upon the firewall you've selected. You need to make yourself an expert on that specific firewall. This isn't particularly difficult anymore, and there's little reason to worry about learning other firewalls once you've selected one.

Terms to Know

Application-layer proxies	proxy server
border gateways	source routing
circuit layer switches	stateful inspection
content blocking	stateless packet filters
demilitarized zone	transparent
firewalls	tunneling
Network Address Translation	virtual private networking
packet filters	virus scanning

Review Questions

1. Firewalls are derived from what type of network component?

2. What is the most important border security measure?

3. Why is it important that every firewall on your network have the same security policy applied?

4. What is a demilitarized zone?

5. Why is it important to deny by default rather than simply block dangerous protocols?

6. What fundamental firewall function was developed first?

7. Why was Network Address Translation originally developed?

8. Why can't hackers attack computers inside a network address translator directly?

9. How do proxies block malformed TCP/IP packet attacks?

Chapter 6

Virtual Private Networks

Virtual Private Networks provide secure remote access to individuals and businesses outside your network. VPNs are a cost-effective way to extend your LAN over the Internet to remote networks and remote client computers. They use the Internet to route LAN traffic from one private network to another by encapsulating and encrypting unrestricted LAN traffic inside a standard TCP/IP connection between two VPN-enabled devices. The packets are unreadable by intermediary Internet computers because they are encrypted and they can encapsulate (or carry) any kind of LAN communications, including file and print access, LAN e-mail, and client/server database access. Think of a VPN as a private tunnel through the Internet between firewalls within which any traffic can be passed securely.

Pure VPN systems do not protect your network—they merely transport data. You still need a firewall and other Internet security services to keep your network safe. However, most modern VPN systems are combined with firewalls in a single device.

Virtual Private Networking Explained

Virtual private networks solve the problem of direct Internet access to servers through a combination of the following fundamental components:

- IP *encapsulation*
- Cryptographic authentication
- Data payload encryption

virtual private network
A packet stream that is encrypted, encapsulated, and transmitted over a nonsecure network like the Internet.

All three components must exist in order to have a true VPN. Although cryptographic authentication and data payload encryption may seem like the same thing at first, they are actually entirely different functions and may exist independently of each other. For example, *Secure Sockets Layer (SSL)* performs data payload encryption without cryptographic authentication of the remote user, and the standard Windows logon performs cryptographic authentication without performing data payload encryption.

IP Encapsulation

encapsulation
The insertion of a complete Network layer packet within another Network layer packet. The encapsulated protocol may or may not be the same as the encapsulating protocol and may or may not be encrypted.

Secure Sockets Layer (SSL)
A public key encryption technology that uses certificates to establish encrypted links without exchanging authentication information. SSL is used to provide encryption for public services or services that otherwise do not require identification of the parties involved but where privacy is important. SSL does not perform encapsulation.

When you plan to connect your separated LANs over the Internet, you need to find a way to protect the data traffic that travels between them. Ideally, the computers in each LAN should be unaware that there is anything special about communicating with the computers in the other LANs. Computers outside your virtual network should not be able to snoop on the traffic exchanged between the LANs, nor should they be able to insert their own data into the communications stream. Essentially, you need a private and protected tunnel through the public Internet.

An IP packet can contain any kind of information: program files, spreadsheet data, audio streams, or even other IP packets. When an IP packet contains another IP packet, it is called IP encapsulation, IP over IP, or IP/IP. Encapsulation is the process of embedding packets within other packets at the same Network layer for the purpose of transporting them between the networks where they will be used. For example, you may want to connect two Novell networks that use IPX together over the Internet, so you could encapsulate the IPX packets within IP packets to transport them. The end router would remove the IP packets and insert the IPX packets into the remote network.

Why encapsulate IP within IP? Because doing so makes it possible to refer to a host within another network when the route does not exist. For example, you can't route data to a computer inside the 10.0.0.0 domain because the Internet backbone is configured to drop packets in this range. So connecting your branch office in Chicago (10.1.0.0 network) to your headquarters in San Diego (10.2.0.0 network) cannot be accomplished over the Internet. However, you can encapsulate data exchanged between the two networks over the Internet by connecting to the routers (which have valid public IP addresses) and configuring the destination router to remove the encapsulated traffic and forward it to the interior of your network. This is called clear-channel tunneling.

When the 10.0.0.0/8, 172.16.0.0/12, and 192.168.0.0/16 private network blocks were assigned, routing rules were created to ensure that they could not be routed over the Internet backbone. This provides a good measure of security and prevents conflicts with other networks using the same address block. Private networks should always use these ranges for their internal networking and use Network Address Translation or proxying to access the public Internet.

──────── **NOTE** ────────

IP encapsulation can make it appear to computers inside the private network that distant networks are actually adjacent—separated from each other by a single router. But they are actually separated by many Internet routers and gateways that may not even use the same address space because both internal networks are using address translation.

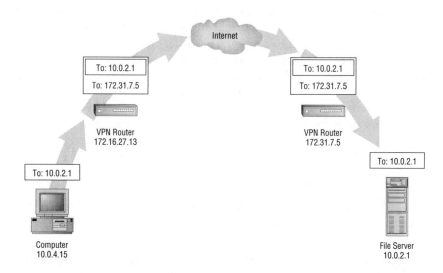

The tunnel endpoint—be it a router, firewall, VPN appliance, or a server running a tunneling protocol—will receive the public IP packet, remove the internal packet contained within it, decrypt it (assuming that it's encrypted—it doesn't have to be), and then apply its routing rules to send the embedded packet on its way in the internal network.

Cryptographic Authentication

Cryptographic authentication is used to securely validate the identity of the remote user so the system can determine what level of security is appropriate for that user. VPNs use cryptographic authentication to determine whether or not the user can participate in the encrypted tunnel and may also use the authentication to exchange the secret or public key used for payload encryption.

Many different forms of cryptographic authentication exist, and the types used by VPNs vary from vendor to vendor. In order for two devices from different vendors to be compatible, they must support the same authentication and payload encryption algorithms and implement them in the same way. Your best bet for determining compatibility is to perform a Web search to make sure all the devices you want to use are actually compatible.

Data Payload Encryption

wide area networks (WANs)
Networks that span long distances using digital telephony trunks like dedicated leased lines, Frame Relay, satellite, or alternative access technologies to link local area networks.

Data payload encryption is used to obfuscate the contents of the encapsulated data without relying on encapsulating an entire packet within another packet. In that manner, data payload encryption is exactly like normal IP networking except that the data payload has been encrypted. Payload encryption obfuscates the data but does not keep header information private, so details of the internal network can be ascertained by analyzing the header information.

Data payload encryption can be accomplished using any one of a number of secure cryptographic methods, which differ based on the VPN solution you chose.

In the case of VPNs, because the "real" traffic is encapsulated as the payload of the tunnel connection, the entire private IP packet, header and all, is encrypted. It is then carried as the encrypted payload of the otherwise normal tunnel connection.

Characteristics of VPNs

local area networks (LANs)
High-speed (short distance) networks existing (usually) within a single building. Computers on the same local area network can directly address one another using Data Link layer protocols like Ethernet or Token Ring and do not require routing in order to reach other computers on the same LAN.

When you consider establishing a VPN for your company, you should understand the advantages and disadvantages of VPNs when compared with traditional *local area networks (LANs)* and *wide area networks (WANs).*

VPNS are cheaper than WANS. A single dedicated leased line between two major cities costs many thousands of dollars per month, depending on the amount of bandwidth you need and how far the circuit must travel. A company's dedicated connection to an ISP is usually made with a leased line of this sort, but the circuit is much shorter—usually only a few miles—and an IP connection is usually already in place and budgeted for. With a VPN, only one leased line to an ISP is required, and it can be used for both Internet and VPN traffic. ISPs can be selected for proximity to your operation to reduce cost.

dedicated leased lines
Digital telephone trunk lines leased from a telephone company and used to transmit digitized voice or data.

VPNs are easier to establish. It typically takes at least two months to get a traditional WAN established using *dedicated leased lines* or *Frame Relay*, and a lot of coordination with the various telecommunications companies is usually involved. In contrast, you can establish a VPN wherever an Internet connection exists, over any mix of circuits, and using whatever technology is most cost effective in each locale.

VPNs are slower than LANs.   You will not get the same performance out of your VPN that you would with computers that share the same LAN. Typical LANs transfer data at 10 or 100Mbps, while the Internet limits VPNs to the slowest of the links that connect the source computer to the destination computer. Of course, WANs are no different; if you linked the same LANs directly via *T1 leased lines,* you would still have a 1.5Mbps (each way) bandwidth limit. Furthermore, you will find that Internet congestion between your VPN endpoints may put a serious drag on your network. The best way to take care of this problem is to use the same national or global ISP to connect your systems. This way, all your data will travel over its private network, thus avoiding the congested *commercial Internet exchange* network access points.

VPNs are less reliable than WANs.   Unexpected surges in Internet activity can reduce the bandwidth available to users of your VPN. Internet outages are more common than Telco circuit outages, and (recently) hacking and Internet worm activity has begun to eat up a considerable amount of bandwidth on the Internet, creating weather-like random effects. How susceptible your VPN is to these problems depends largely on the number of ISPs between your systems.

VPNs are less secure than isolated LANs or WANs.   Before a hacker can attack your network, there must be a way for the hacker to reach it. VPNs require Internet connections, whereas WANs don't, but most networks are connected to the Internet anyway. A VPN is marginally more vulnerable to network intrusion than a LAN or WAN that is connected to the Internet because the VPN protocol's service port is one more vector for the hacker to try to attack.

Frame Relay
A Data Link layer packet-switching protocol that emulates a traditional point-to-point leased line. Frame Relay allows the telephone companies to create a permanent virtual circuit between any two points on their digital networks by programming routes into their Frame Relay routers.

T1 leased lines
The traditional designator for the most common type of digital leased line. T1 lines operate at 1.544Mbps (as a single channel, or 1.536Mbps when multiplexed into 24 channels) over two pairs of category 2 twisted-pair wiring.

commercial Internet exchange (CIX)
One of an increasing number of regional datacenters where the various tier-1 ISPs interconnect their private networks via TCP/IP to form the nexus of the Internet.

Common VPN Implementations

Although theoretically any cryptographically strong algorithm can be used with some form of IP encapsulation to create a VPN, a few market-leading implementations have arisen—because they are easy to splice together from existing separate tools, because they are the agreed upon standards of numerous small vendors, or because a large vendor implemented them and incorporated them for free into ubiquitous products like operating systems. The common VPN implementations are as follows:

- IPSec tunnel mode
- L2TP
- PPTP
- PPP/SSL or PPP/SSH

Each of these common implementations is detailed in the following sections.

IPSec

security association (SA)
A set of cryptographic keys and protocol identifiers programmed into a VPN endpoint to allow communication with a reciprocal VPN endpoint. IKE allows security associations to be negotiated on-the-fly between two devices if they both know the same secret key.

IPSec is the IETF's standard suite for secure IP communications that relies on encryption to ensure the authenticity and privacy of IP communications. IPSec provides mechanisms that can be used to do the following:

◆ Authenticate individual IP packets and guarantee that they are unmodified.

◆ Encrypt the payload (data) of individual IP packets between two end systems.

◆ Encapsulate a TCP or UDP socket between two end systems (hosts) inside an encrypted IP link (tunnel) established between intermediate systems (routers) to provide virtual private networking.

IPSec performs these three functions using two independent mechanisms: Authenticated Headers (AH) to provide authenticity and Encapsulating Security Payload (ESP) to encrypt the data portion of an IP Packet. These two mechanisms may be used together or independently.

NetBEUI
Microsoft's original networking protocol that allows for file and resource sharing but which is not routable and is therefore limited to operation on a single LAN. As with any protocol, NetBEUI can be encapsulated within a routable protocol to bridge distant networks.

Authenticated Headers work by computing a checksum of all of the TCP/IP header information and encrypting the checksum with the public key of the receiver. The receiver then decrypts the checksum using its secret key and checks the header against the decrypted checksum. If the computed checksum is different than the header checksum, it means that either the decryption failed because the key was wrong or the header was modified in transit. In either case, the packet is dropped.

NOTE

Because NAT changes header information, IPSec Authenticated Headers cannot be reliably passed through a network address translator (although some network address translators can perform translation automatically for a single internal host). ESP can still be used to encrypt the payload, but support for ESP without AH varies among implementations of IPSec. These variations account for the incompatibilities between some vendors' IPSec VPN implementations.

Internet Key Exchange (IKE)
A protocol that allows the exchange of IPSec security associations based on trust established by knowledge of a private key.

With Encapsulating Security Payload, the transmitter encrypts the payload of an IP packet using the public key of the receiver. The receiver then decrypts the payload upon receipt and acts accordingly.

IPSec can operate in one of two modes: transport mode, which works exactly like regular IP except that the headers are authenticated (AH) and the contents are encrypted (ESP), or tunnel mode, where complete IP packets are encapsulated inside AH/ESP packets to provide a secure tunnel. Transport mode is used for providing secure or authenticated communication over public IP ranges between any Internet-connected hosts for any purpose, while tunnel mode is used to create VPNs.

Because IPSec has problems traversing NATs, and because NATs have become ubiquitous, the deployment of IPSec as a common VPN platform is stalling. Vendors have come up with various solutions, the most common of which is to further encapsulate entire VPN sessions inside UDP packets that can be network address translated. These solutions are proprietary and do not necessarily work well across different device vendors. An emerging standard for UDP encapsulation of IPSec VPN traffic is helping to sort out these problems, but it will be a few years before all vendors are compatible with the standard.

Internet Key Exchange

IPSec uses the concept of the *security associations (SAs)* to create named combinations of keys, identifiers of cryptographic algorithms, and rules to protect information for a specific function. The policy (rule) may indicate a specific user, host IP address, or network address to be authenticated, or it may specify the route for information to take.

In early IPSec systems, public keys for each SA were manually installed via file transfer or by actually typing them in. For each SA, each machine's public key had to be installed on the reciprocal machine. As the number of security associations a host required increased, the burden of manually keying machines became seriously problematic—IPSec was used primarily only for point-to-point systems because of this.

The *Internet Key Exchange (IKE)* protocol obviates the necessity to manually key systems. IKE uses private key security to validate the remote firewall's authority to create an IPSec connection and to securely exchange public keys. IKE is also capable of negotiating a compatible set of encryption protocols with a destination host, so administrators don't have to know exactly which encryption protocols are supported on the destination host. Once the public keys are exchanged and the encryption protocols are negotiated, a security association is automatically created on both hosts and normal IPSec communications can be established. With IKE, each computer that needs to communicate via IPSec needs only to be keyed with a single private key. That key can be used to create an IPSec connection to any other IPSec host that has the same private key.

L2TP

Layer 2 Tunneling Protocol (L2TP) is an extension to the *Point-to-Point Protocol (PPP)* that allows the separation of the Data Link layer endpoint and the Physical layer network access point. PPP is the protocol used when you dial into the Internet with a modem—it transfers data from your computer to a remote access server at your ISP, which then forwards the data on to the Internet.

The separation between Data Link layer endpoints and Physical layer endpoints means that, for example, you could outsource a *dial-up modem bank* to your phone company and have it forward the data in the modem conversation to you so that your own routers can extract it and determine what to do with it. You save the cost of expensive telephone banks while retaining the ability to connect directly to dial-up users.

Layer 2 Tunneling Protocol (L2TP)
An industry-standard protocol for separating the Data Link layer transmission of packets from the flow control, session, authentication, compression, and encryption protocols. L2TP is typically used for remote access applications and is the successor to PPP.

Point-to-Point Protocol (PPP)
A protocol originally developed to allow modem links to carry different types of Network layer protocols like TCP/IP, IPX, NetBEUI, and AppleTalk. PPP includes authentication and protocol negotiation as well as control signals between the two points, but does not allow for addressing because only two participants are involved in the communication.

dial-up modem bank
A collection of modems that are connected to a high-speed network and are dedicated to the task of answering calls from the modems of end users, thereby connecting them to the network.

Internetwork Packet Exchange (IPX)
The routable LAN protocol developed by Novell for its NetWare server operating system. IPX is very similar to TCP/IP, but it uses the Data Link layer Media Access Control (MAC) address for unique addressing rather than a user-configured address and is therefore easier to configure. IPX routes broadcasts around the entire network and is therefore unsuitable in larger networks.

Like PPP, L2TP includes a mechanism for secure authentication using a number of different authentication mechanisms that can be negotiated among the connecting computers. L2TP is a tunneling protocol—its purpose is to embed higher-layer packets into a protocol that can be transported between locations. Unlike pure IPSec tunneling, L2TP can support any interior protocol, including *Internetwork Packet Exchange (IPX)*, *AppleTalk*, and *NetBEUI*, so it can be used to create links over the Internet for protocols that are not Internet compatible. L2TP packets can also be encrypted using IPSec.

L2TP is also not a transport protocol—it can be transported over any Data Link layer protocol (ATM, Ethernet, etc.) or Network layer protocol (IP, IPX, etc.). LT2P is essentially an "any-to-any" shim that allows you to move any protocol over any other protocol in a manner that can be negotiated between compatible endpoints.

AppleTalk
The proprietary file and resource sharing mechanism for Apple Macintosh computers. Recent versions of the Mac OS are also compatible with the Windows (SMB) file sharing protocol.

You may have noticed that L2TP supports the three requisite functions to create a VPN: authentication, encryption, and tunneling. Microsoft and Cisco both recommend it as their primary method for creating VPNs. It is not yet supported by most firewall vendors, however, and does not transit network address translators well.

PPTP

Asynchronous Transfer Mode (ATM)
A packet-switched Data Link layer framing protocol used for high-speed digital circuits that is compatible across a wide range of physical circuit speeds. ATM is typically used for intercity and metropolitan area circuits.

PPTP was Microsoft's first attempt at secure remote access for network users. Essentially, PPTP creates an encrypted PPP session between two TCP/IP hosts. Unlike L2TP, PPTP operates only over TCP/IP—L2TP can operate over any packet transport, including Frame Relay and *Asynchronous Transfer Mode (ATM)*. PPTP does not use IPSec to encrypt packets—rather it uses a hash of the user's Windows NT password to create a private key between the client and the remote server. This (in the 128-bit encrypted version) is salted with a random number to increase the encryption strength. Because PPTP does not use authenticated headers, it passes through network address translators easily and is quite simple to forward from a public address to an interior PPTP server on the private network. All versions of Windows, all common distributions of Linux, and the latest versions of Mac OS X include PPTP clients that operate as part of the operating system and are exceptionally easy to configure. Because of its ubiquity, routing flexibility, and ease of use, it is probably the most common form of VPN.

NOTE

L2TP is the successor to PPTP—it is more generalized in that it works over any packet transport, and its encryption strength is far stronger thanks to IPSec encryption. PPTP should be used for legacy compatibility, but new installations should favor L2TP for secure remote access.

Open-source developers for Unix implementations including Linux and the various *open source* BSD derivatives have implemented PPTP to support inexpensive encrypted tunnels with Windows clients. Both client-side and server-side implementations are available that interoperate well with Microsoft's implementation of PPTP. So, while IPSec is still the future of VPNs, PPTP is a pragmatic "here now" solution to cross-platform VPN interoperability.

PPP/SSL or PPP/SSH

PPP (Point to Point Protocol) over Secure Sockets Layer (SSL) or *Secure Shell (SSH)* are two common methods that Unix and open-source operating system administrators employ to create VPNs "on-the-fly." Both methods, which might be considered "hacks" in the Windows world, employ a clever combination of an existing encrypted transport (SSL or SSH) and an existing tunnel provider, PPP.

PPP

Point-to-Point Protocol was originally designed to support multiprotocol transport over serial lines. Originally, the dial-up access world was clearly split into operating system–specific camps; Windows, which supported only Net-BIOS connections over modem links; Macintosh, which supported only Apple-Talk connections; Unix, which supported only Serial Line Internet Protocol (SLIP) connections; and NetWare, which supported only IPX connections to NetWare servers. PPP was developed originally to abstract the protocol away from the connection so that a serial line connection could be established that would then be able to carry any Network layer protocol. So, essentially, PPP creates a Data Link layer connection between endpoints over which a Network layer protocol can be transported—or, in other words, a tunnel.

Because of its flexibility, PPP can be used to create a connection between any two IP systems and then transport IP over the PPP connection. This is an easy way to create IP/IP tunnels without specific operating system support for tunneling. But PPP performs no encryption, so while tunneling is useful, it's not secure.

open source
Software produced by a free association of programmers who have all agreed to make their work available at no cost along with the original source code. Actual licensing terms vary, but generally there are stipulations that prevent the code from being incorporated into otherwise copyrighted software.

SSL

Secure Sockets Layer is a public key encryption protocol developed by Netscape to support secure web browsing. SSL does not perform authentication—its only purpose is to encrypt the contents of a connection between a client and a public server. So SSL performs an essentially "pure" public key exchange—when a client connects to the SSL port on a server, the server transmits an encryption key that the client uses to encrypt its data stream. The client does the same thing, so a bidirectional secure stream can be established. This stream is used to exchange a pair of randomly generated secret keys so that high-speed encryption algorithms can be used.

Secure Shell
A secure version of Telnet that includes authentication and encryption based on public keys.

SSH

SSH is the Unix secure shell, which was originally designed to shore up the serious security flaws in Telnet. Telnet allowed users to connect to a Unix host and establish a remote text console from which the host could be operated. Because Telnet hails from those early days when hackers did not have access to the Internet, it performs no encryption and only simple unencrypted password challenges. SSH shores this up by performing secure authenticated logons using perfect forward secrecy and then by encrypting the communication session between the client and the host. Like most Unix applications, SSH can accept redirection to and from other running applications by correctly constructing "pipes" on the Unix command prompt. Unlike SSL, SSH uses secret key encryption so both parties must know the secret key in advance to establish a connection.

Securing PPP

Given the PPP command built into most modern implementations of Unix and either SSH or SSL, it's a simple task to construct a command that can direct the establishment of an encrypted tunnel and pipe its input and output streams to the PPP command. This, in essence, creates a virtual network adapter on each host system that is connected via PPP to the remote host, which is in turn encrypted by either SSH or SSL.

The security of a system like this is based mostly on the security of the underlying cryptosystem—SSL or SSH. If the administrator has done his homework and knows for certain the identity of the hosts involved in the connection, these connection methods can be as secure as PPTP or L2TP.

NOTE   **Although the implementation differs in the way authentication is handled, PPTP is analogous to PPP over SSL and provides basically equivalent security.**

VPN Best Practices

Virtual private networks are convenient, but they can also create gaping security holes in your network. The following practices will help you avoid trouble.

Use a real firewall.   As with every other security component, the best way to ensure that you have comprehensive security is to combine security functions on a single machine. Firewalls make ideal VPN endpoints because they can route translated packets between private systems. If your VPN solution weren't combined with your NAT solution, you'd have to open some route through your firewall for the VPN software or the NAT software, either of which could create a vector for attack.

Real firewalls are also most likely to use provably secure encryption and authentication methods, and their vendors are more likely to have implemented the protocol correctly. Ideally, you'd be able to find an open-source firewall whose source code you (and everyone else) could inspect for discernable problems.

Secure the base operating system.   No VPN solution provides effective security if the operating system of the machine is not secure. Presumably, the firewall will protect the base operating system from attack, which is another reason you should combine your VPN solution with your firewall.

Implementing any sort of VPN endpoint on a server without also implementing strong filtering is asking for trouble—without a secure base operating system, the VPN can be easily hacked to gain access to your network from anywhere.

Use a single ISP.   Using a single ISP to connect all the hosts acting as tunnel endpoints will increase both the speed and security of your tunnel because ISPs will keep as much traffic as they possibly can on their own networks. This means that your traffic is less exposed to the Internet as a whole and that the routes your ISP uses will avoid congestion points in the Internet. When you use multiple ISPs, they will most likely connect through the commercial Internet exchange network access points—the most congested spots on the Internet. This practically guarantees that your VPN tunnel will be slow, often uselessly slow for some protocols.

Choose an ISP that can also provide dial-up service to your remote users who need it. Alternatively, you may choose a local ISP that is downstream from your national ISP because they are also on the national ISP's network and many national ISPs don't provide dial-up service.

Use packet filtering to reject unknown hosts.   You should always use packet filtering to reject connection attempts from every computer except those you've specifically set up to connect to your network remotely. If you are creating a simple network-to-network VPN, this is easy—simply cross-filter on the foreign server's IP address and you'll be highly secure. If you're providing VPN access to remote users whose IP address changes dynamically, you'll have to filter on the network address of the ISP's dial-up TCP/IP domain. Although this method is less secure, it's still considerably more secure than allowing the entire Internet to attempt to authenticate with your firewall.

Use public key encryption and secure authentication.   Public key authentication is considerably more secure than the simple, shared secret authentication used in some VPN implementations—especially those that use your network account name and password to create your secret key the way PPTP does. Select VPN solutions that use strong public key encryption to perform authentication and to exchange the secret keys used for bulk stream encryption.

Microsoft's implementation of PPTP is an example of a very insecure authentication method. PPTP relies upon the Windows NT account name and password to generate the authentication hash. This means that anyone with access to a valid name and password (for example, if one of your users has visited a malicious website that may have initiated a surreptitious password exchange with Internet Explorer) can authenticate with your PPTP server.

Compress before you encrypt. You can get more data through your connection by stream compressing the data before you put it through your VPN. Compression works by removing redundancy. Since encryption salts your data with nonredundant random data, properly encrypted data cannot be compressed. This means that if you want to use compression, you must compress before you encrypt. Any VPN solution that includes compression will automatically take care of that function for you.

Secure remote hosts. Make sure the remote access users who connect to your VPN using VPN client software are properly secured. Hacking Windows home computers from the Internet is depressingly easy and can become a vector directly into your network if that home computer is running a VPN tunnel to it. Consider the case of a home user with more than one computer who is using a proxy product like WinGate to share their Internet connection and also has a VPN tunnel established over the Internet to your network. Any hacker on the planet could then proxy through the WinGate server directly into your private network. This configuration is far more common than it should be.

The new breed of Internet worms that exploit bugs in operating systems are running rampant on the cable modem and DSL networks of home users right now. Here they find a garden of unpatched default installations of Windows. These clients are suddenly the Typhoid Marys of the corporate world, propagating worms to the interior of corporate networks through their VPN connections.

Alert users to the risks of running a proxy or web server (or any other unnecessary service) software on their home machines. Purchase personal firewall software or inexpensive DSL/cable routers to protect each of your home users; remember that when they're attached to your network, a weakness in their home computer security is a weakness in your network security.

WARNING Be especially vigilant about laptops—they travel from network to network and easily pick up worms from unprotected connections. Use strong software firewalls such as Norton Internet Security to protect them.

Prefer compatible IPSec with IKE VPNs. To achieve the maximum flexibility in firewalls and remote access software, choose IPSec with IKE VPN solutions that have been tested to work correctly with each other. IPSec with IKE is the closest thing to a standard encryption protocol there is, and although compatibility problems abound among various implementations, it is better than being locked into a proprietary encryption protocol that in turn locks you into a specific firewall vendor.

IPSec users may have problems connecting from hotels and clients that are behind their own firewalls. To solve this problem, use IPSec implementations that can encapsulate IPSec within UDP, or fall back to using PPTP, which has no problems with network address translation.

Terms to Know

AppleTalk	local area network (LAN)
Asynchronous Transfer Mode (ATM)	NetBEUI
commercial Internet exchange (CIX)	open source
dedicated leased lines	Point-to-Point Protocol (PPP)
dial-up modem bank	Secure Shell (SSH)
encapsulation	Secure Sockets Layer (SSL)
Frame Relay	security associations (SA)
Internet Key Exchange (IKE)	T1 leased lines
Internetwork Packet Exchange (IPX)	virtual private network (VPN)
Layer 2 Tunneling Protocol (L2TP)	wide area network (WAN)

Review Questions

1. What are the three fundamental methods implemented by VPNs to securely transport data?

2. What is encapsulation?

3. Why are VPNs easier to establish than WANs?

4. What is the difference between IPSec transport mode and IPSec tunnel mode?

5. What functions does IKE perform?

6. What common sense measure can you take to ensure the reliability and speed of a VPN?

7. What is the most common protocol used among VPN vendors?

8. What's the primary difference between L2TP and PPP?

9. What encryption algorithm is specified for L2TP?

Chapter 7

Securing Remote and Home Users

In This Chapter

- The two major problems with remote access
- How to protect remote machines
- How to protect your network against remote users

Just as a web browser can connect from a home computer to any web server on the planet, so can any network-enabled computer connect to any other type of server over the Internet. This means that home users can technically connect from their home computers directly to servers at work, just as if they were at work (with, however, a slower connection). In the security-naïve early days of the Internet, many users did just this.

Since the Internet is simply a big network, there are no inherent restrictions on any type of use. Users from home could technically have direct access to files on a file server, could print to a network printer at the office, and could connect a database client directly to a database server.

But the requirement that the company's information technology assets be secured against hackers also secures them against remote home users. The firewalls that drop hackers' connection attempts will also drop remote users' attempts to connect to the network.

By establishing a VPN, you can both secure the transmission and enforce strong authentication, thus ensuring that remote home users will have access while hackers will not.

But VPNs are just the beginning of the real security problem.

The Remote Security Problem

There are two major problems with allowing legitimate remote users to access your network:

♦ Hackers can easily exploit home computers and use those computers' VPN connections to penetrate your network. Worms (which are just automated hackers) do the same thing.

♦ Thieves can steal laptops containing VPN software and keys and use them to connect to your network.

The next two sections explain these problems in detail.

Virtual Private Security Holes

Many companies use VPNs to allow authorized users to securely transit firewalls—the practice has become increasingly common in the last two years due to the convenience and efficiency it allows.

But this seriously undermines your network security policy. The problem is that hackers can quite easily exploit home computers that have not themselves been secured. And if that home computer has a VPN connection to your network, hackers can relay through the home computer and through the firewall via the virtual private tunnel. Most businesses do not attempt to enforce any sort of security requirements for remote home users because they don't own the equipment and they can't really prevent users from circumventing security measures on their own computers.

This means that, in effect, every remote VPN connection you allow into your network is a potential vector for hackers to exploit.

Laptops

Laptops are an extraordinary convenience, especially for users who travel extensively. But they suffer from two very serious security problems.

First, laptops are the Typhoid Marys of the computer world. They connect to networks all over the place, within your organization and the organizations of your business partners, at Internet cafes and hotels, and on home networks. Any worms in these locations can easily jump to laptops, hibernate there, and then infect your network when the laptop is again attached to it. Infection by worms brought in on laptops or transferred from home computers over a VPN is now the most likely way that infections slip past corporate firewalls.

Second, an amazing number of laptops are stolen every year. We all know that airports, hotels, taxis, and rental cars are obvious places from which a laptop may be stolen, but according to the FBI, 75 percent of all computer theft is perpetrated by employees or contractors of the business that experiences the loss. In 2000, nearly 400,000 laptops were stolen in the United States. Generally, 1 out of every

14 laptops will be stolen within 12 months of purchase, and 65 percent of companies that use laptops have reported that at least one of their laptops has been stolen. The FBI reports that 57 percent of corporate crimes (of all sorts) are eventually traced back to a stolen laptop that contained proprietary secrets or provided both the means and the information necessary to remotely penetrate the corporate network. While losing the hardware is an expensive inconvenience, losing the data can often be devastating. Loss of work done is bad enough, but the loss of proprietary secrets can potentially ruin a company.

But, when a laptop is stolen, worse than all of that is losing control of security keys and VPN software that could allow the thief to directly access your network. Many people never consider that "one-click" convenience to attach to the VPN using stored keys means that their laptop is essentially a portal into the network for anyone. Keep in mind that passwords in Windows 2000 and NTFS file system permissions are really just user-grade security efforts that any Windows administrator or competent hacker could easily defeat.

Protecting Remote Machines

Protecting remote machines from exploitation is actually pretty easy, but it requires diligence and constant monitoring. Diligence because you must protect every remote computer that you allow to connect to your machine. Just one unprotected machine connecting to your network allows a potential vector in, and with the contemporary threat of automated Internet worms, it's likely that every computer that can be exploited will be exploited—it's just a matter of time.

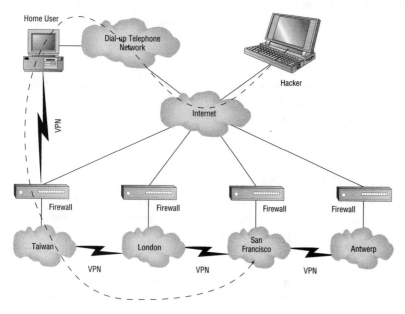

Monitoring is required to discover when a remote machine has become unprotected for some reason. The easiest way to monitor remote networks is to use the same tools that hackers use to find them: port scanners. By setting up a scriptable port scanner to constantly check for ports that a hacker might exploit across the entire range of remote computers, you can discover and close those ports. For machines that do not have fixed IP addresses, a clever administrator could create a script that receives the VPN client's public IP address, scans it, and then drops the VPN connection if the machine might be exploitable.

Due Diligence

A perfect example of the necessity for constant diligence is my own failure to protect my laptop. Even though I completely understand the risks of unprotected Internet access, I once forgot to enable a software firewall on my laptop when I was connected to an unprotected Internet connection. Frankly, I was so used to working behind a firewall that I forgot that the Internet connection at my ISP's co-location facility was not secure. During just the 15 minutes that I was using this connection, before I remembered that it was not secure, my computer had already been scanned and was in the process of uploading the Code Red worm when I stopped it and enabled its software firewall. It was only the unusual activity of the hard disk light that alerted me to the fact that something was going on. So I've since mandated that firewalling software should be left enabled by default on all laptops at my firm, except when the laptops are being used for network sniffing and ping scanning (which the firewall software will interfere with if enabled).

VPN Connections

You need to provide the same sort of firewall protection for remote users that you provide to your network in order to properly secure a computer that will be connecting to your network via VPN.

There are two methods you can use: provide an actual firewall for home users, or provide software firewall applications.

Software Firewall Applications

personal firewall applications
Software programs that protect an individual computer from intrusion by filtering all communications that enter through network connections.

Software-based PC *personal firewall applications* like Symantec's Norton Internet Security and ZoneAlarm are excellent ways to prevent direct intrusion into a client computer. But they can cause problems for users because they get in the way of file sharing and can cause other similar problems for those who want to use networking at home.

VPN *software clients,* which are required to connect to the company network and must operate on the same computer as the software firewall filters, are notoriously hard to use and glitchy. They are usually difficult to set up, and they frequently cause problems for the host operating system because the software tends to require very specific versions of certain operating system files. It's likely that upgrading to a new service pack will cause problems for these programs, and it's certain that upgrading to a new operating system will. They also tend to not play well with software firewall filters because the filters block the protocols that the VPN software requires to establish the connection.

The only way to figure out exactly what's going to work and what isn't is to take the VPN software client software that allows remote users to connect to your company firewall and test it with various software firewall applications that you are considering to protect remote users. Firewall applications vary widely in both software quality and feature set. Many of them aren't as secure as they seem, and some cause serious problems for the computers that they are installed upon. Testing is crucial to uncovering these problems before the software is deployed to end users.

VPN software client
A software application for individual computers that creates VPN connections to VPN servers or devices.

Firewall Devices for Home Users

A vastly better (but slightly more expensive) solution is to simply use a real device-based firewall for every home user. This device category is becoming very broad, with entries from firewall vendors like SonicWALL and WatchGuard that are below the $500 mark and include VPN connectivity. These devices are true firewalls and support features like NAT, VPN, and sophisticated filter setup. When you connect these firewalls to a home user's broadband Internet connection, you are ensuring their security with the same level of protection that you use to ensure your company's security.

But $500 can be expensive when multiplied by the number of remote users you need to support. Fortunately, devices called *NAT routers* made by companies like Linksys, NETGEAR, and D-Link can provide very strong firewall security for less than $100. These devices were originally devised as a way to share a single broadband Internet connection. They are NAT devices, so they automatically block all inbound connections because there's no route to the interior private network. Because they are devices in general, they don't require any software setup on the protected computers and won't interfere with file sharing for interior machines. The latest versions of these devices support IPSec pass-through for a single connection, which allows remote users to use VPN software from a machine protected by the NAT device. Most of these devices contain an embedded web server for administration, so you just point your web browser to their LAN address to manage them.

Linksys has many versions of its very popular NAT router that are well under $100 and include a full IPSec client, so they can be directly connected to your company LAN to provide all the computers in a home office or even a small branch office with a true VPN connection. They work with almost all IPSec firewalls. When you consider that VPN client software typically runs $70 per client,

NAT routers
Small routers that provide the network address translation function of a firewall. Originally used to share a single IP connection for home users, they have recently become more important for home computer security because they are natural firewalls. These devices are frequently marketed as "cable-DSL routers."

and a firewall application costs $40 per client, paying for a VPN-enabled NAT router that requires less administration, causes fewer problems, and is highly reliable makes sense.

Data Protection and Reliability

The laptops of traveling users can't be secured with NAT routers very conveniently, especially if the laptop users frequently use modem connections. For these users, there's little choice but to use VPN clients and software firewall applications.

flash memory
Flash memory is a nonvolatile permanent storage device that is exceptionally reliable and is now used in almost every computing device on the market to store upgradeable boot loaders or operating systems. Flash memory is also used to make a wide variety of convenient memory storage for cameras, PDAs, and laptops in various forms.

To mitigate the loss of control over information when a laptop is stolen, use encryption software like ScramDisk (my personal favorite), Windows 2000 Encrypting File Service, encrypted disk images in Mac OS X, or any of a number of other encryption services. Most of these services work by creating a single large encrypted volume that is mounted like a normal hard disk drive once you enter the key phrases. The Encrypting File Service encrypts individual files and directories based on a key stored in the Registry, which could theoretically be retrieved unless you use Microsoft's Syskey utility for encrypting the Security Accounts Manager portion of the Registry and configure it to request a password at boot time. In any case, any reasonable type of encryption will prevent most hackers and thieves from retrieving anything of value from your computer.

WARNING

You must configure Syskey to ask for a password during the boot process in order for it to remain secure because its default mode (with a key stored in the Registry) is only one iteration of obscurity beyond the SAM itself, and it has already been cracked.

To prevent files from being lost when a laptop is damaged by dropping it, store your documents on a *flash memory* device like a PCMCIA card, Card-Flash, Smart Media, Memory Stick, Secure Digital or MultiMedia Card, or USB Flash memory fob. These devices are solid state and impervious to normal failure and most accidental damage. An easy way to achieve true data protection is to encrypt the contents of the flash device so that if the memory card is lost or stolen, it won't compromise your information.

Backups and Archiving

Laptops almost never get backed up because it's exceptionally difficult to attach a tape drive to them and most other forms of removable media are too inconvenient to bother with.

I break with tradition on this problem and recommend that you don't bother trying to enforce a backup policy for laptops. Rather, it is most effective for users to simply keep their working documents in the laptop on removable flash memory, which isn't going to fail when the hard disk fails.

Separation of Security

My company uses USB keychain flash memory to store secure information. Our laptops have the encryption software, and the file containing the encrypted disk is stored on the USB keychain, which is kept with each user's car keys. This way, encrypted data isn't lost when the laptops are stolen or broken, and the keychains don't suffer from hard disk failure because they're solid state. Also, the USB interface is ubiquitous (unlike PCMCIA, CardFlash, Memory Stick, or Smart Media memory solutions) and can be mounted on any computer with the encryption software. The encryption software we use performs steganography, so our encrypted disk stores are actually large sound files that remain playable with encrypted data in them, thus fooling anyone who happens to find the keychain into thinking that it's just a dongle with a song on it.

This doesn't protect against theft or accidental loss, however. To protect against those problems, teach users to remove the flash memory whenever they aren't actually using the laptop and store it somewhere safe and not along with the laptop. I recommend using USB keychain–style flash memory for this purpose because people never forget to remove their keychain from the laptop when they're done and they're good about keeping track of their keys.

You might also consider automatically synchronizing user data with an Internet server running the WebDAV protocol when users are connected to the Internet. This is something you could set up to work through your VPN to a server inside your company. On the server side, you only need Microsoft's IIS web server or the Apache server to set up a WebDAV-compatible file storage area. On the client side, use file synchronization software like Iomega's file sync package, or you could use a service like Apple's iDisk service if you use a Mac. Synchronizing user files up to an Internet server when they change keeps a backup copy automatically that your end users never have to think about.

Protecting against Remote Users

Despite all of these security precautions, it remains impossible for you to truly control what happens to computers that are outside of your network. A coworker's child may download a video game demo that contains a Trojan horse that connects back to a hacker and allows them access to your VPN. Or, even more likely, you may click yes to a download request on a web site thinking that it's necessary to view content when the download is actually spyware. Chapter 8 discusses spyware in depth. No firewall device or personal firewall application can prevent these sorts of problems because home users will circumvent the highly restrictive policies that would be required to mitigate them.

Windows Terminal Services
A service of Windows that implements the Remote Data Protocol (RDP), which intercepts video calls to the operating system and repackages them for transmission to a remote user (as well as receiving keystrokes and mouse pointer data from the remote user), thus enabling a low-bandwidth remotely controlled desktop environment in which any applications can be run.

So you have to ask yourself whether allowing VPN access from home users is necessary and wise considering your security posture. You may very well be better off allowing controlled access for specific protocols through your firewall than providing the wide open unencumbered access that a VPN provides. While hackers could attempt to exploit your open protocols, securing a single known open protocol is far easier than securing against the wide range of exploits that could be perpetrated through a VPN.

If users really only need a single protocol to perform their work and that protocol doesn't suffer from known exploits and provides strong authentication, it's a good candidate for simply passing through your firewall.

An example of a protocol that could be reliably used in this manner is *Windows Terminal Services*. Terminal servers provide a broad range of services to users very efficiently and are commonly used to provide low-bandwidth users with access to a network's data.

Secure Shell (SSH)
A secure encrypted version of the classic Telnet application. SSH uses public key cryptography to authenticate SSH connections and private key encryption with changing keys to secure data while in transit.

As long as passwords aren't easily guessed, exposing Terminal Services to the Internet is a lot more secure than opening up VPN connections to your network. Viruses cannot automatically transit through a Terminal Services connection because there's no file services connection. A hacker who has exploited a home user's computer doesn't have any more access to the terminal server than they would have from their own home because they would still need the account name and password for the remote network in order to log in.

Once remote users have logged into Terminal Services, they will have just as much access to applications and just as much ability to perform work as they would have if they were in the building. The relative richness of the protocol is what makes it a good candidate to simply replace VPN accessibility for remote users.

Other protocols that could be candidates for opening to the Internet are *Secure Shell (SSH)*—for text-based applications on Unix machines—and secure web-enabled applications (as long as proper web server security measures have been implemented).

Terms to Know

flash memory	Secure Shell (SSH)
NAT routers	VPN software client
personal firewall applications	Windows Terminal Services

Review Questions

1. Why are VPN connections potentially dangerous?

2. What threats are presented to network security by laptop users?

3. Why are laptops the most likely source of virus infection in a protected network?

4. What percentage of corporate crimes has the FBI traced back to stolen laptops?

5. What software should be used to protect laptops from hackers?

6. What is the best way to protect home computers from hackers?

7. How should you reduce the risk posed by lost information when a laptop is stolen?

8. What is the best way to prevent the loss of data from a damaged or stolen laptop?

9. Are VPNs always the most secure way to provide remote access to secure networks?

Chapter 8

Malware and Virus Protection

In This Chapter

- How viruses operate in your network
- How viruses propagate
- Common types of virus attacks
- How to protect your network from viruses

Malware is a relatively new term that describes software that deliberately behaves in ways that are detrimental to the user of a computer. The term encompasses several types:

- Viruses
- Worms
- Trojan horses
- Spyware

Malware can cause all sorts of unexpected behavior like system crashes, strange pop-up messages, and the deletion of important files. Some extremely clever worms copy themselves using the Internet and can absorb so much bandwidth that they interfere with the proper operation of your Internet connections. Even completely benign viruses that have no apparent ill effects expand the size of executable files and macro-enabled documents like barnacles encrusting a ship's hull.

Understanding Malware

Computer viruses are *self-replicating* malicious programs that attach themselves to normal application programs and documents without the user's awareness or consent. Your system "catches" a virus by running a program that contains one. They are one of the most feared causes of data loss—but, as it turns out, they have more of a reputation than they deserve. More than 90 percent of viruses are completely harmless aside from the computing resources that they waste by propagating. You are much more likely to lose data due to a hardware failure or by human error than due to a virus infection.

Computer worms are automated hacking programs that use one or more specific attacks against running services on a computer to gain access to it. Once the worm has access to the computer, it copies itself over to it and then attempts to propagate from there. Unlike viruses, worms fully deserve the reputation they have. Because they spread so quickly, they can use up bandwidth on a scale that can slow down the entire Internet. User activity (like clicking a download or opening an e-mail) is not required to activate them, so they can spread like water breaking open a dam. And because they work silently behind the scenes, they can easily bring much larger payloads with them—usually a Trojan horse that will allow hackers to manually exploit computers infected by the worm after it has infected the machine. Finally, because worms usually run in the protected memory area used by the operating system rather than the user area used by virus-infected applications, worms are far more likely to cause system crashing.

Trojan horses are programs that listen for connections from hackers and provide ways for the hacker to control your computer. Often, these are simply regular administrative tools like VNC or Telnet that are embedded in a virus or worm. Or they are programs specifically written to listen for a hacker and perform specific tasks on your system.

Spyware is technically legitimate software. Its creators entice users to download it from the Web by claiming that it performs some useful function (such as providing pretty cursors or a feature to keep your system clock adjusted to atomic time), but they omit the fact that it will pop up ads while you work, block the websites of the creator's competition, or collect personal information about you such as your name and e-mail address. Worse, spyware is notoriously poorly written and usually makes such a mess of your system by plugging itself into your browser and operating system that your computer becomes noticeably slower and begins crashing regularly. It also typically does not provide end users with any way to automatically remove it.

Understanding Viruses

To combat viruses effectively, you need to understand how they propagate and what defenses are available.

Computers store two entirely different types of information: *executable code* and *data*. Code specifies how the computer should operate, while data provides the information on which the operation is performed. For example, in the equation 1+1=2, the 1, 1, and 2 are the data and the + and = are code. The difference between code and data is crucial to virus defense because only code is susceptible to virus infection. Viruses can corrupt data but cannot propagate using pure data because data does not provide an execution environment for viruses to run in.

But it's not always clear what is data and what is code. Is a Word document code or data? It's mostly data, but because Word documents can contains *macros* that Word interprets in order to perform complex operations, it can also contain code. The same goes for any macro-enabled application that stores a mixture of code and data in a single document. Applications that look at data and then perform wide-ranging operations based on that data are called *execution environments, interpreters,* or *scripting hosts.*

You could consider any use of data to be interpretation, but for viruses to propagate, the execution environment needs to be complicated enough to allow for self-replication. This is a very high-level function that is typically only available when a scripting host running an interpreted computer language is built into an application.

What does all this really mean? Simple. You don't have to worry about viruses in pictures, audio files, online movies, and other programs that merely edit or display content, but you do need to worry about programs that use content to control the program's behavior. If the control mechanisms are complex enough to allow self-replication to occur, the application could host viruses.

When you search the Web, you'll often see the term *virii* used as the plural for virus. Since *virus* comes from Greek and not Latin, its correct plural is *viruses*, not *virii*. But most hackers don't know that, so they use the term "virii" for the plural.

NOTE

Virus Operation

Viruses have two separate and distinct modes of operation to perform the separate functions of self-replicating and attacking the host:

♦ Propagation code is required for viruses to copy themselves. Without a *propagation engine,* viruses would just be normal programs.

♦ Attack code is included in viruses that have some specific malicious activity to perform, such as erasing data, installing a Trojan horse for further direct attacks, or displaying a message on the screen.

Benign viruses only have propagation code and exist (usually) because hackers are testing a propagation engine and want to determine how far it will spread. Since the virus doesn't do anything, it's likely nobody will discover it, so the virus protection industry won't capture its signature and prevent its movement.

execution environments
Any environment that interprets data as actions and performs those actions. An execution environment might be a microprocessor, a virtual machine, or an application that interprets a script or macro.

interpreter
A programming language application that loads scripts as data and then interprets commands step-by-step rather than by compiling them to machine language.

scripting hosts
Execution environments that can be called from applications in order to execute scripts contained in the application's data.

propagation engine
The code used by a virus to self-replicate.

benign viruses
Viruses that do not destroy data. Benign viruses may display a simple message or may simply propagate without performing any other function.

malignant viruses
Viruses that contain attack code that performs some malicious act.

Malignant viruses include attack code that performs some annoying or damaging act, like deleting files, changing filenames, and so forth. Many malignant viruses are not immediately triggered but lie dormant waiting for a date or an event to occur before executing so that they can propagate before they damage their host.

A Brief History of Viruses

Believe it or not, viruses were invented by accident. Two men who owned a computer store in Pakistan devised a clever on-screen advertisement for their store. They wrote the advertisement so that it would propagate by copying itself to whatever program was loaded until it reached the boot sector, at which point it would flash its advertisement on the screen and copy itself to subsequently loaded files.

This advertisement eventually infected a hacker's computer. The hackers immediately understood the virus's potential to propagate mischief, and thus the Pakistani Brain virus was invented. That same virus engine was modified to become the infamous Stoned virus, as well as the Friday the 13th virus, and a host of others. Each of these viruses relied upon the sharing of programs via floppy disk in order to propagate.

The panic caused by these viruses spawned the virus protection industry. At first, it appeared that the virus makers would forever have the edge, because in the early days of the computer industry, software piracy was somewhat the norm—an environment in which viruses flourished. A lack of understanding and an ignorance of the damage caused by viruses led to a hysteria that was never really justified by the actual threat—oddly parallel to epidemics of biological viruses, which served only to strengthen the analogy between the two.

But as antivirus software became better and protection manufacturers became more savvy, the tide began to turn. And once businesses became more willing to treat antivirus software like a true tool and purchase it, the virus epidemic subsided. With the widespread use of permissions-based operating systems like derivatives of Windows NT and Unix, it's no longer possible for viruses to propagate "up the chain" to the operating system where they can be spread to other applications. In these environments, they sit dormant and can't spread. Since virus protection manufacturers now have far more development manpower than hackers, it's unlikely that old-fashioned executable computer viruses will ever again reach epidemic proportions.

But when new methods of virus propagation appear, it takes virus protection manufacturers days to detect and respond to the new threat. This gives time for the virus to spread without inhibition. So viruses that can spread quickly—by using the Internet and automatic methods like exploiting e-mail programs with scripting hosts (Microsoft Outlook)—can span the globe before the virus scanners are updated. Further complicating the problem is the fact that many users never update their virus protection software, so new types of viruses are not detected.

Understanding Virus Propagation

When you launch a program on any computer, you are directing an existing running program to launch it for you. In Windows, this program is (usually) Windows Explorer. It could technically be many other programs, like the command prompt or Internet Explorer (if you download the program and choose to open it from its current location). On a Macintosh it's usually the Finder, and in Unix it's the command shell or the X Windows manager. The important concept is that every program is started by another program in an unbroken chain all the way back to the initial bootstrap code stored permanently in the computer's motherboard.

So how do viruses wedge themselves into this process? How do they know which programs will spread them and which will simply cause them to lie dormant? Usually, they don't. Viruses only know the program that was running when they were first executed (like Internet Explorer) and the program that started that program. When a virus is first executed, it attaches itself to the beginning of the current program. The next time that program is run, the virus takes the information about the program that started the current program to determine what file it should infect next and attaches itself to the beginning of that program. In this way, the virus propagates one step closer to the beginning of the chain each time the programs in the startup chain are launched.

Viruses also attach themselves to each program that the current program launches. In most cases this is nothing—most applications can't launch other programs. But some do, and when those applications are found, the virus automatically spreads. The graphic that follows shows how a virus attached to Internet Explorer can propagate back to the program that launched it (Word), then back to Windows Explorer, and from there to other applications.

worms
Viruses that spread over a network automatically without human intervention.

It's important to note that viruses require human activity—booting a floppy, executing a program, or opening an attachment—in order to activate and spread. Viruses that can spread without human activity are referred to as *worms.* Worms typically exploit buffer overrun attacks against common Internet services like mail or web.

NOTE

Common Types of Virus Attacks

Types of viruses are defined mostly by the propagation method they use. In many cases, an entire class of viruses is composed of permutations of just a single virus, so they're nearly equivalent. Viruses are categorized by their ultimate target, as described in the following sections.

Boot Sector Viruses

boot sector
The first executable code that is stored on a disk and is used to load the operating system.

Boot sector viruses were the original viruses, and they spread by the only common means of sharing information in the early days of computers—on floppy disks. Twenty years ago, networks were uncommon. Most data was shared by copying it to floppy disks. It was common at that time to boot floppy disks for special purposes like playing games or simply because the floppy had been left in the drive when the computer was turned off. Boot sector viruses would copy themselves to the boot sector of the host when the floppy was booted and then subsequently infect every floppy that was inserted into the computer.

Thanks to the proliferation of networks, these viruses are practically extinct.

Executable Viruses

shell
A command-line interface to an operating system.

Executable viruses infect the startup code for programs and propagate back to the *shell* or desktop application of the computer in order to infect all programs launched from it.

Because of the native immunity to this activity in modern permissions-based operating systems, these viruses have become rare, except in places where older operating systems are common.

Macro Viruses

macro virus
Viruses that exist in the interpreted code embedded in Office documents. These viruses are not capable of escaping the confines of their interpreted environment, so they cannot infect executables.

Macro viruses are written in a higher-level language, such as the Visual Basic scripting language built into Microsoft Office, so they are related to other interpreted language viruses like those that can infest Java applications. Macro viruses attach themselves to document templates and can spread to other documents that are saved after opening the infected one. They spread like wildfire through corporate networks where users share documents indiscriminately.

Luckily, most Office document macro viruses are relatively harmless, and Microsoft has worked to close the security holes in the Office macro languages (the most common macro viruses are specific to Word and Excel). The latest version of Office ships with immunity enabled by default, so macro viruses will become obsolete when this software becomes widespread.

E-Mail Viruses

Unfortunately, the same application language has been built into Microsoft Outlook, the e-mail software that comes with Office (and its free-with-the-operating-system sibling, Outlook Express). Viruses written for Outlook can automatically read your list of contacts from the Address Book or Contacts folder and mail themselves to everyone you know, thus propagating extremely rapidly. Currently, Outlook e-mail viruses are by far the fastest spreading and largest threat in the virus world.

E-mail viruses are rarely completely automatic (although there are some suscep-
tibilities in Outlook that could allow this to happen). They almost always rely upon
the recipient to click the embedded attachment to execute it and then immediately
propagate by scanning that user's address book and e-mailing itself to everyone that
the user knows. Once they've propagated, they execute their attack code.

The latest versions of Outlook are automatically immune to most of these
attacks, but since these attacks rely upon human psychology to activate the virus,
it's likely that they will never completely go away.

Virus Protection

There are three ways to keep computers virus free:

- Prevention
- Natural Immunity
- Protection

Each method is an important part of total defense, and you should implement
policies to encourage all of them. Of course, the best way to prevent viruses is to
avoid risky behavior and programs altogether.

Prevention

There was a time when you could avoid viruses by never pirating software and
avoiding free downloadable software from the Internet. Unfortunately, with the
advent of e-mail viruses, you now also must ensure that you don't know anybody
who does this either, which is basically impossible.

Macro viruses took the corporate world by storm because virus-scanning software wasn't prepared for them. When they first appeared, scanning software only
checked executable code, not documents, and people were used to indiscriminately
trading documents. Although these viruses could infect only Office documents,
they wreaked havoc because the primary job of many corporate computers is to
run Office applications.

Prevention today means the following:

- Being very selective about software you install from the Internet
- Never opening e-mail attachments that you didn't ask for
- Configuring programs like Outlook to automatically quarantine executable attachments according to the instructions at the
  `www.Microsoft.com/security` website
- Disabling macro execution in Office applications unless you absolutely
  need it
- Configuring your computer's BIOS to lock the boot sector, except when
  you are reinstalling your operating system

These measures will go a very long way in preventing you from getting a virus. In the two decades since viruses first appeared, no computer of mine has been infected or spread a virus to others, and I've never run virus software to protect them (although after catching an attempted worm infection in progress, I now run a personal firewall on my laptop to prevent Nimda infections).

Natural Immunity

Due to its inherent security, versions of Windows based on the NT kernel (Windows NT, Windows 2000, and Windows XP—hereafter referred to as NT to distinguish them from those based on the Windows 95 platform) are immune to executable file viruses as long as you use the NTFS and are not logged in as the administrator when you install software. However, NT cannot prevent the spread of viruses that infect nonexecutable files—like Office documents that normal users must have Write access to.

For a virus to spread to the program that loaded it, the user loading the program must have Write access to the executable file doing the loading. As soon as you hit an actual system file, the NT kernel will pop up with an Access Denied message, usually aborting the executable load. You may not know what's happening (and you may blame the operating system), but virus propagation is stopped cold by the NT kernel's inherent security.

However, users who store files on your NT-based server but run them on their Windows 95/98/Me–based computers have no such protection. Just because a virus can't spread to your server doesn't mean your server can't host it. Client operating systems see a server as just a big shared hard disk, so any executable files containing viruses they copy to your server will still contain viruses. You won't be able to run them on the server, but other users will be able to load them on other client computers running Windows 95/98/Me, MS-DOS, Apple Macintosh, or other simpler client operating systems. This is somewhat analogous to a carrier organism that is itself immune to the effects of a virus but is still contagious to other organisms.

Active Protection

virus scanner
Software that scans every executable file on a computer searching for virus signatures.

Virus scanners provide the only way to actually recover from a virus infestation. Virus software works by scanning through every executable file looking for the *signatures* (unique code sequences) of viruses. The process is much like spell-checking a Word document—the scanner reads through the file looking for any virus signature in its dictionary of viruses. When a virus is found, the file is examined and the virus is removed from the file. After scanning all your mass storage devices, all viruses will be removed from your system.

Many viruses cause corruption to files beyond simply attaching to them, and frequently virus scanners can remove the virus but cannot fix the specific corruption that the virus caused. In this case, check the virus vendor's website for a special program that can repair the corruption caused by a specific virus. Some viruses also cause such widespread damage that special virus removal programs are required to completely eradicate them. If this is the case, your virus scanner should tell you that it was unable to remove a virus.

Most modern virus-protection software also comes with *inoculators* that check software as it is loaded and interrupts the load process if a virus is found. This can be very convenient because it keeps infestation from happening in the first place. Inoculators can get in the way of bulk file transfers, so turn them off during backups and large copy operations.

Unfortunately, viruses tend to bounce around in network environments. Eliminating a network virus infestation is difficult because people often reintroduce viruses from machines that aren't yet clean. The only way to prevent this is to either disconnect all computers from the network and disallow their re-attachment until they've been cleaned or to use enterprise virus-scanning software that can be centrally deployed and simultaneously scans all computers on the network.

signature
A short sequence of codes known to be unique to a specific virus and indicates that virus's presence in a system.

inoculator
Antivirus software that scans data files and executables at the moment they are invoked and blocks them from being loaded if they contain a virus. Inoculators can prevent viruses from spreading.

Understanding Worms and Trojan Horses

Worms are viruses that spread automatically, irrespective of human behavior, by exploiting bugs in applications that are connected to the Internet. You've probably heard the names of the most widely successful ones in the mainstream media: Code Red, Nimda, and Slammer. From an infected machine, the worm scans the network searching for targets. It then contacts the target, initiates a benign exchange, exploits a bug in the receiver's server software to gain control of the server momentarily, and uploads itself to the target. Once the target is infected, the process starts again on it.

Worms usually carry a Trojan horse along with them as payload and set up a listening service on the computer for hackers to connect to. Once a worm is in the wild, hackers will begin port scanning wide ranges of computers looking for the port opened up by the worm's listening service. When a hacker (let's call him Sam) finds a compromised computer, he will typically create an administrative account for himself and then clean up the worm and patch the computer against further exploits—to keep other hackers out so that he can reliably use the computer in the future. The computer is now "owned" by Sam and has become his "zombie," in hacker terms. Because this all happens behind the scenes (and often at night), the real owner of the computer often never knows. But like a parasitic symbiote, people who have been "owned" are sometimes better off having a knowledgeable hacker protecting their zombie from further attacks.

Your computer has probably already been hacked if you have a broadband Internet connection and you don't have a cable/DSL router or a software firewall. It wouldn't show up on a virus scan because the hacker would have cleaned up the worm within a few hours of infection. To take back ownership of your computer, change the passwords on every account on the machine.

Hackers like to collect from a few dozen up to (in some cases) a few thousand zombies so that they can perpetrate attacks from many different IP addresses on the Internet. Some hackers actually sell (using auction sites, believe it or not) large banks of zombies to spammers who use them to transmit bulk spam. Anti-hacking researchers leave unprotected computers out on the Internet to allow them to be exploited so that they can track down hackers by watching the activity on the exploited computers, so hackers will typically "bounce" through multiple zombies before perpetrating an attack to throw investigators off their trail. This is going on all around you on the Internet, right now.

Worms are basically impossible for end users to prevent, and they typically exploit newly found bugs that are either unpatched or not widely patched in a vendor's code. When they attack extremely common systems like Windows or Linux, they spread very quickly and can cause enormous damage before they're stopped.

Here are some suggestions to defend against worms:

♦ Avoid software that is routinely compromised, like Microsoft Internet Information Server and Internet Explorer. (Mozilla, a free download from `www.mozilla.org` is an excellent replacement for IE on Windows computers.)

♦ Stay up-to-date on patches and security fixes for all your public computers. Strongly consider using automatic updates for any public server, and schedule them for a nightly reboot to make sure that patches become effective as quickly as possible.

♦ Keep client computers behind firewalls or cable/DSL routers.

♦ Run only those services you intend to provide on public servers—don't just install everything for the sake of convenience when you set up a public server.

♦ Use firewalls to prevent worms from reaching the interior of your network from the Internet.

♦ Keep your virus-scanning software updated.

But even with all these precautions, you can only be protected against worms that the vendors know about, and it's quite likely that a worm will infest your public servers at some point, so keep good backups as well.

Protecting Against Worms

There are two common ways to protect against worms. Firewalling services that you don't use is the primary method. However, some services (like web and e-mail) must be open to the Internet and usually cannot be protected against by a firewall.

In this case, using software specifically designed to filter the protocol—such as a proxy-based firewall, a supplemental security service like e-eye Secure IIS, or simple URL filtering on the characters used by hackers to insert buffer overruns—can stop the attacks before they get to the firewall. For mail servers, simply putting a mail proxy server from a different operating system in front of your actual mail server will prevent the interior mail server from being affected by any buffer overrun that can affect the proxy.

Finally, virus scanners receive signatures that allow them to recognize and (sometimes) clean worms that have already infected a server. In cases where the virus scanner cannot automatically clean up the worm, antivirus software vendors will provide a downloadable tool that will clean up the infection. Unfortunately, this method doesn't stop worm infection; it merely removes it.

Implementing Virus Protection

Although it used to be possible to avoid viruses by avoiding software downloads and avoiding opening e-mail attachments, it's no longer feasible to think that every user will always do the right thing in the face of the rampant virus propagation going on now. Especially with e-mail viruses and Internet worms (which you can receive irrespective of how you behave), you can no longer guarantee that you'll remain virus free no matter what you do.

You must implement virus scanners in order to protect your computer and your network from virus attack. But purchasing software once is not sufficient for staying up-to-date with the virus threat because new viruses crop up every day. All major virus protection vendors offer subscription services that allow you to update your virus definitions on a regular basis. Whether or not this process can be performed automatically depends on the vendor, as does the administrative difficulty of setting up automatic updating.

Frequent (hourly) automatic updates are a mandatory part of antivirus defense, so don't even consider virus scanners that don't have a good automatic update service. Worms can spread through the entire Internet in less than one day now, so you should check for updates on an hourly basis for the best defense possible. Critical gateway machines like mail servers and public web servers should update every 15 minutes.

TIP

Virus scanners can be effectively implemented in the following places:

- On each client computer
- On servers
- On e-mail gateways
- On firewalls

Larger enterprises use virus scanners in all of these places, whereas most small businesses tend to go with virus protection installed on individual computers. Using all of these methods is overkill, but which methods you choose will depend largely on how you and your users work.

Client Virus Protection

Client-based virus protection is the traditional method of protecting computers from viruses. Virus scanners are installed like applications, and once installed they begin protecting your computer from viruses. There are two primary types, which are combined in most current packages.

Virus scanners The original type of virus protection. In the days of MS-DOS and Windows 3.1, these programs ran during the boot process to scan for viruses and disinfected your computer each time you booted it. They did not protect you from contracting or spreading viruses, but they would make sure that a virus would not affect you for long.

Inoculators A newer methodology that wedges itself into the operating system to intercept attempts to run programs or open files. Before the file can be run or opened, the inoculator scans the file silently in the background to ensure that it does not contain a known virus. If it does, the inoculator pops up, informs you of the problem, disinfects the file, and then allows you to proceed to use the file. Inoculators cannot find dormant viruses in unused files that may have been on your computer before you installed the scanner or in files that are mounted on removable media like Zip disks or floppy drives.

Both types are required for total virus defense on a computer, and all modern virus applications include both.

The dark side of client-side virus protection software is the set of problems it can cause. Besides the obvious problems of buggy virus software, all virus software puts a serious load on your computer. Inoculators that scan files that are being copied can make transporting large amounts of data between computers extremely time intensive. Virus scanners will also interfere with most operating system upgrade programs and numerous setup programs for system services. To prevent these problems, you will probably have to disable the virus inoculators before installing many software applications on your computer.

Another problem with client-side virus protection is ubiquity: all the clients have to be running virus protection for it to remain effective. Machines that slip through the cracks can become infected and can transmit viruses to shared files, causing additional load and recurring corruption for users that do have virus applications.

Client-side virus scanners are good enough to keep most smaller businesses virus free. Even if dormant viruses exist on the server, they will be found and cleaned when they are eventually opened, and if the files are never again opened, the virus is irrelevant.

Spyware Protection

Spyware is a slightly different problem than the other types of malware (all of which are picked up by virus scanners) because the users have legally agreed to download the software when they clicked "yes" to the download dialog that offered them whatever freebie the software said it did. Symantec lost a court case to a spyware company, so antivirus vendors cannot include signatures to detect and remove spyware.

If you think a computer has a spyware problem (because ads pop up randomly or the computer has suddenly become very slow), then you can download and run any one of a number of programs that will scan for and remove spyware from your computer.

The following list includes the three most commonly used programs:

- Ad-aware, which is the market leader and the most comprehensive, costs about $30 per computer.
- Spysweeper has a $30 commercial version as well as a limited free download.
- Spybot is a free download that works well to detect most spyware applications.

Server-Based Virus Protection

Server-based virus protection is basically the same as client-side protection but it runs on servers. In the server environment, the emphasis is on virus scanning rather than inoculation because files are not opened on the server; they're merely copied to and from it. Scanning the network streams flowing into and out of a busy server would create far too much load, so server-based virus protection invariably relies upon scanning files on disk to protect against viruses. Servers themselves are naturally immune to viruses as long as administrators don't run applications indiscriminately on the servers while they are logged in with administrative privileges.

Server-side scanners are normally run periodically to search for viruses, either nightly (the preferred method) prior to the daily backup, or weekly, as configured by the administrator.

Server-based virus protection does not disinfect clients, so it alone is not sufficient for total virus protection. It is effective in eliminating the "ping-pong" effect where some clients that don't have virus protection continually cause problems for clients that do.

E-Mail Gateway Virus Protection

E-mail gateway virus protection is a new but important method of controlling viruses. Since nearly all modern virus infections are transmitted by e-mail attachments, scanning for viruses on the e-mail gateway is an effective way to stop the vast majority of virus infestations before they start. Scanning the e-mail gateway can also prevent widespread transmission of a virus throughout a company that can occur even if most (but not all) of the clients have virus protection software running.

E-mail gateway virus protection works by scanning every e-mail as it is sent or received by the gateway. Because e-mail gateways tend to have a lot more computing power than they actually need, and because e-mail is not instantaneous anyway, scanning mail messages is a very transparent way to eliminate viruses without the negative impact of client-side virus scanning.

Modern e-mail scanners are even capable of unzipping compressed attachments and scanning their interior contents to make sure viruses can't slip through disguised by a compression algorithm.

Like all forms of server-based virus protection, e-mail gateway virus protection does not disinfect clients, so it alone is not sufficient for total virus protection. However, since the vast majority of viruses now come through e-mail, you can be reasonably secure with just e-mail gateway virus protection, a firewall to block worms, and prudent downloading practices.

TIP

Rather than installing client-side virus protection for computers behind a virus-scanned e-mail server and a firewall, I just use Trend Micro's free and always-up-to-date Web-based virus scanner to spot-check computers if I think they might be infected. Check it out at housecall.antivirus.com. **Symantec also provides Web-based file scanning.**

Firewall-Based Virus Protection

Some modern firewalls include a virus-scanning function that actually scans all inbound communication streams for viruses and terminates the session if a virus signature is found. This can prevent infection via e-mail and Internet downloads.

Like all forms of server-based virus protection, e-mail gateway virus protection does not disinfect clients, so it alone is not sufficient for total virus protection.

Unlike e-mail gateway–based virus scanners, firewall scanners cannot unzip compressed files to check their contents for viruses. Since most downloaded programs are compressed, these scanners won't catch embedded viruses in them either.

Enterprise Virus Protection

Enterprise virus protection is simply a term for applications that include all or most of the previously discussed functions and include management software to automate the deployment and updating of a client's virus protection software.

A typical enterprise virus scanner is deployed on all clients, servers, and e-mail gateways and is managed from a central server that downloads definition updates and then pushes the updates to each client. The best ones can even remotely deploy the virus-scanning software automatically on machines that it detects do not already have it.

Symantec's Norton AntiVirus for Enterprises is (in my opinion) the best enterprise virus scanner available. It works well, causes few problems, automatically deploys and updates, and is relatively inexpensive.

Terms to Know

benign viruses	malignant viruses
boot sector	propagation engine
data	scripting hosts
executable code	self-replicating
execution environments	shell
inoculator	signature
interpreter	virus scanner
macro	worms
macro virus	

Review Questions

1. Where do viruses come from?

2. Can data contain a virus?

3. Do all viruses cause problems?

4. What is a worm?

5. Are all applications susceptible to macro viruses?

6. What is the only family of e-mail clients that are susceptible to e-mail viruses?

7. If you run NT kernel–based operating systems, do you still need antivirus protection?

8. What two types of antivirus methods are required for total virus defense?

9. How often should you update your virus definitions?

10. Where is antivirus software typically installed?

Chapter 9

Creating Fault Tolerance

In This Chapter

- The most common causes of data loss
- Improving fault tolerance
- Backing up your network
- Testing the fault tolerance of your system

Security means more than just keeping hackers out of your computers. It really means keeping your data safe from loss of any kind, including accidental loss due to user error, bugs in software, and hardware failure.

Systems that can tolerate hardware and software failure without losing data are said to be fault tolerant. The term is usually applied to systems that can remain functional when hardware or software errors occur, but the concept of fault tolerance can include data backup and archiving systems that keep redundant copies of information to ensure that the information isn't lost if the hardware it is stored upon fails.

Fault tolerance theory is simple: Duplicate every component that could be subject to failure. From this simple theory springs very complex solutions, like backup systems that duplicate all the data stored in an enterprise, clustered servers that can take over for one another automatically, redundant disk arrays that can tolerate the failure of a disk in the pack without going offline, and network protocols that can automatically reroute traffic to an entirely different city in the event that an Internet circuit fails.

fault tolerance
The ability of a system to withstand failure and remain operational.

Causes for Loss

To correctly plan for *fault tolerance,* you should consider what types of loss are likely to occur. Different types of loss require different fault tolerance measures, and not all types of loss are likely to occur to all clients.

At the end of each of these sections, there will be a tip box that lists the fault tolerance measures that can effectively mitigate these causes for loss. To create an effective fault tolerance policy, rank the following causes for loss in the order that you think they're likely to occur in your system. Then list the effective remedy measures for those causes for loss in the same order, and implement those remedies in top-down order until you exhaust your budget.

NOTE

The solutions mentioned in this section are covered in the second half of this chapter.

Human Error

User error is the most common reason for loss. Everyone has accidentally lost information by deleting a file or overwriting it with something else. Users frequently play with configuration settings without really understanding what those settings do, which can cause problems as well. Believe it or not, most computer downtime in businesses is caused by the activities of the computer maintenance staff. Deploying patches without testing them first can cause servers to fail; performing maintenance during working hours can cause bugs to manifest and servers to crash. Leading-edge solutions are far more likely to have undiscovered problems, and routinely selecting them over more mature solutions means that your systems will be less stable.

TIP

A good archiving policy provides the means to recover from human error easily. Use permissions to prevent users' mistakes from causing widespread damage.

Routine Failure Events

Routine failure events are the second most likely causes for loss. Routine failures fall into a few categories that are each handled differently.

Hardware Failure

Hardware failure is the second most common reason for loss and is highly likely to occur in servers and client computers. Hardware failure is considerably less likely to occur in devices that do not contain moving parts, such as fans or hard disk drives.

The primary rule of disk management is as follows: Stay in the mass market—don't get esoteric. Unusual solutions are harder to maintain, are more likely to have buggy drivers, and are usually more complex than they are worth.

Every hard disk will eventually fail. This bears repeating: Every hard disk will eventually fail. They run constantly in servers at high speed, and they generate the very heat that destroys their spindle lubricant. These two conditions combine to ensure that hard disks wear out through normal use within about five years.

Early in the computer industry, the *mean time between failures (MTBF)* of a hard disk drive was an important selling point.

The real problem with disk failure is that hard disks are the only component in computers that can't be simply swapped out because they are individually customized with your data. To tolerate the failure of your data, you must have a copy of it elsewhere. That elsewhere can be another hard disk in the same computer or in another computer, on tape, or on *removable media*.

Some options don't work well—any backup medium that's smaller than the source medium will require more effort than it's worth to swap. Usually this means you must use either another hard disk of equivalent or greater size or tape, which can be quite capacious.

Solutions for hardware failure include implementing RAID-1 or RAID-5 and strong backup and archiving policies. Keeping spare parts handy and purchasing all of your equipment from the same sources makes it easier and faster to repair hardware when problems occur.

Software Failures

Software problems cause a surprising amount of data loss. Server applications that place all of their data in a single file may have unknown bugs that can corrupt that file and cause the loss of all data within it. These sorts of problems can take years to discover and are especially likely in new applications. Another class of problems comes from misconfiguration or incompatibility between applications installed on the same server.

The solution to software failure is to perform rigorous deployment testing before deploying software on production servers. Test software compatibility without risking downtime by using servers that are configured the same way as production servers but are not used to provide your working environment.

Power Failure

Unexpected power failures have become relatively rare in the United States, as advances in power delivery have made transmission systems themselves very fault tolerant. Unfortunately, poor planning has created a situation in many parts of the world where demand for power very nearly exceeds capacity. In California, rolling blackouts have been used to manage power crises, and will likely be used again,

mean time between failures (MTBF)
The average life expectancy of electronic equipment. Most hard disks have an MTBF of about five years.

NOTE

removable media
Computer storage media that can be removed from the drive, such as floppy disks, flash cards, and tape.

TIP

TIP

causing the most reliable power transmission systems in the world to fail despite their fault tolerance systems.

Even when power failures are rare, power line problems such as surges, brownouts, and poorly regulated power cause extra stress on power supplies that shortens their lives. Computer power supplies always last longer behind a UPS than they do plugged into line power directly.

TIP **The solution to power failure problems is to use uninterruptible power supplies and, when necessary, emergency power generators.**

Data Circuit Failure

Circuit failures are rare, but they do happen, and when they do, networks can be cut off from their users. Circuit failure is especially critical to public websites that depend upon access for their revenue, but they are also problematic for branch offices that rely on services at their headquarters site.

TIP **The solution to circuit failure is to have multiple redundant circuits from different ISPs and to configure your routers to balance across the circuits and route around them in the event of failure.**

Crimes

As a group, crimes are the third most likely cause for loss of data in a network. As the level of hacking activity on the Internet increases, this category is currently increasing dramatically as a cause for loss and may soon surpass routine failures as the second most likely cause for loss in a network.

Hacking

If hackers gain access to your systems, especially if they are able to gain administrative privileges, they can wreak serious havoc, sabotaging anything they please. Even simple attacks can cause the denials of service similar to those caused by a circuit failure.

circuit
In the context of information technology, a circuit is a data network connection between two points, usually different facilities. The term *circuit* traditionally applies to high-capacity telephone trunk lines.

That said, most hacking does not significantly damage systems because most hackers are not motivated to maliciously destroy data. Most hackers are either joyriding to simply gain access to systems or looking to steal information. Like common criminals, they don't want to get caught, so they usually don't do anything to make their presence known.

However, younger naïve hackers, those with a chip on their shoulder, or ideological hackers with an agenda may cause extreme damage to your systems in order to cause you as many problems as possible.

The solutions to hacking problems are presented throughout this book. Strong border security, the use of permissions to restrict access to individual accounts, and *offline* backups can eliminate this problem.

Virus or Worm Outbreak

Internet-based worms and viruses have become a major cause of downtime in the last few years as operating system vulnerabilities have been routinely exploited to create worms that spread rapidly.

Fast-spreading worms and viruses cause direct problems on the machines they infect and have the secondary effect of using up so much Internet bandwidth to spread that they can choke backbone connections on the Internet.

The solution to worm and virus outbreaks is to keep all clients (including home computers connected through VPNs) on a network that is kept up-to-date with patches automatically and to check for virus updates on an hourly basis.

Theft

We all know that laptops are routinely stolen, but servers and datacenter equipment aren't immune to theft either. Expensive servers are worth about 10 percent of their retail value on the black market, so your $15,000 server can pay a thief's rent for a month. If you've got a datacenter full of servers that someone could back a truck into, you could be a target for theft.

Who would know about your expensive systems? According to the FBI, most computer thefts are inside jobs either perpetrated or facilitated by employees and contractors, like cleaning crews and other service providers. Typically, an employee or contractor acts as a "spotter," identifying high-value systems and providing copies of keys or security codes and instructions for how to find valuable systems. Then, while the inside accomplice is performing some public activity that provides a strong alibi, the employee's criminal associates will perpetrate the theft of equipment.

Offline data
Data that is not immediately available to running systems, such as data stored on tape.

The solution to physical theft of equipment is strong physical security and offsite backups. Measures like live security guards or video surveillance can eliminate equipment theft as a serous concern. Offsite backups allow for quick restoration in the event of a burglary.

Sabotage

Sadly, sabotage by system users is rather common. Sabotage can be as subtle as one user sabotaging another by deleting files for some personal reason or as blatant as an employee deliberately physically destroying a computer.

Disgruntled employees can cause a tremendous amount of damage—more so than any other form of loss—because employees know where valuable data is stored and they usually have the access to get to the data.

TIP **The solution to sabotage is strong physical security to restrict access and provide evidence, proper permissions to restrict access, auditing to provide evidence and proof of activity, and offsite backups to restore information in the worst case. If employees know that there's no way for them to get away with acts of sabotage, they are far less likely to attempt it.**

Terrorism

Acts of war or terrorism are exceptionally rare, but they should be planned for if you expect your business to survive them. Because the specific events might take any form, they should be planned for as you would for earthquakes.

TIP **Solutions to acts of war and terrorism are offsite distant backups (preferably in another country) and offsite distant clustering, if you expect to be able to continue business operations through these types of events.**

Environmental Events

Environmental events are the least likely events to occur, but they can be devastating because they usually take people by surprise.

Fire

Fires are rare, but they are a potential problem at most sites. Fires destroy everything, including computers and onsite backups. Being electrical equipment, it's possible that computers might even start fires; failing power supplies in computers can start small fires.

Fires create a situation in which the cure is just as bad as the illness. Computers that may have survived a fire are certain to be ruined by water damage when the fire is put out. Sprinkler or chemical fire suppression systems can destroy computers and may be triggered by small fires that would not have seriously damaged a computer on its own.

TIP **The solution to fire damage for computers is sophisticated early fire detection and high-technology gas-based fire suppression systems. Offsite backups are also necessary to restore data in the event that computers are completely destroyed. For continuity of business, distant offsite clustering is required.**

Flooding

Flooding, while relatively rare, is a surprisingly common source of computer failures. It only takes a small amount of water to destroy a running computer. Leaky roofs can allow rain to drip into a computer, HVAC units or other in-ceiling plumbing may leak onto a computer, a flooding bathroom in a floor above a server room may drain down into machines. Finally, minor fires may set off sprinkler systems that can destroy computers even though the fire itself is not a threat.

A source of water damage that most people fail to consider is the condensation caused by taking computers from cool air-conditioned offices outside to high-temperature humid air. This can cause just enough condensation in electrical equipment to short out power supplies or circuit cards, and this is why most electrical equipment has maximum operating humidity specifications.

The solution to flooding is offsite backups and, for continuity of business, offsite clustering. If flooding is a major concern, clustering can often be performed in the same building as long as the clustered servers are on a different floor.

TIP

Earthquake

We all know that earthquakes can potentially destroy an entire facility. While earthquakes of this magnitude are very rare, they're much more common in certain parts of the world than others. Consult your local government for statistics on the likelihood of damage-causing earthquakes.

Those in areas where earthquakes are common should employ multicity fault tolerance measures, where backups and clustered solutions exist in different cities. You can easily weather moderate earthquakes by using rack-mounted computers in racks that are properly secured to walls.

TIP

Fault Tolerance Measures

The following fault tolerance measures are the typical measures used to mitigate the causes of loss listed in the first part of this chapter. Some of these measures are detailed here, while others that are covered in other chapters are merely mentioned here along with a reference to the chapter in which they're covered.

Backups

Backups are the most common specific form of fault tolerance and are sometimes naïvely considered to be a cure-all for all types of loss. Backups are simply snapshot copies of the data on a machine at a specific time, usually when users are not using the system. Traditionally, backups are performed to a tape device, but as disks have become less expensive, they have begun to replace tape as backup devices.

Backup Methods

Traditional backup works like this: Every night, you insert a fresh tape into your server. The next morning when you arrive at work, you remove the tape, mark the date, and store it in your tape vault. At larger companies, you'll never use that tape again—it's a permanent record of your network on that date. In smaller companies, that's the same tape you use every Wednesday, and you only keep tapes made over the weekend or perhaps you reuse them once a month.

Nearly all operating systems, including all Microsoft operating systems and all versions of Unix, support a backup methodology called *archive marking,* which is implemented through a single bit flag attached to every file as an attribute. The archive bit is set every time a file is written to and is only cleared by archive software. This allows the system to retain a memory of which files have changed since the last backup.

Windows and Unix both come with simple tape backup solutions that are capable of performing full and incremental system backups to tape or disk (except Windows NT prior to Windows 2000, which can only back up to tape) on a regularly scheduled basis. In Windows, the tool is called NTBACKUP.EXE, and in UNIX the tool is called "tar" (Tape Archive—tar is also commonly used to distribute software in the Unix environment). Both applications work similarly; they create a single large backup file out of the set of backed-up directories and files and write it to tape or to a file on disk.

With effort, you can do anything you need with the built-in backup tools for these operating systems. But the preference for larger sites is to automate backup procedures with enterprise backup software that can automatically back up multiple servers to a central archive server.

archive marking
A method used by operating systems to indicate when a file has been changed and should thus be included in an incremental backup.

TIP

You can script your own custom backup methodology using file copy programs like tar (Unix) and XCOPY (Windows) to back up files as well. Both programs can be configured to respect archive marking.

Most backup software offers a variety of backup options:

Full Backup   Archives every file on the computer and clears all the archive bits so that all future writes will be marked for archiving.

Copy Backup   Archives every file on the computer without modifying the archive bit flags. Copy operations proceed faster and can archive read-only files since the file does not have to be opened for write operations to reset the archive bit flag.

Incremental Backup   Archives every file that has its archive bit set (meaning it has changed since the last backup) and resets the bit so that the next incremental backup will not re-archive the file.

Differential Backup   Archives every file that has its archive bit set, but it does not reset the bit; therefore, every differential backup tape includes the complete set of files since the last full system backup.

Periodic Backup   Archives all files that have been written to since a certain date.

Because software vendors have begun to realize how badly traditional solutions perform for restoration, a new type of tape backup called image backup has become available. In an image backup, a complete sector copy of the disk is written to tape, including all the information necessary to reconstruct the drive's partitions. Because the backup occurs below the file level, image archives are capable of archiving open files.

Restoration is where an image backup shines. The image backup software will create a set of boot floppies (or boot CDs) for emergency restoration. When the emergency restore boot floppy and an image tape are inserted, the computer will boot a proprietary restore program that simply copies the image on the tape back to disk. One reboot later and you're looking at your old familiar computer.

Image backup is not for archiving—file access is not as good as traditional backup software, and in some cases it's not available at all. But there's no reason you can't use different software for archiving and backup.

Tape Hardware

Tape devices range from simple single cartridge units to sophisticated robotic tape changers. Tape auto-changers are devices that use some mechanical method to change tapes among a library of installed cartridges. When one tape is filled to capacity, the next tape in the changer is installed and the archive operation proceeds. With auto-changers, literally any amount of data can be archived. They suffer from the problem that the archive operation takes as long as there are cartridges to be used, because the operation is sequential and the mechanical devices used to change tapes are (as are all moving devices) subject to failure. Auto-changers frequently can take more time to perform an archive than is allotted because of the volume of information involved and their sequential nature.

Redundant Array of Independent Tapes (RAIT) is the latest development in archiving technology. This technology, also called TapeRAID, is an adaptation of disk RAID technology. RAIT uses as many tape devices in parallel as the size of your backup set requires. RAIT is usually cheaper and always faster than tape auto-changers because auto-changers are low-volume devices that are always expensive and individual tape units are relatively inexpensive. They are faster because the archival operation operates simultaneously. It takes only the time that a single tape archive takes, no matter how many devices are involved.

Problems with Tape Backup

The problem with using tape for archiving and backup is that it is not reliable—in fact, it's highly unreliable. You may find this shocking, but two-thirds of attempts to completely restore a system from tape fail. That's an awfully high number, especially considering how many people rely upon tape as their sole medium of backup.

Humans are the major cause of backup failure. Humans have to change that tape every day. This means that in any organization that doesn't have a dedicated tape archivist, the overburdened IS team is bound to forget. And if you've tried to train a non-IS employee to change the tape, you probably feel lucky if it happens at all.

One of two things will occur when the backup software detects that the tape has not been changed. Poorly designed or configured software will refuse to run the backup in a misguided attempt to protect the data already on the tape. Better-configured software will simply overwrite the tape assuming that a more recent backup is better than no backup at all. So in many cases, the same tape may sit in a server (wearing out) for days or weeks on end, while business goes by and everyone forgets about the backup software.

NOTE

An individual tape cartridge is only reliable for between 10 and 100 uses—and unless you verify your backups, you won't know when it has become unreliable. Be certain that your tape rotation policy specifies reusing tapes only 10 times (or the manufacturer-recommended amount) before they are discarded.

It is a combination of tape wear, truculent backup software, and this human failure component that contributes to the high failure rate of tape restorations.

A typical restore operation is very problematic. Assuming the worst—you lost your storage system completely—here's what you have to look forward to: After installing new hard disks, you must reinstall Windows or Unix from scratch. Then you must reinstall your tape backup software. Once you've finished these tasks (after a frantic search for the BackupExec or ARCserve installation code that is required to reinstall the tape software and a panicked call to their tech support to beg forgiveness, mercy, and a new code number), you're ready to completely overwrite the installation effort with a full restoration from tape. You now get to sit in front of your server providing all the base system tapes, then the Monday incremental tape, the Tuesday incremental tape, and so forth until you hit the current day of the week—the whole time cursing your decision to use daily incremental backups. Once you're completely finished, and assuming that all six tapes involved worked flawlessly, you're ready to reboot your server—an entire workday after you began the restore operation.

Backup Best Practices

Backup is a critical security component of any network. Allocate a large enough budget to do it correctly.

Use tape devices and media large enough to perform an entire backup onto a single tape. In the event that this is not possible, use RAIT software to allow the simultaneous unattended backup of the entire system.

Always set your tape backup software to overwrite media that may have been left in the machine without having to ask you to change or overwrite.

Choose image backup software rather than file-based backup software. Restorations are far easier and faster with this software.

Turn off disk-based catalogs. They take up far more space than they're worth, and they're never available when the computer has crashed. Use media-based catalogs that are stored on tape.

Sony has a new advanced tape system that stores file catalogs in flash memory on the tape cartridge, providing instance catalog access with the media and eliminating the need for disk-based storage.

TIP

Perform a full-system backup every day. Differential, incremental, and daily backups that don't create a complete image cause headaches and complications during a restoration operation and increase the likelihood of failure by adding more components to the process. If your backup system is too slow to back up your entire data set in the allotted time, get a new one that is capable of handling all your data in this time frame.

Use software with an open-file backup feature to back up opened files or force them to close if you perform your backup at night. Use the Windows "force system logoff" user policy to shut down user connections at night and force all files to close just prior to the backup.

If you reuse tapes, mark them each time they've been written to. Discard tapes after their 10th backup. Saving a few dollars on media isn't worth the potential for loss.

If you haven't implemented online archiving, pull out a full system backup once a week (or at the very least once a month) and store it permanently. You never know when a deleted file will be needed again.

Test your backups with full system restores to test servers at least once per quarter. This will help you identify practices that will make restoration difficult in an emergency.

Don't bother backing up workstations. Rather, get users comfortable with the idea that no files stored locally on their computers will be backed up—if it's important, put it on a network file server. This reduces the complexity of your backup problem considerably. Workstations should contain operating system and application files only, all of which can be restored from the original software CD-ROMs.

Use enterprise-based backup software that is capable of transmitting backup data over the network to a central backup server. Watch for network capacity, though, because that much data can often overwhelm a network. Schedule each server's transmission so it doesn't conflict when running over the same shared media as other servers do. You should put your archive server on your backbone or at the central point of your network.

You don't have to spend a lot of money on esoteric archive servers, even for large environments. When you consider that a medium capacity tape is going to cost $2,000, adding another $1,000 for a motherboard, hard disk, RAM, network adapter, and a copy of your operating system isn't all that big of a deal. The software you have to install is likely to cost more than all the hardware combined anyway. So feel free to have six or eight computers dedicated to large backup problems. They can all run simultaneously to back up different portions of your network without investing in expensive RAIT software or auto-loading tape devices. You'll save money and have a more standard solution that you can fix.

Uninterruptible Power Supplies (UPSs) and Power Generators

Uninterruptible power supplies (UPSs) are battery systems that provide emergency power when power mains fail. UPSs also condition poorly regulated power, which increases the life of the computer's internal power supply and decreases the probability of the power supply causing a fire.

Use uninterruptible power supplies to shut systems down gracefully in the event of a power failure. UPSs are not really designed to run through long power outages, so if power is not restored within a few minutes, you need to shut your servers down and wait out the power failure. UPSs are very common and can be purchased either with computers or through retail channels anywhere. Installing them is as simple as plugging them into the power mains, plugging computers into them, connecting them to computers using serial cables so they can trigger a shutdown, and installing the UPS monitoring software on your computers.

It's only really necessary to use UPSs on computers that store data. If you've set up your network to store data only on servers, you won't need UPSs on all your workstations. Remember to put UPSs on hubs and routers if servers will need to communicate with one another during the power failure event.

If the system must be operational during a power failure, you need emergency power generators, which are extremely expensive. Emergency power generators are machines based on truck engines that are designed to generate power. They are started within a few minutes after the main power failure, while computers are still running on their UPS systems. Once the power generators are delivering power, the UPS systems go back to their normal condition because they're receiving power from the generators. When main power is restored, the generators shut down again.

Once you have UPSs and power generators in place, it's imperative that you test your power failure solution before a power event actually occurs. After working hours, throw the circuit breakers in your facility to simulate a power event and ensure that all the servers shut down correctly. When power is restored, you can usually configure servers to either restart automatically or remain off until they are manually started, as you prefer.

Redundant Array of Independent Disks (RAID)

Redundant Array of Independent Disks (RAID) technology allows you to add extra disks to a computer to compensate for the potential failure of a disk. RAID automatically spreads data across the extra disks and can automatically recover it in the event that a disk fails. With hot-swappable disks, the failed drive can be replaced without shutting the system down.

RAID
A family of related technologies that allows multiple disks to be combined into a volume. With all RAID versions except 0, the volume can tolerate the failure of at least one hard disk and remain fully functional.

RAID works in a number of different ways referred to as RAID levels. They are explained in the following sections.

RAID Level 0: Striping

Disk striping allows you to create a single volume that is spread across multiple disks. RAID-0 is not a form of fault tolerance because the failure of any single disk causes the volume to fail. RAID-0 is used to increase disk performance in engineering and scientific workstations, but it is not appropriate for use in a server.

RAID Level 1: Mirroring

Mirrors are exact copies of the data on one disk made on another disk. Disk mirroring is considered a fault tolerant strategy because in the event of a single disk failure, the data can be read and written to the still-working mirror partition. Mirroring also can be used to double the read speed of a partition because data can be read from both disks at the same time.

RAID-1 requires two disks, and both disks should be exactly the same model. Using disks of different models is possible but will likely cause speed synchronization problems that can dramatically affect disk performance.

Mirroring can be implemented in hardware with a simple and inexpensive RAID-1 controller, or it can be implemented in software in Windows NT Server, Windows 2000 Server (all versions), and most popular versions of Unix including Linux and BSD. Implementing software mirroring in Unix is easily performed during the initial operating system installation. In Windows, mirroring is implemented using the disk manager at any time after the completion of the operating system installation. Both software and hardware mirroring are highly reliable and should be implemented on any server as a minimum protective measure against disk failure.

RAID Level 5: Striping with Parity

disk packs
Multiple identical hard disk drives configured to store a single volume in a RAID set.

RAID-5 allows you to create disk sets or *disk packs* of multiple drives that appear to be a single disk to the operating system. A single additional disk provides the space required for parity information (which is distributed across all disks) that can be used to re-create the data on any one disk in the set in the event that a single disk fails. (RAID-4 is a simpler form of RAID-5 that puts all parity information on the extra disk rather than distributing it across all drives, but it is now obsolete.)

The parity information, which is equal to the size of one drive member of the set, is spread across all disks and contains the mathematical sum of information contained in the other stripes. The loss of any disk can be tolerated because its information can be re-created from the information stored on the other disks and in the parity stripe.

Online data
Data that is immediately available to running systems because it is stored on active disks.

For example, if you have six 20GB disks, you could create a RAID-5 pack that provides 100GB of storage (5×20+20GB for parity information). RAID-5 works by using simple algebra: In the equation A×B×C×D×E=F, you can calculate the value of any missing variable (failed disk) if you know the result (parity information). RAID-5 automatically detects the failed disk and re-creates its data from the parity information on demand so that the drive set can remain *online*.

Windows NT Server, Windows 2000 Server, and Linux support RAID level 5 in software, but software RAID-5 is not particularly reliable because detecting disk failure isn't necessarily easy for the operating system. Windows is not capable of booting from a software RAID-5 partition; Linux is.

Basic Input/Output System (BIOS)
The low-level program built into the computer's motherboard that is used to configure hardware and load the operating system.

Serious fault tolerance requires the use of hardware-based RAID-5, which is considerably more reliable and allows booting from a RAID-5 partition. RAID-5 controllers can be purchased as an option in any built-to-purpose server. Configuration of RAID-5 packs must be performed prior to the installation of the operating system and is performed through the RAID-5 adapter's *BIOS* configuration menu during the boot process.

RAID 0+1: Striping with Mirroring

RAID 0+1 (also referred to as RAID-10) is a simple combination of RAID-0 striping and RAID-1 mirroring. RAID-10 allows you to create two identical RAID-0 stripe sets and then mirror across them.

For example, if you had a stripe set of three 20GB disks to create a 60GB volume, RAID-10 allows you to mirror that stripe set to an identical set of three 20GB disks. Your total storage remains 60GB. In theory, a RAID-10 set could withstand the failure of half of the disks (one of the sets), but in practice, you would replace the disks as they failed individually anyway.

Using the same six disks, RAID-5 would allow 100GB of storage with equal fault tolerance. However, hardware RAID-5 controllers are expensive because a microprocessor must be used to recalculate the parity information. RAID-10 controllers are cheap because, as with mirroring, no calculation is required for redundancy.

Permissions

Permissions become a fault tolerance measure when they are used to prevent user error or sabotage. Judicious use of permissions can prevent users from accidentally deleting files and can prevent malicious users from destroying system files that could disable the computer.

Implementing permissions is covered in Chapters 10 and 11, and for further reading, I'd recommend *Mastering Windows Server 2003* by Mark Minasi (Sybex, 2003) and *Linux Network Servers* by Craig Hunt (Sybex, 2002).

Border Security

Border security is an extremely important measure for preventing hacking. Border security is covered in Chapter 5, and you can read more detail in my book *Firewalls 24seven* (Sybex, 2002).

Auditing

Auditing is the process of logging how users access files during their routine operations. It is done for the purpose of monitoring for improper access and to make sure there is evidence in case a crime is committed. Windows has strong support for auditing, and auditing measures can be implemented in Unix.

Implementing auditing is covered in Chapters 10 and 11.

Offsite Storage

Offsite storage is the process of removing data to another location on a regular basis so that if something disastrous occurs at the original facility, the backups or archives are not destroyed along with the online systems.

There are two ways to implement offsite storage: Physically moving backup media such as tapes to another location on a regular basis, and transmitting data to another facility via a network of data circuits.

You can outsource a tape pickup or storage service from companies like Iron Mountain or Archos. These companies will stop by your facility periodically to pick up tapes that are then stored in their secure bunkers and can be retrieved at any time with one day's notice. Outsourcing is far more reliable than relying on employees to take tapes offsite.

Of the two methods, transmitting data automatically over network links is far more reliable, because it can be automated so that it doesn't rely on unreliable human activity. Establishing automated offsite backups or archiving is as simple as copying a backup file across the network to a store located at another facility. You must ensure that you have enough bandwidth to complete the operation before the next operation queues up, so testing is imperative. You can use sophisticated file synchronization software to reduce the amount of data transmitted to changes only, which will allow you to use slower circuits to move data.

Archiving

archiving
The process of retaining a copy of every version of files created by users for the purpose of restoring individual files in case of human error.

Archiving is the process of retaining a copy of every file that is created by users on the system, and in many cases, every version of every file. The difference between backup and archiving is that with archiving, only user files are copied, whereas with backup, everything is copied. Archiving cannot be used to restore entire systems, but systems can be rebuilt from original sources and an archive copy.

Archiving and backup are not the same thing. Archiving refers to the permanent storage of information for future reference, whereas backup refers to the storage of information for the sole purpose of restoration in the event of a failure. The effective difference is that you can reuse backup tapes but not archive tapes.

Backup and archiving are most effectively approached separately—solutions that do both will do neither well. For example, image backup software is better for backups and restoration in an emergency, and file-based backup software is better for archiving permanently on cheap tape or CD-R media. There is no reason to choose one or the other when you can have both.

file synchronization
The process of comparing files in different locations and transmitting the differences between them to ensure that both copies remain the same. Synchronization is only easy if you can guarantee that the two files won't change on both ends at the same time. If they can, then decisions must be made about which version to keep, and it may not be possible to automate the decision-making process depending upon the nature of the information.

Archiving is designed to respond to human error more than machine failure, which is covered more effectively by backup. Archiving allows you to solve the "I deleted a file four months ago and I realize that I need it back" problem or deal with users who say, "I accidentally overwrote this file four days ago with bad data. Can we get the old version back?" Because archiving permanently keeps copies of files and is usually implemented to keep all daily versions of files, you can easily recover from these sorts of problems. Trying to find individual files on tapes when you don't know the exact date is a long and tedious process akin to searching for a needle in a haystack.

Archives can be kept on online stores on special archive servers, which also run the archiving software and search other servers and computers for changed files. Archiving can be implemented by using various *file synchronization* packages, but software written specifically to do it is uncommon.

Deployment Testing

Deployment testing is the process of installing software and simulating normal use in order to discover problems with the software or compatibility before they affect production systems. Implementing deployment testing is as simple as maintaining a test server upon which you can create clones of existing servers by restoring a backup tape to it and then performing an installation of the new software.

Despite how simple it is to perform software deployment testing, it's actually rarely performed in smaller to medium-sized environments, which is unfortunate because it could eliminate a major source of downtime.

Using tools like vmware (from vmware corporation) or VirtualPC (from Microsoft) make deployment testing very easy. By restoring the most recent backup of the server in question into a virtual machine, you can make the configuration changes and software installation in a virtual environment and test for proper operation without having to dedicate a real machine to the problem—and even better, you can typically do the testing on your laptop.

Circuit Redundancy

Circuit redundancy is implemented by contracting for data circuits from separate Internet service providers and then using sophisticated routing protocols like the Interior Gateway Routing Protocol (IGRP) or the Exterior Gateway Routing Protocol (EGRP), both of which are capable of detecting circuit failure and routing data around it. They can also be configured to load-balance traffic between multiple circuits so that you can increase your available bandwidth. Proper circuit redundancy requires a complex router configuration, so you will probably need to bring in consultants who specialize in routing unless you have routing experts on staff.

Physical Security

Physical security is the set of security measures that don't apply to computers specifically, like locks on doors, security guards, and video surveillance.

Without physical security there is no security. This simply means that network security and software constructs can't keep your data secure if your server is stolen.

Centralization is axiomatic to security, and physical security is no exception. It's far easier to keep server and computer resources physically secure if they are located in the same room or are clustered in rooms on each floor or in each building. Distributing servers throughout your organization is a great way to increase overall bandwidth, but you need to be sure you can adequately protect workgroup servers from penetration before you decide to use a distributed architecture.

Physical security relies upon locks. The benefits of a strong lock are obvious and don't need to be discussed in detail, but there are some subtle differences between locking devices that are not immediately apparent. Key locks may have unprotected copies floating around. Combinations are copied every time they're told to someone. Choose biometric sensors like handprint scanners if you can afford them because they prove identity rather than simple possession of a device or code in order to allow access.

A secure space has secure lock mechanisms on each door, locks that can't simply be removed from the door, doors that can't be removed from outside the space, and no available access except doors. A secure space doesn't have glass windows, a drop ceiling adjoining other rooms, flimsy walls, or ventilation ducts large enough to crawl through.

combination
A numeric code used to open a physical lock.

Alarm systems add to the functionality of electronic locks by integrating them into a system capable of detecting unauthorized entry and alerting a monitoring agency. Most alarm systems are enabled and disabled with a keypad based on a *combination*—avoid these. Combinations are no more secure for alarm systems than they are for locks, and since most companies outsource their alarm monitoring, they're even less secure because at least one other agency has access to your codes. Good alarm systems can automatically call the police, integrate with fire alarms, and page responsible employees when alarms go off. Alarm systems add considerably to the security of a facility.

Finally, if you think that crime is a serious consideration for your business, security guards are a very effective deterrent to direct intrusion attempts. Businesses with security guards are far less likely to suffer from an insider-assisted theft than businesses that are unguarded.

Clustered Servers

Clustering is running a single application on multiple machines at one time. This allows you to apply the resources of many machines to one problem, and when properly implemented, it is an excellent way to handle large problems like problems with enterprise databases, commercial websites, and serious scientific applications.

There are actually two different technologies that fall in the clustering definition: fail-over clustering and load balancing.

Fail-Over Clustering

fail-over clustering
A fault tolerance method whereby a server can assume the services of a failed server.

Fail-over clustering, also called server replication, is the process of maintaining a running spare server that can take over automatically in the event that the primary server fails. Typically, these solutions use disk systems that can be switched from one machine to another automatically or they mirror changes to the disk from the primary server to the secondary server so that if something happens to the primary server, the secondary server can take over immediately.

Fail-over clustering does not allow multiple servers to handle the same service at the same time; rather, responsibility for clients is switched among members of the cluster when a failure event occurs.

These solutions are not without their problems—information stored in RAM on the servers is not maintained, so although the server can switch over, open network sessions will be dropped unless they are *stateless protocols* like HTTP. This would happen anyway if the primary server failed and was not replicated, and sessions can usually be automatically reestablished on the new server for file sharing protocols without difficulty. But fail-over clustering must be specifically supported by application services like SQL Server and messaging servers because those applications maintain responsibility for moving data among the members of the cluster.

stateless protocol
A protocols that does not maintain any information about the client session on the server side. Stateless protocols can be easily clustered across multiple machines without fear of data loss or side effects because it does not matter which server the client connects to from one instance to the next.

Fail-over clustering is the form implemented natively by Windows 2000 Advanced Server.

NOTE

Load-Balancing

There is another form of clustering that works well for certain problems: load balancing. *Load balancing* is quite simple; it allows multiple machines to respond to the same IP address and balances the client load among that group. For problems such as a web service, this makes all the servers appear to be one server that can handle a massive number of simultaneous connections. Both Windows and Unix support this type of clustering.

Load balancing
A clustering mechanism whereby individual client sessions are connected to any one of a number of identically configured servers so that the entire load of client sessions is spread evenly among the pool of servers.

Load balancing doesn't work for file service, database, or e-mail problems because there's no standard way to replicate data stored on one server to all the rest of the servers. For example, if on your first session you stored a file to the cluster (meaning one of the machines in the cluster) and then connected to the cluster at a later date, there's only a small chance that you would connect again to the machine that had your file. Stateless clustering works only with applications that don't maintain any data transmitted by the client—you can think of them as "output only" applications. Examples of this sort of application are web and FTP services.

There is a solution to even that problem, though—all the clustered machines can transmit their stored data to a single back-end storage or database server. This puts all the information in one place, where any user can find it no matter which clustered server they're attached to. Unfortunately, it also means that the cluster is no faster than the single machine used to store everything.

Stateless clustering works well in the one environment it was designed for: web service for large commercial sites. The amount of user information to store for a website is usually miniscule compared to the massive amount of data transmitted to each user. Because some websites need to handle millions of simultaneous sessions, this method lets designers put the client-handling load on frontline web servers and maintain the database load on back-end database servers.

Simple Server Redundancy

High availability and clustering solutions are all expensive—the software to implement them is likely to cost as much as the server you put it on. There are easy ways to implement fault tolerance, but they change depending on what you're doing and exactly what level of fault tolerance you need. I'll present a few ideas here to get you thinking about your fault tolerance problems.

Vendors traditionally calculate the cost of downtime using this method:

Employees × Average Pay Rate × Down Hours = Downtime Costs

Sounds reasonably complete, but it's based on the assumption that employees in your organization become worthless the moment their computers go down. Sometimes that's the case, but often it's not. I'm not advocating downtime; I'm merely saying that the assumptions used to cost downtime are flawed and that short periods of downtime aren't nearly as expensive as data loss or the opportunity cost of lost business if your business relies on computers to transact.

If you can tolerate 15 minutes of downtime, a whole array of less expensive options emerges. For example, manually swapping an entire server doesn't take long, especially if the hard disks are on removable cartridges. For an event that might occur once a year, this really isn't all that bad.

The following inexpensive methods can achieve different measures of fault tolerance for specific applications.

The DNS service can assign more than one IP address to a single domain name. If there's no response from the first address, the client can check, in order, each of the next addresses until it gets a response (however, depending on the client-side address caching mechanism, it may take a few minutes for the client to make another DNS attempt). This means that for web service, you can simply put up an array of web servers, each with its own IP address, and trust that users will be able to get through to one of them. With web service, it rarely matters which server clients attach to; as long as they're all serving the same data, you have fault tolerance.

Another way to solve the load-balancing problem is with firewalls. Many firewalls can be configured to load-balance a single IP address across a group of identical machines, so you can have three web servers that all respond to a single address behind one of these firewalls.

Fault tolerance for standard file service can be achieved by simply cross-copying files among two or more servers. By doubling the amount of disk space in each server, you can maintain a complete copy of all the data on another machine by periodically running a script to copy files from one machine to another or by using a mechanism like the Windows File Replication Service. In the event that a machine has crashed, users can simply remap the drive letter they use for the primary machine to the machine with the share to which you have backed everything up. By using the archive bit to determine which files should be copied, you can update only those files that have changed, and you can make the update fairly frequently—say, once per hour.

There is a time lag based on the periodicity of your copy operation, so this method may not work in every situation. Since it's not completely automatic (users have to recognize the problem and manually remap a drive letter), it's not appropriate for every environment. You reduce the automation problem by providing a desktop icon that users can click to run a batch file that will remap the drive.

Fault tolerance doesn't mean you have to spend a boatload of money on expensive hardware and esoteric software. It means that you must think about the problem and come up with the simplest workable solution. Sometimes that means expensive hardware and esoteric software, but not always.

Terms to Know

archive marking	file synchronization
archiving	load balancing
BIOS (Basic Input/Output System)	mean time between failures (MTBF)
circuit	offline
combination	online
disk packs	RAID
fail-over clustering	removable media
fault tolerance	stateless protocol

Review Questions

1. What are the four major causes for loss, in order of likelihood?

2. What is the best way to recover from the effects of human error?

3. What is the most likely component to fail in a computer?

4. What is the most difficult component to replace in a computer?

5. What is the easiest way to avoid software bugs and compatibility problems?

6. How can you recover from a circuit failure when you have no control over the ISP's repair actions?

7. What are the best ways to mitigate the effects of hacking?

8. What is the most common form of fault tolerance?

9. What is the difference between an incremental backup and a differential backup?

10. What causes the majority of failures in a tape backup solution?

11. Why is RAID-0 not appropriate as a form of fault tolerance?

12. RAID-10 is a combination of which two technologies?

13. If you create a RAID-5 pack out of five 36GB disks, how much storage will be available?

14. What are the two methods used to perform offsite storage?

15. What is the difference between backup and archiving?

16. What are the two common types of clustering?

Chapter 10

Windows Security

This chapter will provide you with all the information you need to understand the major Windows security mechanisms in the Windows NT/2000/XP/2003 family, along with some management advice and practical walk-throughs.

But no single chapter, and perhaps not even a single book, could cover the wide array of Windows security mechanisms in complete detail. Once you've read this chapter and used the information presented herein to design a security architecture for your network, consult the Internet RFCs upon which most of these standards are based for technical details of their operation. Microsoft's Resource Kits and Training Kits are the authoritative source for the Microsoft implementation of these mechanisms and should be consulted for configuration-specific information.

Windows Local Security

Windows security is based on user authentication. Before you can use a Windows computer, you must supply a username and a password. The *logon prompt* (provided by the WinLogon process) identifies you to the computer, which then provides access to resources you are allowed to use and denies access to things you aren't. This combination of a user identity and password is called a *user account.*

logon prompt
The interface through which users identify themselves to the computer.

> **NOTE**
>
> **Windows 95/98/Me has no significant security mechanisms to speak of, and these systems are not in themselves secure, so no information in this chapter applies to them.**

user account
The association between a user account name, a password, and a security identifier.

It is possible for a computer to be set up to automatically log on for you, using stored credentials or an account that has an empty password (as is the case by default in Windows XP Home), but an account is still logged on, and the security that applies to that account is used to manage permissions for that user session.

security group
A construct containing a security identifier (SID) that is used to create permissions for an object. User accounts are associated with security groups and inherit their permissions from them.

Windows also provides *security groups*. When a user account is a member of a security group, the permissions that apply to the security group also apply to the user account. For example, if a user is a member of the Financial security group, then the permissions of the Financial security group are available to the user account. User accounts may be members of any number of security group accounts, and they accumulate the sum of the permissions allowed for all of those groups.

> **NOTE**
>
> **Allowing multiple people to log in using a single account invalidates the concept of accountability that is central to Windows security. Even when a group of people do the same job, each user should have an individual account so that when one user violates security, you can track the violation back to a specific user rather than a group of people. If you want to control security for a group of people, use security groups rather than shared accounts.**

User and group accounts are valid only for the Windows computer on which they are created. These accounts are local to the computer. The only exception to this rule is computers that are members of a domain and therefore trust the user accounts created in the Active Directory on a domain controller. Domain security is discussed later in this chapter. Computers that are members of a domain trust both their own local accounts and Active Directory accounts (Windows 2000) or the primary domain controller's (PDC's) accounts (Windows NT).

> **WARNING**
>
> **The most common Windows security flaw I see is administrators who strongly secure domain accounts yet forget about the local administrator account on workstations and member servers. Their passwords are rarely changed from the installation default, which is frequently left blank or set to something simple during the operating system installation! Always set very strong local administrative account passwords.**

Each Windows computer has its own list of local user and group accounts. The WinLogon *process* (which logs you on and sets up your computing environment) passes your credentials to the *Local Security Authority (LSA)* when you log in. The LSA determines whether you are attempting to log in using a local account or a domain account.

If you're using a local account, the LSA invokes the *Security Accounts Manager (SAM),* which is the Windows operating system component that controls local account information. The SAM will refer to the database (stored in the *Registry*) and return the account information to the WinLogon process.

If you are logging in with a domain account, the Local Security Authority will query the NetLogon process on the domain controller and return the validated logon information (the security identifier) to the WinLogon process so that an access token can be created.

Irrespective of the source of authentication, access is allowed only to the local computer by the computer's Local Security Authority (LSA).

When you access other computers in the same domain, the local computer's LSA establishes your credentials automatically with the LSA on the foreign computer by passing the access token held by your LSA, effecting a logon for each computer you contact. To gain access to a foreign computer, that computer must trust the credentials provided by your computer.

When you access other computers in a foreign domain running operating systems other than Windows, through Internet Explorer, or by using the workgroup mechanism, your account name and hashed password are transmitted to the foreign computer where you are logged in using whatever native mechanism exists if a matching account name is found. This is called transparent background authentication. If a matching account name is not found, a logon dialog will appear asking for credentials on the local machine.

Security Identifiers

Security principles, like user accounts and *computer accounts,* are represented in the system as *security identifiers (SIDs).* The SID is a serial number that uniquely identifies the security principle to all the computers in the domain, much the way that a Social Security number uniquely identifies national citizens. When you create an account using the User Manager (Windows NT) or the Local Users and Groups snap-in (Windows 2000/XP), a new SID is always created, even if you use the same account name and password as a deleted account. The SID will remain with the account for as long as the account exists. You may change any other aspect of the account, including the username and password, but you cannot change the SID under normal circumstances—if you did, you would create a new account.

---

process
A running program.

Local Security Authority (LSA)
The process that controls access to secured objects in Windows.

Security Accounts Manager (SAM)
The process that controls access to the user account database in the Registry.

Registry
A hierarchical database local to each Windows computer and used for storing configuration information.

security principle
A user, computer, or security group account.

computer accounts
Security identifiers that uniquely identify computers in a domain and authenticate their participation in the domain.

security identifier (SID)
A unique serial number used to identify user, computer, and security group accounts.

Security group accounts also have SIDs, which are unique identifiers that are created when the group is created. The rules that apply to account SIDs also apply to group SIDs.

Logging In

When you log in, you identify yourself to the computer. The process of logging in is managed by the WinLogon mechanism of the Local Security Authority.

The LSA is a part of the kernel through which all access to secured objects is routed. When you request access to a file, the request is passed through the LSA for authentication before it is passed to the file system. The LSA is the gatekeeper of local security in Windows NT–based operating systems.

New Technology LAN Manager (NTLM)
The network authentication protocol used prior to Kerberos in Windows NT. NTLM is a much simpler authentication protocol that does not support transitive trusts and stores domain user accounts in the SAM of the primary domain controller.

The WinLogon process checks your username and password (or smartcard, if so configured) to determine if you should be allowed to access the computer. If the name supplied in the logon box is the local computer name, the WinLogon process checks the account against the local SAM stored in the Registry. Otherwise, the WinLogon process contacts a domain controller for the domain name specified and uses Kerberos (Windows 2000/XP) or *NTLM* (Windows NT) authentication to authenticate the user, depending upon the client operating system.

access token
A combination of security identifiers that represents the user account and the security groups that it belongs to. Access tokens are passed from the initial logon to all user-mode programs executed subsequently.

If the account name is valid and the password's hash matches the stored hash (thus indicating that the password is correct), the WinLogon process will create an *access token* for you. The access token is composed of the account SID, the SIDs of the groups the account belongs to, and a *locally unique identifier (LUID)*, which indicates a specific logon session (to differentiate between two simultaneously logged in sessions).

NOTE

An access token is created each time you log on to Windows. This is why you must log off and then log back on again after making changes to your user account—you need a new access token that will reflect the changes you have made.

locally unique identifier (LUID)
An identifier that is created for each logged-on instance of a user account to differentiate it from other logon sessions.

The WinLogon process then launches the program that is configured in the Registry as the shell, usually Windows Explorer, and passes your access token to it. Windows Explorer then provides the access token to the LSA whenever it needs access to a secured object, like a file. The file's Discretionary Access Control List (DACL) is then compared to the access token to determine if access should be granted.

When Explorer launches another program, it passes the access token to it as well, so it can provide credentials to the LSA when it subsequently accesses secured objects.

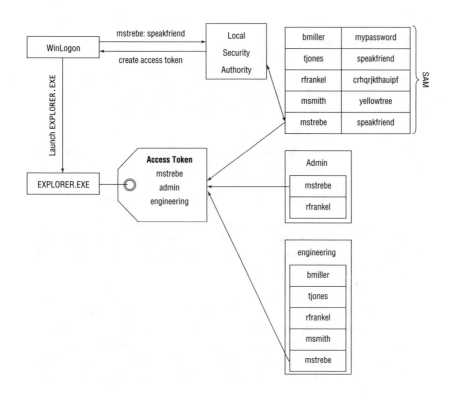

Resource Access

Whenever a program is started in Windows, the program that launches it (usually *Windows Explorer*) provides it with an access token based on its own access token. This way, every program has an access token that will always match the identity of the person who originally logged in, and it can then provide the access token to the system in order to gain access to secured resources. The forwarded access token is a copy of the one originally passed to Windows Explorer by the WinLogon process.

The WinLogon process was started from a user-generated interrupt (the Ctrl+Alt+Del keyboard interrupt) and is special in that it does not inherit an access token from its parent process; rather, it can create new access tokens by querying either the local Security Accounts Manager or the NetLogon Service, which in turn queries the *Directory Services Agent (DSA)* on an Active Directory domain controller or the SAM on a Windows NT domain controller. The WinLogon process and the Run As service are the only processes that are able to create access tokens.

Windows Explorer
The shell program in Windows from which most user-mode programs are launched.

Directory Services Agent (DSA)
The service that communicates between the Local Security Authority and the Active Directory in order to authenticate domain users.

> ### Mandatory Logons
>
> The foundation of Windows security is the mandatory login. Unlike in some networking systems, there is no way for a user to do anything in Windows without a user account name and password. Although you can choose to automatically log in with credentials provided from the Registry, a user account logon still occurs.
>
> Although it's not the friendliest of keystrokes, there's a very good reason Windows requires the Ctrl+Alt+Del keystroke to log in, and it's one of the reasons Windows is considered secure. Because the computer handles the Ctrl+Alt+Del keystroke as a hardware interrupt, there's literally no way to for a clever programmer to make the keystroke do something else without rewriting the operating system.
>
> Without this feature, a hacker would be able to write a program that displayed a fake login screen and collected passwords from unsuspecting users. However, since the fake screen wouldn't be able to include the Ctrl+Alt+Del keystroke, users familiar with Windows would not be fooled.
>
> It is possible to set passwords to be blank. In this case, you need only indicate your username in order to login. A mandatory logon has still occurred; it's just not very secure because no password is required. This is the method used by default in Windows XP Home. Users merely click on an icon representing their identity and are not required to enter a password, unless they configure the operating system to require it. Microsoft seems committed to sacrificing security for the sake of user convenience.

Through this method, every program that is started after a user has logged on will have the access token that represents the user. Because programs must always provide that token to access resources, there is no way to circumvent Windows 2000 resource security.

Since the access token is passed to new programs when the programs are started, there is no further need to access the SAM database locally or the Active Directory on a domain controller for authentication once a user has logged on.

Objects and Permissions

permission
An access control entry in an object's Discretionary Access Control List.

In order for a user to perform an action on a secured entity like a file or directory, the user must have permission. In this case, a *permission* is an access control entry that links the action to be performed to the security identifier of the user account attempting the operation. If the link exists, the operating system executes the action; otherwise, it will deny access and display an error message.

Windows maintains security for various types of *objects* including (but not limited to) directories, files, printers, processes, and network shares. Each object exposes services that the object allows to be performed upon it—for example, open, close, read, write, delete, start, stop, print, and so on.

The security information for an object is contained in the object's *security descriptor*. The security descriptor has four parts: owner, group, *Discretionary Access Control List (DACL)*, and *System Access Control List (SACL)*. Windows uses these parts of the security descriptor for the following purposes:

Owner   This part contains the SID of the user account that has ownership of the object. The object's *owner* may always change the settings in the DACL (the permissions) of the object, irrespective of whether or not the owner has permission to access the file.

Group   This part is used by the POSIX subsystem of Windows. Files and directories in Unix operating systems can belong to a group as well as to an individual user account. This part contains the SID of the group this object belongs to for the purposes of POSIX compatibility. Windows does not use this field for any other purpose. Don't be confused by the name: Windows security groups cannot be owners of a resource. Group security and permissions are managed through the DACL, not through this field.

Discretionary Access Control List   The DACL contains a list of user accounts and group accounts that have permission to access the object's services. The DACL has as many access control entries as there are user or group accounts that have been specifically given access to the object.

System Access Control List   The SACL also contains *access control entries (ACEs)*, but these ACEs are used for auditing rather than for permitting or denying access to the object's services. The SACL has as many ACEs as there are user or group accounts that are specifically being audited.

Access to a resource will be allowed if an access token contains any SID that matches a permission in the DACL that corresponds to the type of access requested. For example, if an individual account is allowed Read access and the user account is a member of a group account that is allowed Write access, then the access token for that logged-on user will contain both SIDs and the LSA will allow Read and Write access to the object because the DACL contains an entry that matches each type of access. Deny ACEs still override any accumulation of permission.

For example, if user mstrebe wants to access a file called `ADDRESS.TXT`, then the system (actually a component called the Security Reference Monitor) will compare the access token of his running the `WINWORD.EXE` program to the DACL associated with `ADDRESS.TXT`. If `ADDRESS.TXT` has any SID in common with the access token for `WINWORD.EXE` that allows Read access, then he can open the file, otherwise access is denied.

---

objects
Data structures in a computer environment, such as files, directories, printers, shares, and so forth.

security descriptor
Information stored with each object that specifies the owner and contains the access control list.

owner
The user account that created an object or was otherwise assigned ownership. The owner of an object has the right to change its permissions irrespective of user account's permissions.

Discretionary Access Control List (DACL)
The access control list that is used to allow or deny access to an object.

access control entry (ACE)
An entry in an access control list that joins a security identifier to a type of allowed or denied access.

System Access Control List (SACL)
An access control list used to determine how to audit objects.

deny ACE

An access control entry that specifically denies permissions in order to override other permissions that might allow access to an account.

A special type of ACE, called a *deny ACE,* indicates that the account identified by the SID will be denied all access to the object. A deny ACE overrides all other ACEs. Windows implements the No Access permission using the deny ACE.

The access control entries in the SACL are formed the same way as the ACEs in the DACL (they are composed of a SID and an access mask), but the access mask, in this case, identifies those services of the object for which the account will be audited.

Not every object has a security descriptor. The FAT file system, for example, does not record security information, so file and directory objects stored on a FAT volume lack owners, DACLs, and SACLs. When a security descriptor is missing, any user account may access any of the object's services. This is not the same as when an object has an empty DACL. In that case, no account may access the object. When there is no SACL for an object, that object may not be audited. An existing but empty SACL indicates that an object can be but is not currently being audited.

Rights versus Permissions

There are activities that do not apply to any specific object but instead apply to a group of objects or to the operating system as a whole. Shutting down the operating system, for example, affects every object in the system. To perform operations of this nature, the user is required to have *user rights*.

Earlier in this chapter, I mentioned that the Local Security Authority includes a locally unique identifier (LUID) when it creates an access token. The LUID describes which of the user rights that particular user account has. The Local Security Authority creates the LUID from security information in the Security Accounts Manager database. The SAM database matches users with rights. The LUID is a combination of the rights of a specific user account and the rights of all the groups of which that account is a member.

Rights take precedence over permissions. That's why the Administrator account can take ownership of a file even though the owner of the file has set the No Access to Everyone permission; the Administrator has the Take Ownership of Files or Other Objects right. The Windows operating system checks the user rights first, and then (if there is no user right specifically allowing the operation) the operating system checks the ACEs stored in the DACL against the SIDs in the access token.

User accounts have the right to read or write to an object the user account owns even in the case of a *No Access permission*. The owner may also change the permissions of an object irrespective of the object's existing permissions.

NTFS File System Permissions

The *NTFS* file system is the bastion of Windows security. Being the platform upon which a secure Windows computer runs, NTFS is the gatekeeper of persistent security.

The LSA makes sure that running programs cannot violate each other's memory space and that all calls into the kernel are properly authorized. But access to files on disk must also be controlled, since running programs are loaded from disk files that could potentially be changed to anything. NTFS prevents unauthorized access to disk files, which is required for a truly secure system.

NTFS works by comparing a user's access token to the ACL associated with each file requested before allowing access to the file. This simple mechanism keeps unauthorized users from modifying the operating system or anything else they're not given specific access to.

Unfortunately, the default state of Windows is to provide full control to the Everyone group at the root of all drives so that all permissions inherited by files created therein are accessible by everyone. In order to receive any real benefit from NTFS file system security for applications and user-stored files, you must remove the Full Control for Everyone permission and replace it with the appropriate user or group.

NOTE

Windows Server 2003 is far more serious about default security than Windows 2000 or prior versions of Windows NT. However, you must still manage permissions explicitly for your environment if security is important.

Using Windows Explorer, you can only replace permissions on existing files, which means that if you perform a permissions change across a large group of objects, the result will be that they all have the same permissions. Using the CACLS command prompt tool, you can edit a large body of objects to insert or remove specific permissions without affecting the other existing permissions on the objects.

Managing NTFS File System Permissions

inherit
To receive a copy of security information from the launching program, containing folder, or other such precursor.

Managing NTFS file system permissions in Windows is simple. To change security permissions on a file or folder, browse to the file or folder object using the Windows Explorer, right-click the file or folder, select the Permissions tab, select the appropriate group or user account, and make the appropriate settings in the Access Control Entry list.

When a new file or directory is created, it receives a copy of the containing folder's (or drive's, if the object is created in the root) permissions (the DACL). In this way, objects are said to *inherit* permissions from their *parent*.

parent
The preceding process (for programs) or containing folder (for objects, directories, and files).

Inheritance is handled slightly differently in Windows 2000 than it is in Windows NT. In Windows NT, inherited permissions are simply the same as the parent objects and can be immediately modified. In Windows 2000, if the object is inheriting its permissions from a containing folder object, you'll have to uncheck the Allow Inheritable Permissions check box in order to create a copy of the inherited permissions and then modify the existing permissions. You can create new ACEs without overriding the inheritance setting.

Encrypting File System (EFS)

Encrypting File System (EFS) is a file system driver that provides the ability to encrypt and decrypt files on-the-fly. The service is very simple to use: users need only check the encrypted attribute on a file or directory to cause the EFS service to generate an encryption certificate in the background and use it to encrypt the affected files. When those files are requested from the NTFS file system driver, the EFS service automatically decrypts the file for delivery.

The biggest problem with EFS is that it only works for individual users. That fact alone makes it useful only on client computers. Encryption certificates for files are created based on a user identity, so encrypted files can only be used by the account that created them.

NOTE

This is extremely shortsighted on Microsoft's part. If encryption certificates could be assigned to group objects rather than just accounts, encryption could be used to protect general files stored on a server.

EFS also has numerous accidental decryption problems that can occur when files are printed, when temporary files are created, and when files are moved. For these reasons, you should consider a third-party encryption package if you truly require encrypted storage on your system.

Windows Network Security

Windows network security is based on a few principle services:

◆ Active Directory

◆ Kerberos

◆ Group Policy

◆ Share security

◆ IPSec

All of these services work together to form a coherent whole: IPSec is defined by group policies, which are stored in the Active Directory and can be configured to use Kerberos for automatic private key exchange. Share security is based on user identity as proven by Kerberos authentication based on password hashes stored in the Active Directory. Managing security policy through the Active Directory allows administrators to create group policies that can be automatically applied throughout the organization.

Active Directory

Active Directory is not a security service, but nearly all the security mechanisms built into Windows rely upon the Active Directory as a storage mechanism for security information like the domain hierarchy, trust relationships, crypto keys, certificates, policies, and security principle accounts.

Because nearly all of Windows's security mechanisms are integrated within Active Directory, you'll use it to manage and apply security. Most of the technologies covered in the sections to follow could be considered components of Active Directory because they're so tightly integrated with it.

Although Active Directory is not a security service, it can be secured: Active Directory containers and objects have ACLs just as NTFS files do. In Active Directory, permissions can be applied to directory objects in much the same way as they can be applied to files by NTFS.

Unlike NTFS file system permissions, you can set permissions for the fields inside specific objects so that different users or security groups can be responsible for portions of an object's data. For example, while you wouldn't want to give

Active Directory

A database that is distributed among the domain controllers in a domain or tree and contains user accounts, machine accounts, and other administrative information concerning the network.

a user the ability to change anything about their own user account, allowing them to update their contact information is a good idea. This is possible using Active Directory permissions.

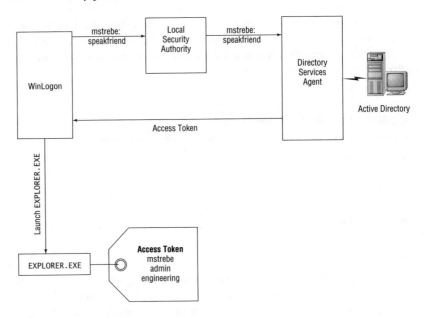

Kerberos Authentication and Domain Security

Kerberos
An authentication protocol that allows for a transitive trust between widely diverse domains. The primary authentication protocol for Windows 2000 and many Unix distributions.

Key Distribution Center (KDC)
In Kerberos, a computer that manages user accounts. Domain Controllers perform the KDC function in Windows.

Kerberos authentication was developed by the Massachusetts Institute of Technology (MIT) to provide an inter-computer trust system that was capable of verifying the identity of security principles like a user or a computer over an open, unsecured network. Kerberos does not rely on authentication by the computers involved or the privacy of the network communications. For this reason, it is ideal for authentication over the Internet and on large networks.

Kerberos operates as a trusted third-party authentication service by using shared secret keys. Essentially, a computer implicitly trusts the Kerberos *Key Distribution Center (KDC)* because it knows the same secret the computer knows, a secret that must have been placed there as part of a trusted administrative process. In Windows, the shared secret is generated when the computer joins the domain. Since both parties to a Kerberos session trust the KDC, they can be considered to trust each other. In practice, this trust is implemented as a secure exchange of encryption keys that proves the identities of the parties involved to one another.

Kerberos authentication works like this. A requesting client requests a valid set of credentials for a given server from the KDC by sending a plaintext request containing the client's name (identifier).

The KDC responds by looking up both the client and the server's secret keys in its database (the Active Directory) and creating a *ticket* containing a random session key, the current time on the KDC, an expiration time determined by policy, and optionally, any other information stored in the database. The ticket is then encrypted using the client's secret key. A second ticket called the session ticket is then created; the session ticket comprises the session key and optional authentication data that is encrypted using the server's secret key. The combined tickets are then transmitted back to the client. It's interesting to note that the authenticating server does not need to authenticate the client explicitly because only the valid client will be able to decrypt the ticket.

Once the client is in possession of a valid ticket and session key for a server, it can initiate communications directly with the server. To initiate a communication with a server, the client constructs an authenticator consisting of the current time, the client's name, an application-specific checksum if desired, and a randomly generated initial sequence number and/or a session subkey used to retrieve a unique session identifier specific to the service in question. Authenticators are only valid for a single attempt and cannot be reused or exploited through a replay attack because they are dependent upon the current time. The authenticator is then encrypted using the session key and transmitted along with the session ticket to the server from which service is requested.

When the server receives the ticket from the client, it decrypts the session ticket using the server's shared secret key (which secret key, if more than one exists, is indicated in the plaintext portion of the ticket). It then retrieves from the session key the ticket and uses it to decrypt the authenticator. The server's ability to decrypt the ticket proves that it was encrypted using the server's private key known only to the KDC, so the client's identity is trusted. The authenticator is used to ensure that the communication is recent and is not a replay attack. Tickets can be reused for a duration specified by the domain security policy, not to exceed 10 hours. This reduces the burden on the KDC by requiring ticket requests as few as once per workday. Clients cache their session tickets in a secure store located in RAM and destroy them when they expire.

Kerberos uses the reusability property of tickets to shortcut the granting of tickets by granting a session ticket for itself as well as for the requested target server the first time it is contacted by a client. Upon the first request by a client, the KDC responds first with a session ticket for further ticket requests called a Ticket Granting Ticket (TGT) and then with a session ticket for the requested server. The TGT obviates further Active Directory lookups by the client by pre-authenticating subsequent ticket requests in exactly the same manner that Kerberos authenticates all other requests. Like any session ticket, the TGT is valid until it expires, which depends upon domain security policy.

Kerberos is technically divided into two services: the TGT service (the only service that actually authenticates against the Active Directory) and the Ticket Granting service, which issues session tickets when presented with a valid TGT.

ticket
In Kerberos, encrypted time and identity information used to authenticate access between computers.

Trust Relationships between Domains

Kerberos works across *domain* boundaries. (Domains are called realms in Kerberos terminology—the two terms are equivalent.)

The name of the domain that a security principle belongs to is part of the security principle's name (e.g., titanium.sandiego.connetic.net). Membership in the same Active Directory tree automatically creates inter-domain keys for Kerberos between a parent domain and its child domains.

The exchange of inter-domain keys registers the domain controllers of one domain as security principles in the trusting domain. This simple concept makes it possible for any security principle in the domain to get a session ticket on the foreign KDC.

What actually happens is a bit more complex. When a security principle in one domain wants to access a security principle in an adjacent domain (one domain is the parent domain, one is the child), it sends a session ticket request to its local KDC. When the KDC determines that the target is not in the local domain, it replies to the client with a referral ticket, which is a session ticket encrypted using the inter-domain key. The client then uses the referral ticket to request a session ticket directly from the foreign KDC. The foreign KDC then decrypts the referral ticket because it has the inter-domain key, which proves that the trusted domain controller trusts the client (or it would not have granted the referral key), so the foreign KDC grants a session ticket valid for the foreign target server.

The process simply reiterates for domains that are farther away. To access a security principle in a domain that is two hops away in the Active Directory domain hierarchy, the client requests a session ticket for the target server against its KDC, which responds with a referral ticket to the next domain away. The client then requests the session ticket using the referral ticket just granted. That server will simply reply with a referral ticket that is valid on the next server in line. This process continues until the local domain for the target security principle is reached. At that point, a session key (technically, a TGT and a session key) is granted to the requesting client, which can then authenticate against the target security principle directly.

The Ticket Granting Ticket authentication service is especially important in inter-domain ticket requests. Once a computer has walked down the referral path once, it receives a TGT from the final KDC in the foreign domain. This ensures that subsequent requests in that domain (which are highly likely) won't require the referral walk again. The TGT can simply be used against the foreign KDC to request whatever session tickets are necessary in the foreign domain.

The final important concept in Kerberos authentication is delegation of authentication. Essentially, delegation of authentication is a mechanism whereby a security principle allows another security principle with which it has established a session to request authentication on its behalf from a third security principle. This mechanism is important in multitier applications, such as a database-driven website. Using delegation of authentication, the web browser client can authenticate with the web

domain
A collection of computers that trust the same set of user accounts. Domain accounts are stored in the Active Directory.

server and then provide the web server with a special TGT that it can use to request session tickets on its behalf. The web server can then use the forwarded credentials of the web client to authenticate with the database server. This allows the database server to use appropriate security for the actual web client rather than using the web server's credentials, which would have completely different access than the actual client.

Group Policy

Group policy is Windows' primary mechanism for controlling the configuration of client workstations for security as well as administrative purposes. Policies in general are simply a set of changes to the default settings of a computer. Policies are usually organized in such a way that individual policies contain changes that implement a specific goal—for example, disabling or enabling file system encryption or controlling which programs a user is allowed to run.

Group Policies are polices that are applied to groups like security groups or the members of an Active Directory container like a domain or organizational unit. Group Policy is not strictly a security mechanism—its primary purpose is change and configuration management—but it allows administrators to create more secure systems by limiting users' range of actions.

Group policies can be used to control the following for computer policies:

- Registry settings related to security configuration and control
- Windows Installer package distribution
- Startup/shutdown scripts
- Services startup
- Registry permissions
- NTFS permissions
- Public key policies
- IPSec policies
- System, network, and windows components settings

Group policies can be used to control the following for user policies:

- Windows Installer
- Internet Explorer settings
- Logon/logoff scripts
- Security settings
- Remote Installation Service
- Folder redirection
- Windows components

Group Policy

A collection of computer and user configuration policies that are applied to computers based upon their association within an Active Directory container like a domain or organizational unit.

- Start menu, Taskbar, Desktop, and Control Panel settings
- Network settings
- System settings

Mechanics of Group Policy

Group Policy objects and any supporting files required for a Group Policy are stored on domain controllers in the SysVol share. Group Policy objects are essentially custom Registry files (and supporting files like .msi packages and scripts) defined by policy settings that are downloaded and applied to domain member client computers when the computer is booted (computer policy) and when a user logs in (user policy). Multiple group policies can be applied to the same computer, each policy overwriting the previous policy settings in a "last application wins" scenario—unless a specific policy is configured not to be overwritten.

Each Group Policy object has two parts: *computer policy* and *user policy*. You can configure both user and computer settings in a single group policy object, and you can disable the computer or user portion of a Group Policy object in the policy's Properties panel. I recommend splitting all policies to apply to either users or computers because the policies are downloaded at different times and because the configuration requirements for the two types of security principles are highly likely to diverge over time, requiring the application of a different policy anyway.

Computer policies are applied at system initialization before a user logs in (and during periodic refreshes). Computer policies control the operating system, applications (including the Desktop Explorer), and startup and shutdown scripts. Think of computer policies as applying to the HKEY_Local_Machine portion of the Registry. Computer policies usually take precedence over user policies in the event of a conflict. Use computer policies whenever a configuration is required regardless of who logs on to the computer. You easily can apply a company-wide policy to computer policies.

User policies are applied after a user logs in but before they're able to work on the computer, as well as during the periodic refresh cycle. User policies control operating system behavior, desktop settings, application settings, folder redirection, and user logon/logoff scripts. Think of user policies as applying to the HKEY_Current_User portion of the Registry. Use user policies whenever a configuration is specific to a user or group of users, even if those users always use the same computers. By applying security-related settings to users rather than computers, you can ensure that those settings travel with the user in the event that they use someone else's computer—and that those policies don't apply to administrative or support personnel who may need to log on to the computer. (Of course, security group membership could be used to filter settings for support personnel as well.)

Group policies are called group policies because they're applied based on membership in Active Directory container security groups. Group policies are

computer policy
The portion of a Group Policy that is applied irrespective of which user account logs on.

user policy
The portion of Group Policy that applies to the logged-on user.

also hierarchical in nature; many policies can be applied to a single computer or user, and they are applied in hierarchical order. Furthermore, later policies can override the settings of earlier policies, so group change management can be refined from the broad policies applied to large groups to narrowly focused policies applied to smaller groups.

Group polices are configured at the following levels and in the following order:

Local Machine   Local Group Policy is applied first so that it can be overridden by a domain policy. Every computer has one local Group Policy that it is subject to. Beyond the local Group Policy, Group Policy objects are downloaded from the Active Directory depending upon the user's and computer's location in the Active Directory.

Site   These group policies are unique in that they are managed from the Active Directory Sites and Services snap-in. Site policies apply to sites, so they should be used for issues relating to the physical location of users and computers rather than for domain security participation. If your organization has only one site, this may not be obvious, but you should still apply policies this way because your organization may someday have multiple physical sites.

Domain   These group policies apply to all users and computers in the domain and should be the primary place where you implement global policies in your organization. For example, if your company has a security policy document that requires specific configuration of logon passwords for all users, apply that policy to the domain.

Organizational Unit   These group policies apply to organizational unit (OU) member users and computers. Group policies are applied from top to bottom (parent then child) in the OU hierarchy.

You cannot apply group policies to generic folders or containers other than those listed here. If you need to create a container for a Group Policy, use an organizational unit.

Group Policy objects are either all or nothing in their application—you cannot specify that only part of a policy will be applied. If you need to implement variations on a policy theme for different users, simply create one policy for each variation and apply the variants to the appropriate Active Directory container or security group.

A single Group Policy can be applied to more than one container in the Active Directory because group policies are not stored in the Active Directory at the location where you apply them. Only a link to the Group Policy object is stored—the objects themselves are actually stored in the replicated SysVol share of the domain controllers in the domain.

Share Security

Shares are directories or volumes made available from a workstation or server for access by other computers in the network. Shares can be publicly available, or they can be given a list of users or groups with permission to access them. Shares use share-level security, which allows you to control permissions for shared directories but not for anything contained within the directory. File-level security is superior to share-level security, but it can only be used on NTFS volumes.

Although you can set up a reasonably secure small network with shares, share security techniques don't really scale well for larger networks and environments where security is required because a new share must be created whenever security requirements change and because multiple shares with different security levels can be applied to the same directories.

Using and Securing Shares

File sharing is one of the most important uses of a network. Any directory on any workstation or server in the network can be set up as a shared directory. Although shares don't have the same level of security as NTFS directories on a dedicated server, Windows does provide a simple set of security features for shared directories.

Creating a Share

You can create a share with any volume or any directory within a volume. You can create shares in either NTFS or FAT partitions, although shares in NTFS partitions can be made more secure. To create a share, right-click a drive or a directory in an Explorer window and select the Sharing option. The Sharing Properties dialog box is displayed.

From this dialog box you can specify these options:

Not Shared/Shared As   Specify whether the volume or directory should be shared.

Share Name   Choose a name for the share. This name will appear as a directory name when users view a directory listing for the server. If the share will be accessed by users running Windows 3.*x* or if your users use DOS applications, be sure to use a DOS-compatible name for the share (eight or fewer characters).

Comment   Enter a description of the share's purpose, or other information. (This is optional.) The contents of this field are displayed in the Explorer window to the right of the share name if the user selects the Details view.

User Limit   If Maximum Allowed is selected, the number of users accessing the share is limited only by the Windows NT license. If a number is specified, only that many concurrent users can access the share.

Permissions   Clicking this button displays a dialog box that allows you to change permissions for the share, as described later in this chapter.

Caching   Click this button to configure caching options for this share. Offline caching allows users to store the file locally on their hard disk so it's available even if they're not online or if the server is unavailable.

When a directory or drive is shared, it is listed in Explorer with a special icon that shows a hand underneath the drive or folder icon.

Accessing Shares

Although a server might have several shares configured—some entire volumes, some directories several levels deep—they all appear to users as a single listing under the server's name. Users can navigate to the server name using the My Network Places icon and then open it to display a list of shares. Unfortunately, share names are not shown automatically in the Active Directory when you double-click on a computer—they must be manually added in the Active Directory hierarchy.

As an example, suppose we created several shares, including VOL_F for an entire NTFS volume and IE4 for the `\Program Files\Plus!\Microsoft Internet` directory. A user who navigated to the server through My Network Places or Network Neighborhood would see a flat list of shares.

To make access to shares more convenient for users in the workgroup, you can create Desktop shortcuts to particular directories. You can also map a drive letter on the workstation to the share. This method has the benefit of not only fooling users into thinking it's a local drive, but also fooling DOS and Windows applications that otherwise might not support network access. To map a drive to a share, right-click the My Network Places icon and then select Map Network Drive. Mapping drives is not normally necessary to access files from the Desktop Explorer or from Win32 applications.

To use this dialog box, choose a local drive letter and then choose a server name and path to map the drive to. In Windows NT, the window at the bottom of the dialog box displays a list of servers and shares. In Windows 2000 and XP, you click the Browse button to search for a server and share. Select the Reconnect at Logon option to have the drive mapped each time the user logs on.

As an administrator, you have another option for displaying a list of shares on a server. The Computer Management snap-in's Shared Folders extension allows you to list shares on the local machine, add or remove shares, and monitor users who are currently accessing shares. The tool is available in the Administrative Tools folder and works just like every other MMC snap-in.

Default Shares

Windows automatically creates some shares, called administrative shares, which are accessible only to administrators and the operating system itself. These shares are used for remote administration and communication between systems.

Each drive is automatically given an administrative share, with the share name being the drive letter followed by a dollar sign. The ADMIN$ share is connected to the \WINNT directory on each server. There is also an IPC$ share, used for inter-process communication between Windows NT servers, and a PRINT$ share, which shares printer information between servers. Domain controllers have a SYSVOL$ share used to distribute group policies, scripts, and installation packages.

As you've probably noticed, these shares don't appear in the browse lists that you can view from the Explorer. The only way to list them is with the Computer Management snap-in, which was described in the previous section.

TIP

You can create your own "administrative" shares. Any share name ending with a dollar sign ($) will be hidden from browse lists. Users (administrators or not) can access the share if they know its exact name.

Administrative shares present a potential security risk. A hacker who has gained access to the Administrator account on a single workstation in the workgroup can access the system drives of other workstations, effectively allowing administrator-level access to the entire workgroup.

You can improve security by disabling the administrative shares. You can remove the shares from each drive's Properties window or use the Shared Folder extension's Stop Sharing option. It's best to disable all of these and then add a share for any specific drives or directories that need to be available across the network.

Share versus File Security

Share-level security is similar to file system security, but not nearly as sophisticated (or as secure) because share access control entries can be applied only to the share as a whole. Security cannot be customized within a share.

There is one significant advantage of share-level security: It works with any shared directory, whether it's on an NTFS or FAT volume. Share-level security is the only way to secure FAT directories. However, the share permissions you set affect only remote users. Users logged on to the machine locally can access anything on a FAT volume, shared or not. Share-level security also does not apply to users logged on locally or to Terminal Services clients.

Share Permissions

To set permissions for a share, click the Permissions button from the Sharing Properties dialog box. By default, the Everyone built-in group is given Full Control access to the share—in other words, share security is not implemented by default. The first thing you should do to secure a share is remove the Everyone group from the list. You can then add any number of users or groups and give them specific permissions. The following are the permissions available for shares, and each can be allowed or denied:

Read   Allows users to list contents of the directory, open and read files, and execute programs.

Change   Allows users to create, delete, or modify files, as well as do everything the Read permissions allow.

Full Control   Allows all Read and Change permissions. In addition, users can change permissions and change file ownerships.

IPSec

Windows can be configured to use IPSec to secure communications between computers. Using default IPSec policy rules, you can configure clients to allow encryption and configure servers to request encryption or require encryption. A server that requires encryption will only communicate with hosts that have a valid Security Association (SA) that can be negotiated using Internet Key Exchange (IKE).

Windows 2000 supports both Authenticated Headers (AH) and Encapsulating Security Payload (ESP) in transport mode. Windows 2000 does not support ESP tunnel mode (IP encapsulation). This means that a Windows host cannot act as a bastion host and encrypt the communication stream between two private networks; it can only encrypt communications between itself and other hosts.

Windows 2000 uses IKE to negotiate encryption protocols and keys among hosts. As with any implementation of IKE, a private key is used for IKE authentication. In the case of Windows 2000, the private key can be a valid Kerberos ticket, a certificate, or a manually configured secret key.

Kerberos tickets   Make IPSec authentication seamless among hosts in the same domain, but they only work when all the participants are running Windows 2000 or higher.

Certificates   Are appropriate for use in extranets, in situations in which trust does not transit between domains, in communication with non-Windows hosts that can utilize certificates, or in environments where a Public Key Infrastructure (PKI) is in place.

Manual secret keys   Are useful for encrypting communications between hosts that are not in domains and not in PKI environments where communications with non-Windows hosts are required; they are also useful when compatibility problems prevent the use of Kerberos or certificates.

Windows 2000 creates filters to determine which SA a particular host belongs to in order to encrypt the communications with that host. These filters can be edited by the administrator to fix problems and for further customization or refinement. Automatically created filters tend to have problems if the host has more than one network adapter (as all remote access servers do) and in other situations.

Problems with IPSec

Microsoft believes that IPSec is the future of all communications among hosts in a network and sees it as something of a panacea for security problems. While it certainly could help with a number of problems, it's not compatible with more important security mechanisms like NAT and proxy service, and it prevents firewalls from seeing the interior of TCP and UDP packets, thus eliminating their ability to filter based on packet type. This creates a conundrum for security administrators: If you allow IPSec to transit your firewall, you eliminate the firewall's ability to filter IPSec traffic.

Because IPSec transport mode doesn't play well with firewalls and private addressing allowed by NAT, which are far more important to holistic security, IPSec really only has a purpose in securing administrative connections to public hosts and in environments (like the military) where secure communications are required on the interior of already public networks. For most users, host-to-host IPSec will not significantly improve security and will dramatically increase the administrative burden.

IPSec puts heavy loads on servers (which must maintain numerous simultaneous encrypted streams), so extra processing power is required. In the case of Terminal Services and database servers, CPU power is at a premium, so requiring encryption will reduce the number of users that a server can support.

In sum, these problems mean that host-to-host IPSec is going to remain a network-to-network encryption as implemented by IPSec tunnel-mode VPN devices, not a host-to-host security service as implemented by Windows 2000's IPSec transport mode. Once you have network-to-network communications established, there's little reason for most users to be concerned with additional encryption inside the private network.

Terms to Know

access control entry (ACE)

access token

Active Directory

computer accounts

computer policy

deny ACE

Directory Services Agent (DSA)

Discretionary Access Control List (DACL)

domain

Group Policy

inherit

Kerberos

Key Distribution Center (KDC)

Local Security Authority (LSA)

locally unique identifier (LUID)

logon prompt

No Access permission

New Technology File System (NTFS)

New Technology LAN Manager (NTLM)

objects

owner

parent

permission

process

Registry

Security Accounts Manager (SAM)

security descriptor

security group

security identifier (SID)

security principle

shares

System Access Control List (SACL)

ticket

user account

user policy

user rights

Windows Explorer

Review Questions

1. Upon what foundation is Windows security built?

2. Where is the list of local computer accounts stored?

3. What represents user accounts in Windows security?

4. What process manages logging in?

5. What protocol is used to authenticate a user account in a Windows 2000 domain?

6. How is the user's identity passed on to running programs?

7. When you attempt to access a file, what does the LSA compare your access token to in order to determine whether or not you should have access?

8. What special right does an object's owner possess?

9. For what purpose is the System Access Control List used?

10. What is the difference between a right and a permission?

11. What does the term *inheritance* mean in the context of file system permissions?

12. Where are user accounts stored in a domain?

13. In a Kerberos authentication, can a user in Domain A log on to a computer in Domain C if Domain C trusts Domain B and Domain B trusts Domain A?

14. What is the primary mechanism for controlling the configuration of client computers in Windows?

15. Can more than one Group Policy be applied to a single machine?

16. Does share security work on FAT file system shares?

Chapter 11

Securing Unix Servers

The security mechanisms available in standard UNIX (that being System V version 4), which essentially match those of BSD Unix, are significantly simpler than those in Windows. Unix was originally developed as a "security simplified" alternative to Multics—as such, security is mostly an afterthought designed more to prevent accidental harm by legitimate users than to keep hackers at bay. Microsoft specifically designed the NT kernel to allow for much more expressive configuration of security than Unix in order to out-compete it.

But complexity doesn't equal security—in fact, in most situations, complexity is anathema to security. And, the default configuration of Windows after an installation bypasses most of Windows's sophisticated security mechanisms anyway, whereas Unix security is usually considerably stricter than Windows security out of the box. In practice, Unix security can be configured similarly to Windows's security despite its inherent simplicity.

A Brief History of Unix

Multics

A complex operating system developed in the sixties with many innovative concepts, such as multitasking. Multics was the precursor to the simpler and more portable Unix.

To understand Unix security, it's important to understand why Unix was developed and how it evolved. In the mid-sixties, GE, MIT, and AT&T Bell Labs began development of an operating system that was supposed to become the standard operating system for the U.S. government. This system was called *Multics,* and its primary purpose was to support multiple users, multiple running programs, and multiple security levels simultaneously.

NOTE

In this book, *UNIX* in all uppercase letters refers specifically to AT&T System V version 4, and *Unix* with only an initial uppercase letter refers to all Unix-compatible operating systems generically. Linux is Unix, BSD is Unix, and UNIX is Unix.

Unfortunately, because of its distributed development and the difficult problems it attempted to solve, the Multics development effort became bogged down and fell years behind schedule. In 1969, AT&T pulled out of the Multics development effort. Multics was eventually completed in the early seventies, but it languished on a few government-owned and commercial systems without ever spawning an industry to support it or create applications for it. The last known running installation of Multics was shut down in 2000.

Ken Thompson, one of AT&T's programmers on the Multics team, decided to write a stripped-down version of Multics that threw out the security requirements that had bogged the project down and just allowed for the launching and control of multiple processes at the same time. With the help of Dennis Ritchie (codeveloper of the C programming language), he had a running operating system within a year. Ritchie suggested calling the operating system UNIX as a dig at the overburdened Multics operating system. In a few short years, the system had been completely rewritten in Ritchie's C programming language and included the C compiler, so that programmers had a complete system with which they could develop software.

Because AT&T was prevented by the Communications Act of 1957 from marketing or selling software in order to retain its monopoly status as the telephone provider for the entire country, it allowed Thompson to provide UNIX to whoever wanted it for the price of the tape that stored it. It quickly became popular in academic environments and as an operating system for new computer systems whose designers couldn't afford to develop an operating system.

Berkeley Software Distribution (BSD)

A highly customized version of Unix, originally distributed by the University of California at Berkeley.

In the mid-seventies, some students at Berkeley bought a tape of the operating system, including the source code. Unlike most others who merely used the operating system or, at most, ported it to a new type of computer, the Berkeley students set out to modify and improve the system as they saw fit. When they began distributing their improved version of Unix, they called it the *Berkeley Software Distribution,* or *BSD.* BSD soon incorporated the Mach micro-kernel developed at Carnegie Mellon University, which made the installation and incorporation of device drivers much easier and allowed for more distributed modular kernel development by more parties. By the early nineties, BSD did not contain any code that was developed at AT&T, and Berkeley was able to place the entire distribution into the public domain. It survives today as the BSD 4.4, FreeBSD, NetBSD, and OpenBSD open-source distributions and as the operating system for innumerable network devices.

In 1983, the U.S. government split AT&T up, and the restriction that prevented them from selling UNIX commercially was lifted. AT&T immediately recognized the potential of its operating system and began selling it directly and licensing it to computer manufactures who needed compelling operating systems for their mainframes. AT&T officially licensed UNIX to IBM (who named their version AIX), Hewlett-Packard (who named theirs HP-UX), Digital (who named theirs Digital UNIX and now Compaq Tru64), and many others.

AT&T realized the threat posed by BSD, which was technically superior to UNIX and not controlled by AT&T. AT&T refused to allow the UNIX trademark to be used to describe BSD and convinced its corporate customers that BSD was not well supported and so should not be used in commercial enterprises. Largely, AT&T's tactics worked, and UNIX was pretty much officially split into the academic version (BSD) and the commercial version (AT&T UNIX System V). (Microsoft is now using exactly this tactic against competitive open-source operating systems.)

The only major exception to this division of commercial and open-source versions was Sun Microsystems, which based its SunOS on BSD. After heavy marketing to Sun throughout the eighties, AT&T finally convinced Sun to base a new operating system on System V, and Solaris was born. Solaris attempted to merge the two worlds and was mostly compatible with applications written for BSD and System V.

Microsoft simultaneously developed Xenix, which was based on the earlier AT&T System III UNIX, in the early eighties but sold it to the Santa Cruz Operation (SCO) when it couldn't be successfully marketed. Xenix was the first Unix for Intel microcomputers.

Just after completing its domination of the commercial UNIX world, AT&T decided that its fortunes lay in telecommunications after all and sold UNIX to Novell. Novell completely mishandled the acquisition and wound up selling it to the Santa Cruz Operation less than two years later for about 10 percent of what it paid for it—but not before it opened the term *UNIX* to any operating system that could pass a suite of UNIX-compatibility tests, thus allowing BSD to again be referred to as UNIX. SCO UNIX is now actually the original official AT&T System V version 4.

So, at this point, there really is no "official" Unix, merely a set of standards: BSD 4.4 and AT&T System V version 4. Nearly all versions of Unix are based on one of these two standard platforms.

The one exception is the most important Unix: Linux. In 1993, a Finnish college student named Linus Torvalds developed his own operating system kernel as an experiment in creating lightweight and efficient operating systems for Intel computers. When he uploaded his running kernel to the Internet, thousands of independent developers downloaded it and began porting their software to it. The GNU foundation, a loose consortium of developers who had been attempting to develop their own version of Unix that would be free of license restrictions from AT&T or Berkeley, immediately ported the tools they had written for their as yet uncompleted operating system, and the Linux distributions were born.

Students, developers, hackers, scientists, and hobbyists from around the world began using Linux because it was completely free of all licensing restrictions except one: Anyone who wrote software for Linux had to release the software into the public domain so that Linux would always remain free; nobody would be able to "embrace and extend it" back into a proprietary system by adding compelling features that would out-compete the free alternatives. Because it came with source code, Linux was quickly ported to every computing platform that anybody cared about.

Within five years, Linux became the largest distribution of Unix and was compatible with software written for BSD and AT&T System V. Linux is now the second most widely deployed operating system after Windows, and it's currently installed in more than twice as many commercial installations as UNIX or BSD. Within a few years, Linux is certain to displace most other versions of Unix, except for those that ship with computers like the BSD-based Mac OS X.

NOTE

BSD will always exist, because it is not limited to the restrictions of the GNU Public License (GPL). If you extend Linux, you must publish your extensions for everyone to use. For example, when TiVo developed its Television Personal Video Recorder on Linux, the Free Software Foundation pushed it to publish its source code, and it did so because it was license-bound by the GPL to do so. Because BSD is truly in the public domain, you can do whatever you want with it and sell it to anyone for as much as you want, and keep your code proprietary. For this reason, BSD is a more popular choice for embedded systems developers than Linux. This is one of the reasons that the Mac OS is based on BSD's Mach kernel.

Just because Linux is the most popular Unix does not mean that it is technically superior to other Unix distributions; it's just free. BSD Unix remains faster and more stable than Linux (and even freer, since there are no licensing restrictions at all), and IBM's AIX is still the king of high-speed distributed computing. However, the Linux kernel programmers are moving quickly, and they have adopted a number of BSD's speed enhancements. Very serious UNIX developers like IBM, Silicon Graphics, and HP have also been inserting their code into the Linux code base to effect speed improvements and ensure that their hardware is better supported. It is highly likely that because of the interest in Linux, it will soon outclass all other versions of Unix in any meaningful comparison. Programmers often write for Linux rather than BSD because they can guarantee that by writing for Linux their work won't wind up co-opted into someone's commercial product without their being compensated for it.

Linus Torvalds does not sell or even designate an "official" version of Linux—he merely controls the kernel code. It is up to third parties to create installable operating systems with packages of tools, and there are many of them, all referred to as *distributions*. The Red Hat distribution is the most popular, but other distributions like Debian, Knoppix, Yellow Dog, and SuSe are also popular. These various distributions include a canonical set of tools, various applications, and management tools. They differ mostly in their ease of installation and setup, but some are tuned for various processors or situations. Anyone who wants to can create and market their own Linux distributions, and many institutions have created their own customized distributions of Linux for internal use.

distribution
A specific packaging of a Unix operating system and associated utility files and applications.

Unix Security Basics

Unix security is similar to Windows in that it is entirely permissions based, with user identity being determined by the login *process*. As in Windows, running processes receive their user context either from the logged-in user who launches the process or from a predefined process *owner*.

To understand Unix security, you need to first understand how Unix organizes the various system objects that can be secured, how account security is managed, and how permissions are applied to file system objects.

process
A running program.

owner
The user account that has wide and separate access to a file. Typically, the owner is the user account that created the file.

Understanding Unix File Systems

In Unix, everything is a file system object. This includes print queues, running processes, and devices; even the kernel's memory space is represented as a file in the file system.

Unix implements permission-based security. So, because everything in Unix is a file, file system permissions can be effectively used to control access to devices, processes, and so forth. This simplifies security dramatically and requires fewer methods of checking for security.

The File System

All hard disks and their various *partitions* are *mounted* in a single unified directory in Unix. There are no drive letters or different disk objects as you would find in Windows or many other operating systems. Otherwise, the directory structure is very similar to most other operating systems in that it is a hierarchy of directories that can contain other directories or files.

The root of the file system is referred to as /, so using the following change directory command will take you to the root of the file system:

```
cd /
```

From there, other partitions and disks can be mounted and will appear as directories. For example, the /boot directory is usually a small partition at the

partition
A low-level division of a hard disk. A partition contains a file system.

mount
To make a file system on a block device available. The term comes from the act of mounting a reel of tape on a tape reader.

beginning of the disk that contains the kernel. This convention stems from the fact that many computer boot loaders can load the kernel only from the beginning of a large hard disk because they were written when all disks were relatively small and they can't access disk sectors beyond a limited range. The following graphic shows the typical first-level Linux directory structure.

```
[root@localhost root]# cd /
[root@localhost /]# ls -l
total 118
drwxr-xr-x    2 root     root         2048 Apr 15 16:20 bin
drwxr-xr-x    4 root     root         1024 Apr 15 15:31 boot
drwxr-xr-x   17 root     root        77824 Apr 16 00:08 dev
drwxr-xr-x   46 root     root         4096 Apr 16 00:07 etc
drwxr-xr-x    3 root     root         4096 Feb  6  1996 home
drwxr-xr-x    2 root     root         1024 Jun 21  2001 initrd
drwxr-xr-x    7 root     root         3072 Apr 15 16:25 lib
drwxr-xr-x    2 root     root        12288 Apr 15 14:58 lost+found
drwxr-xr-x    2 root     root         1024 Aug 29  2001 misc
drwxr-xr-x    4 root     root         1024 Apr 15 23:38 mnt
drwxr-xr-x    2 root     root         1024 Aug 23  1999 opt
dr-xr-xr-x   49 root     root            0 Apr 16 01:05 proc
drwxr-x---    2 root     root         1024 Apr 15 23:48 root
drwxr-xr-x    2 root     root         4096 Apr 15 16:18 sbin
drwxrwxrwt    4 root     root         1024 Apr 16 00:14 tmp
drwxr-xr-x   16 root     root         4096 Apr 15 16:33 usr
drwxr-xr-x   20 root     root         1024 Apr 15 16:17 var
[root@localhost /]#
```

CD-ROM drives are typically mounted in the /dev/cdrom directory, so if you change directory to /dev/cdrom/install, you would be mapped to the same location as d:\install if that CD-ROM were mounted in a Windows machine.

Many Unix administrators create the /home directory in a separate partition to ensure that end users can't fill up the system partition where the operating system needs space to run. The /var directory, where log files are kept, is another popular directory to mount in its own partition. None of this is necessary, however—the entire file system can be created in a single partition, in which case these directories would represent just directories, not mounted disks or partitions.

The Unix mount command is used to attach a block device like a hard disk partition or a CD-ROM drive to the file system.

File System Structures

There are three primary file system structures that are used in Unix to manage files:

Inodes   The heart of Unix file systems. *Inodes* contain all the metadata (data about data) that describes the file (except its name)—including the file's location on disk, its size, the user account that owns it, the group account that can access it, and the permissions for the user and group account. Inodes are stored in an array of inodes on the disk.

Directories   Simply files that relate a list of filenames to an inode index number. They contain no information other than the text of the name and the inode that contains details of the file. There can be any number of names that reference an inode, and when there are more than one, they are called

---

inode (index node)

A file descriptor in Unix systems that describes ownership, permissions, and other metadata about a file.

hard links

Multiple filenames for a single inode. Hard links allow a single file to exist in multiple places in the directory hierarchy.

I/O port

An interface to peripherals like serial devices and printers.

hard links. When you delete a file in Unix, you're really just removing a hard link. When the last hard link is removed, the kernel deletes the inode and reclaims the disk space.

File contents   The data stored on disk, such as the text in a text file, or the information being read in or written out to a serial port, TCP/IP socket, named pipe, and so on.

So when I say that in Unix everything is a file, what I really mean is that every process, network socket, *I/O port,* or mass storage device contains a name in the unified file system directory tree and an inode that describes its security permissions. They do not necessarily have actual file content stored on disk.

Inodes

Consider the following mythical directory listing from a Unix machine in the standard format of the ls command:

```
[root@localhost sample]# ls -l
total 1
brw-rw----  2 root   disk   3,   0 Aug 30  2001 blockdevice
crw-------  2 root   root  10,   2 Aug 30  2001 characterdevice
drwxr-xr-x  2 root   root      1024 Apr 16 08:24 directory
-rw-r--r--  1 root   root         0 Apr 16 08:24 file
prw-------  2 root   root         0 Apr 15 23:51 pipe
srw-rw-rw-  2 root   root         0 Apr 16 08:07 socket
[root@localhost sample]# _
```

The various file types shown are as follows:

◆ Standard *files* are data structures stored on disk.

◆ *Directories* are files that map filenames to inode numbers.

◆ *Character devices* are I/O devices that transfer one character at a time, like a serial or parallel port.

◆ *Block devices* are I/O devices that transfer large blocks of data at a time, such as a hard disk drive or network adapter.

◆ *Sockets* are connections made between computers on a network using TCP/IP.

◆ *Pipes* are first in, first out (FIFO) communication streams between processes on the same computer or on computers in a local area network.

This listing displays much of the information contained in an inode, along with the filename that is contained in the directory. Inodes also contain pointers to the actual file data and a few other things, but for our purposes, this listing shows almost everything in an inode that you need to know to understand Unix security.

file
A sequence of data that is permanently stored on a mass-storage device, such as a hard disk, and referenced by a name.

directory
A file that contains the names of other files or directories.

character devices
A class of peripherals that transmit or receive information one byte at a time (i.e., processing occurs for each byte received). Typically, character devices are lower-speed devices like keyboards, mice, and serial ports.

block devices
Peripherals that process large blocks of information per transaction rather than a single byte. Hard disk drives and network adapters are block devices.

socket
A specific TCP or UDP port on a specific IP address, such as, for example, 192.168.0.1:80. Sockets are used to transmit information between two participating computers in a network environment. Sockets are block devices.

pipe
An interprocess communication mechanism that emulates a serial character device.

You can determine the type of a file using the `ls` command by examining the first character of the mode field (the first character of the file.) I've named the files according to their type, so you can see that *d* represents a directory, for example.

Because all I/O devices and communication mechanisms are described by filenames and inodes, all of the standard Unix file processing tools can be used to operate on them. For example, you can cat (list) the contents of a process file and see a textual representation of its memory on screen (although it will be impossible for you to interpret it).

Devices (and most of the other strange file types) are typically mounted in the /dev directory. This is a convention, not a requirement, and it's important to remember that a hacker may attempt to mount a device within their own /home directory.

User Accounts

Unless a more sophisticated authentication mechanism has been configured, user accounts for local security are stored in a plaintext file in the /etc/passwd file. This file is a simple listing of accounts that are available along with some information about each account, as shown in the following screen shot.

```
[root@localhost etc]# cat passwd |more
root:x:0:0:root:/root:/bin/bash
bin:x:1:1:bin:/bin:/sbin/nologin
daemon:x:2:2:daemon:/sbin:/sbin/nologin
adm:x:3:4:adm:/var/adm:/sbin/nologin
lp:x:4:7:lp:/var/spool/lpd:/sbin/nologin
sync:x:5:0:sync:/sbin:/bin/sync
shutdown:x:6:0:shutdown:/sbin:/sbin/shutdown
halt:x:7:0:halt:/sbin:/sbin/halt
mail:x:8:12:mail:/var/spool/mail:/sbin/nologin
news:x:9:13:news:/var/spool/news:
uucp:x:10:14:uucp:/var/spool/uucp:/sbin/nologin
operator:x:11:0:operator:/root:/sbin/nologin
games:x:12:100:games:/usr/games:/sbin/nologin
gopher:x:13:30:gopher:/var/gopher:/sbin/nologin
ftp:x:14:50:FTP User:/var/ftp:/sbin/nologin
nobody:x:99:99:Nobody:/:/sbin/nologin
mailnull:x:47:47::/var/spool/mqueue:/dev/null
rpm:x:37:37::/var/lib/rpm:/bin/bash
xfs:x:43:43:X Font Server:/etc/X11/fs:/bin/false
ntp:x:38:38::/etc/ntp:/sbin/nologin
rpc:x:32:32:Portmapper RPC user:/:/bin/false
rpcuser:x:29:29:RPC Service User:/var/lib/nfs:/sbin/nologin
nfsnobody:x:65534:65534:Anonymous NFS User:/var/lib/nfs:/sbin/nologin
--More--
```

Anyone with access to this file can create or modify accounts in any way they see fit. By default, this file is writeable only by the root administrative account.

The fields in each line in the `passwd` file are separated by a colon:

♦ Name—Account name.

♦ Password—MD5 hash of the account's password. In this case, the password field is merely a placeholder because shadow passwords are in use (explained later in this chapter).

♦ UID—User Identifier

♦ GID—Primary Group Identifier

♦ Display Name—User's full name

♦ Home Directory—Home directory (shell will start here)

♦ *Shell*—Path to the executable that should be loaded after a successful login

User accounts in Unix are represented in the system by simple integers referred to as *User Identifiers, or UIDs.* UIDs merely indicate a unique serial number for user accounts, beginning with 0 for the root account.

Unix UIDs are not unique on every machine: Root on one machine is the same UID as root on another. This can lead to unintentional elevation of privileges when accounts are moved between machines or connected via various authentication systems. Windows SIDs, on the other hand, are unique for every computer, so this security problem doesn't exist in Windows.

Besides editing the `/etc/passwd` file, you can create user accounts easily using these commands:

adduser mstrebe   Adds a user account named mstrebe.

passwd mstrebe   Changes the password for the account named mstrebe. Running `passwd` without specifying a parameter changes the password for the logged-in account.

userdel mstrebe   Removes a user from the system.

Root

In Unix, there is only one specially privileged account: root, so named because it is the owner of the root of the file system.

The *root* account is used by the kernel to bypass permissions checking—permissions are not checked for the root account, so it is fundamentally different than all other user accounts. Root is the first account created by a new system during the installation, and it has a UID of 0.

---

shell
The program launched after a successful login that presents the user environment. Typically, shells allow a user to launch subsequent programs.

User Identifier (UID)
An integer that identifies a user account to the system.

WARNING

root
The Unix superuser administrative account. Permissions are not checked for the root user.

Root is not analogous to the Windows Administrator account, which is merely a normal account with elevated user rights. It is actually equal to the Windows Local-System account, which cannot be logged into (but can be exploited by writing a service that runs as LocalSystem).

Because permissions are not checked for the root account, there is no way to lock the root account out of any file. Root users are all-powerful in Unix, so access to the root account must be strictly controlled.

There's nothing special about the name *root*—it's just a name, and it can be changed. A root account is any account with a UID of 0. Changing the name of the root account will be confusing to administrators of other systems and some software, but it will also confuse hackers, so for security purposes, you should strongly consider changing the name of the root account by editing the /etc/passwd file.

The traditional Unix security warning is that you should never actually log in as root; rather, you should use the su (set user) command after you've logged in normally to obtain root privilege, as such:

```
su root
```

You'll be prompted for a password and receive a new shell. When you exit from this shell, you'll be back in your normal account's shell.

I'm not nearly as religious about this as most people. There's no technical difference between logging in as root and "suing" to root except that you're far less likely to forget about your elevated privileges if you su to root rather than log in as root. For normal users, this could mean something, but I've been a network administrator for so long that I have a hard time remembering why things aren't working when I don't have elevated privileges. I also tend to administer a lot of special purpose machines that don't necessarily have user accounts for normal users, so logging in as root is normal.

My warning is that you should only log in as root when you're actually performing administration. Log in with your normal user account most of the time. If you do that, you'll find that you su more often anyway because it's more convenient.

Groups

Groups in Unix are analogous to user accounts—they are simply named representations of a Group Identifier (GID) as stored in the file /etc/group (most system configuration files are stored in the /etc directory in Unix).

Groups provide a way to elevate the privileges to a file higher than those allowed to everyone but lower than those provided to the owner of the file. Unix maintains three sets of permissions for each file system object: permissions for

```
[root@localhost etc]# cat group !more
root:x:0:root
bin:x:1:root,bin,daemon
daemon:x:2:root,bin,daemon
sys:x:3:root,bin,adm
adm:x:4:root,adm,daemon
tty:x:5:
disk:x:6:root
lp:x:7:daemon,lp
mem:x:8:
kmem:x:9:
wheel:x:10:root
mail:x:12:mail
news:x:13:news
uucp:x:14:uucp
man:x:15:
games:x:20:
gopher:x:30:
dip:x:40:
ftp:x:50:
lock:x:54:
nobody:x:99:
users:x:100:
slocate:x:21:
[root@localhost etc]# _
```

the owner, permissions for the file's group, and permissions for everyone. By setting permissions for the file's group and then making select user accounts members of that group, you can provide more permission to a file for specific users.
You can specify all the members of a group by simply listing them with commas
behind the group name in the group file.

For example, say you have a set of instructions for using a piece of equipment
that you maintain (so you need Write access to it) and you want to provide those
instructions to the people who use that equipment (so they need Read access to
it) but you don't want anyone else to be able to read it. To set these permissions,
you would give the owner (you) Read and Write permissions, set the group permissions to Read only, and set the Everyone permissions to None. You would
then create a group for the users who need to access the file and set the file's GID
to match that group. Finally, add each of the users to that group in order to provide them with access to the file.

You can create and manage groups using the following Unix commands:

groupadd groupname   Allows you to create a group.

newgrp groupname   Allows a user to switch their group context between
the groups that they belong to.

To delete groups and add or remove members, edit the /etc/group file.

Wheel Group

As with user accounts, there is one group, group 0, that has elevated permissions.
This group is often called "wheel," but its name is not nearly as standardized as
root is for UID 0. (In Linux, GID 0 is typically referred to as root.) Members of
the wheel group are like root in that the system does not perform security checks
on their activities, so they are in essence root users. Various utilities in Unix may
operate only for members of the wheel group.

Shadow Passwords

One major problem with Unix security is that the /etc/passwd file must be accessible by various user accounts in order for a number of service logon mechanisms to work correctly, but if it is accessible, users could change their UIDs or groups to elevate their own privileges. The solution to this problem is *shadow passwords.*

The system implements the shadow passwords mechanism by making a copy of the passwd file called "shadow" that contains the same information but is not accessible by users other than root. This file actually stores the passwords used by the system for logons. Because the passwd file does not contain actual passwords, the true password file does not need to be exposed to other processes. The following screen shot shows a listing of the /etc/shadow file. Notice the long string of strange characters after root: those characters are the MD5 hash of the root password. None of the other accounts on this machine have passwords, so they cannot be used to log in.

```
[root@localhost etc]# cat shadow |more
root:$1$bAOcEOfñ$Z0ceFiYNB2ZHAFYTuR/t00:11792:0:99999:7:::
bin:*:11792:0:99999:7:::
daemon:*:11792:0:99999:7:::
adm:*:11792:0:99999:7:::
lp:*:11792:0:99999:7:::
sync:*:11792:0:99999:7:::
shutdown:*:11792:0:99999:7:::
halt:*:11792:0:99999:7:::
mail:*:11792:0:99999:7:::
news:*:11792:0:99999:7:::
uucp:*:11792:0:99999:7:::
operator:*:11792:0:99999:7:::
games:*:11792:0:99999:7:::
gopher:*:11792:0:99999:7:::
ftp:*:11792:0:99999:7:::
nobody:*:11792:0:99999:7:::
mailnull:!!:11792:0:99999:7:::
rpm:!!:11792:0:99999:7:::
xfs:!!:11792:0:99999:7:::
ntp:!!:11792:0:99999:7:::
rpc:!!:11792:0:99999:7:::
rpcuser:!!:11792:0:99999:7:::
nfsnobody:!!:11792:0:99999:7:::
--More--
```

File System Security

Once you understand Unix user accounts and file systems, understanding file system security is simple.

There are four levels of Read, Write, and Execute permissions maintained for every object in the file system:

- The root user (and wheel group) has all permissions; permissions are not checked for the root user.
- The owner of the file object has the permissions specified by the first three access entries in the inode.

- ◆ Members of the file's system object's group have the permissions specified by the second block of three access entries in the inode.
- ◆ Everyone else has the permissions specified by the final block of three access entries in the inode.

In practice, this system can be nearly as expressive as the complex access control list structure used by Windows, except that, rather than creating a large number of access control entries for a few groups of users on a large number of files, you create a large number of groups (one for each file system object, if necessary) to obtain precise control over how users can access files. Because there are no access control lists, file access in Unix is considerably more efficient than it is in other secure file systems.

NOTE

Windows has numerous security problems due to the complexity of its security subsystem. Because there are many ways that various objects might be secured, there are numerous processes that are responsible for security. This means that Microsoft has much more code to comb through than Unix, and there's a greater possibility of error. It also means that users have to understand a lot more about the system and its security features and they are more likely to make mistakes when securing a computer. It's like having a castle with hundreds of small doors to guard instead of one big one.

While most versions of Unix do not implement any analogue to the "deny ACE" in Windows, you can mimic this behavior by allowing wider access to the Everyone group than you allow to the object's group. For example, if you allow Read/Write access to the Everyone group but allow only Read access to the object's group, then members of the object's group will have only Read access.

To change permissions on a file in Unix, use the chmod command. Permissions are grouped into three octal fields, each represented by a digit from 0 to 7. Each digit is a field representing either the Owner (1st) the Group (2nd), or Everyone (3rd) and represents that role by summing the allowed access according to the following table:

1= Allow Execute Access

2= Allow Write Access

4 = Allow Read Access

You add up these values to determine the exact permission, so a 6 equals Read and Write permission. You then conjoin all three values in Owner, Group, Everyone order to come up with the parameter for chmod:

```
chmod filename 0764
```

A 0764 means that owners have Execute, Read, and Write permissions; members of the file's group have Read and Write permission; and everyone else has Read permission only. The preceding 0 indicates that the file's SetUID bit is not set, which is explained in the section on execution permissions.

To change a file's owner, use the chown command:

```
chown filename user
```

Typically, chown can only be executed by the root user.

> **NOTE**
>
> The term *world* is frequently used to describe "everyone" in Unix—so *world writeable* means that all users have write access to a file.

Access Control Lists

Although neither AT&T System V version 4 UNIX, BSD, nor Linux support access control lists, some versions of Unix (HP-UX and AIX specifically) do support the more complex access control list method of permissions checking.

For the most part, ACLs in the various versions of Unix that support them work the same way as they do in Windows: for any given file, a list of permissions for arbitrary users or groups can be used to specify permissions more explicitly than they can be specified using traditional Unix permissions. In Unix, these permissions are essentially stored in a text file stored in an associated file stream that can be edited with a standard text editor or modified using a set of commands to add, delete, or enumerate permissions.

Unfortunately, ACLs are not widely supported in the Unix community, and every implementation of them is different among the various vendors. This lack of conformity ensures that they will never be widely implemented, and because no clear authority remains to define the constitution of standard Unix, it's unlikely that any real uniformity will ever occur. Solaris and Linux have committed to support ACLs in future releases, but that may be overcome by events; most people have realized that permissions alone are not capable of truly protecting information from dedicated hackers and will move instead to a true Public Key Infrastructure.

> **NOTE**
>
> Ultimately, Linux will assimilate and replace most other versions of Unix, so whatever form of ACLs it implements will become the standard.

Execution Permissions

The only other thing you need to know about file system security is that the setuid and setgid flags can be set on an executable permission in order to modify the user account under which the file is executed.

Normally, an executable file inherits its user security context from the user who executes the file. For example, if user postgres launches a database executable, that database inherits the UID of user postgres in order to access files itself.

But this is a problem for executables that launch automatically at boot time. Daemons and services that launch automatically will all be launched under the root context because there is no logged-in user during the boot process. This means that every daemon would have full access to the system, and any flaw or poorly coded daemon that a hacker could exploit would provide full access to the system.

The Unix solution to this is the `setuid` and `setgid` bits contained in the executable file's inode.

If the `setuid` flag is set on an executable file, then the executing program (process) inherits its UID from its own file's UID rather than from the user who started the executable.

This means, for example, that a daemon could have an owner other than root who would only be able to access files that are necessary for the daemon to operate. The `setgid` flag works the same way and causes the file to inherit its GID from its file GID rather than the logged-on user's primary group.

Programs that operate with `setuid` **or** `setgid` **permissions can open very serious holes in your security. Be extremely cautious about using them.**

WARNING

To create a SetUID executable (also referred to as SUID executables), execute the following command:

```
setuid bash root
```

Note that this command will create a shell that always has root permissions— exactly what a hacker would attempt if they could, and what you should never do. If you do this for test purposes, remember to change it back to normal by executing this command:

```
setuid bash -
```

You can do the same thing to a file's group using the `setgid` command, which gives the executable whatever permissions are held by that group.

SetUID Security Problems

There are numerous security problems associated with SetUID programs; obviously, since they can operate as the root, any exploit that can take control of them and cause them to launch a new process (like a shell) effectively has control of the system.

But there are more subtle ways in which SetUID can cause problems. For example, say a user copies a shell executable to a floppy disk on a system that they have root access to and uses SetUID to set the shell to load as root. If they can mount this floppy on a system upon which they are a normal unprivileged user, then by running that shell they will have root access. UID 0 on their machine is the same as UID 0 on every other Unix machine, so because the shell program on the floppy has root execution privilege, it can be used to exploit other machines. In many cases, mount is restricted to normal users for this reason. Some newer versions of Unix can be configured to ignore SetUID bits on removable or networked file systems. You should check this exploit specifically on your system to ensure that it doesn't work.

SetUID Shell scripts

In most versions of Unix, Shell scripts can be marked as SetUID programs and run as the root user. You should avoid doing this to the extent possible because if the text of a script can be modified by anyone, that user can exploit the script to launch a new shell under the root context. Aside from the obvious method of modifying a script, a user could potentially hook into or replace any executable called by the script (or even modify a program in the executable's search path to mimic a normal system executable) to exploit root context.

For example, say a shell script that executes as root changes into a user's directory and then executes a find command. If the user has replaced the find command with another shell script in their own directory, that find command could be executed instead of the system find command and exploited to launch a new shell, modify the user's permissions, or perform any other action on the system. These sorts of exploits have been used in the past to hack into Unix machines with regularity.

Finding SetUID and SetGID Programs

You should regularly monitor your systems for the presence of SetUID and SetGID programs in order to prevent hackers or users from loading them in and using them as Trojan horses. The methods a potential hacker could use to load a SetUID program onto a system are too numerous to enumerate, but you can avoid them all by using the find command to search for SetUID files.

The following system command (when executed as root) will search for executables with their SetUID or SetGID bits set. By running this regularly and comparing the output with prior output, you can determine when new SetUID programs have been loaded onto your system:

```
find / -type f -perm 4000
```

Daemons and Daemon Security

When Unix boots, the boot loader loads the kernel without checking permissions of any sort and starts the kernel. The kernel begins checking file system permissions as soon as the file system is mounted. Once the kernel has loaded, all subsequent processes are loaded in user mode, where their memory is protected from foreign processes by the kernel.

Daemons (services) in Unix are not special applications with a specific service interface as they are in Windows; they are merely executable programs that are launched by a script that is read in at boot time. Daemons launch with the user identity of the user account that owns the executable file system permission.

Many older (and often exploited) daemons require root access to do their work. Sendmail, the standard mail server for Unix, is notorious for its root user context requirements and the many exploits that it has been susceptible to.

Daemons that require root access to operate are almost always examples of lazy programming by programmers or network administrators who don't want to bother really thinking about how a daemon should be using the system. In every case that I can think of, a more secure alternative exists that operates correctly in the context of a user account that is specifically created for it, and these should be chosen over daemons that require root access. For example, Postfix, a simple alternative to sendmail, is more secure, easier to configure, and more feature-rich than sendmail.

To the extent possible, avoid any software that requires running in the root context. You should also avoid installing software to run as root that does not require it but allows you to do so anyway. For example, MySQL can be configured with a root user context, but it also runs perfectly fine in its own user context. The more security-minded programmers of PostgreSQL won't allow it to run in root context and automatically set up a postgres user as part of the normal setup process.

daemon
A Unix executable that is launched automatically at boot time and normally runs at all times. Similar to a service in Windows.

Terms to Know

Berkeley Software Distribution (BSD)	Multics
block devices	owner
character devices	partition
daemon	pipe
directory	process
distributions	root
file	shadow passwords
hard links	shell
I/O port	socket
inode (index node)	User Identifier (UID)
mount	

Review Questions

1. Why is Unix security so simple?

2. Why did AT&T originally give UNIX away to anyone who wanted a copy?

3. Why are there so many variations of Unix?

4. In Unix, every system object is represented and controlled by what primary structure?

5. What is the primary security mechanism in Unix?

6. Which component stores permissions?

7. Where is user account information stored on a Unix system?

8. How are permissions handled for the root user in Unix?

9. What is the GID of the wheel or superuser group?

10. What are the basic permissions that can be set for owners, group members, and everyone else in an inode?

11. Which two commands are typically used to modify ownership and permissions on an inode?

12. What does it mean when an executable has its `setuid` flag enabled?

13. What makes a daemon different than a normal executable in Unix?

Chapter 12

Unix Network Security

This chapter covers the major contemporary Unix network security mechanisms. There are a number of obsolete Unix protocols and security mechanisms that are not discussed here because they are no longer used—either because better alternatives exist now or because their security was weak and is now considered compromised.

This chapter provides an overview of the basic network security mechanisms available to Unix, including their relative merits, security posture, and administrative difficulty. It's not possible to cover the configuration or administration of these protocols in a single chapter, but pointers to other resources for configuring them are provided.

Unix Network Security Basics

Standard Unix (AT&T System V) does not include facilities to implement either single-signon (one password and user account in the network) or pervasive network security. Security accounts are valid only on individual machines, machines do not "trust" other machines' accounts per se, and every network service implements its own security mechanisms. Unix security is similar to Windows "Workgroup" mode security in this respect, where trust among machines does not exist.

Also consider that no true universal network file system exists in Unix. While Windows has had "Windows networking" since its inception to allow for file and print sharing, Unix did not have anything that could be called a standard file sharing mechanism until the early nineties, when NFS became the de facto file sharing standard. Prior to that, FTP was the closest thing to a file sharing standard, but it only allowed for copying files, not mounting and using them remotely.

Without a standard network file sharing mechanism, there was little point in having a single network logon—traversing machines wasn't that much of an issue. But as networks of single-user computers became popular in the late eighties, Unix began to show its age.

Of course, numerous solutions to these problems have cropped up in the 30+ years since Unix was developed. Originally, network access simply meant connecting to a Unix machine using a terminal application and logging in using a local user account. This method is still used by Telnet, remote shell, secure shell, and numerous other *remote logon* protocols.

When Sun developed the *Network File System (NFS)* and *Network Information Service (NIS)*, it simply adapted Unix security to a network environment. In these situations, all machines share a central account database, but they log on locally using these accounts. Because UIDs are synonymous throughout the network (supposedly), this mechanism was relatively seamless, but terribly insecure—any user logged onto a local machine could simply change their UID in their own `passwd` file to match a target account on the NFS server and then log in. The NFS server would simply trust their UID and serve them supposedly secure files.

The first real attempt to create true network security, where one logon account was valid throughout a security domain and where computers could participate in robust trust relationships, was the Athena project at MIT, which evolved into Kerberos. Kerberos solved the problem so well that Microsoft replaced its own relatively sophisticated Windows NT domain model security with Kerberos when it released Windows 2000. While not perfectly secure, Kerberos solves so many different security problems that it will clearly be the standard single logon methodology for quite some time.

Unfortunately, none of the existing network services supported Kerberos, and they had to be modified and recompiled to support it. For proprietary network services, adding support for Kerberos was difficult and in many cases still has not happened.

remote logon

The process of logging on to a remote machine in order to execute software on it.

Network File System (NFS)

A file sharing protocol developed by Sun Microsystems for use in Unix environments. NFS allows clients to mount portions of a server's file system into their own file systems.

Network Information Service (NIS)

A simple distributed logon mechanism developed by Sun Microsystems for Unix, originally to support single-signon for NFS.

Remote Logon Security

Local area networks (LANs) are new to Unix. Unix was developed in the mid-seventies, but LANs didn't come onto the scene until the mid-eighties. Linking computers together seamlessly was an esoteric problem when Unix came out—the major problem originally was linking a large number of *terminals* to a single computer.

This explains why Unix security is so self-centric—Unix was pretty much set in stone before networking computers together was really that much of a problem. Originally, the problem was trying to get enough serial ports connected to a single computer so each user could have their own terminal.

Remote logon allows multiple users to connect to a single computer and run their software on it. Originally, remote logon was accomplished by connecting multiple terminals to their own serial port on the Unix computer. When modems and PCs became popular, administrators began connecting modems on both ends so that remote users could dial in. This mimicked terminal connections over serial lines but replaced the serial lines with phone lines and modems.

When local area networks first came on the scene in the eighties, Unix adapted by adding the Telnet service so that microcomputers connected to the LAN could run a Telnet client and connect remotely over a network as if the network were a serial connection to the host computer. Telnet naïvely transmitted data the same way a serial connection did—in the clear. This meant that anyone with a sniffer on the local network could steal passwords.

The rlogin service is similar to Telnet, but it does not prompt for a username—rather, user and security information are read in from the Unix machine's /etc/rhosts file. It also sends passwords in the clear. Another service, rsh, is a similar service that executes commands on the remote host without providing a login shell, and it suffers from the same security problems.

Secure Shell (SSH) solves all of these remote logon problems by integrating public-key security to authenticate both users and machines and thus eliminates the possibility of man-in-the middle and other redirection or emulation attacks. SSH is also capable of encrypting the entire communication stream to eliminate all security vulnerabilities except the possibility of bugs in the server service.

To solve the remote logon problem, use only SSH for remote logon connections. For dial-up users, set up your Unix server as a remote access server that accepts PPP connections and run SSH over the PPP connection. This will ensure that all communications and password exchanges are encrypted.

You can find out more about SSH at www.ssh.com. **All modern versions of Unix come with SSH clients and servers built in. You can download a free SSH client for windows called "putty" from** www.chiark.greenend.org.uk/~sgtatham/putty/.

local area network (LAN)
A network in which all participants can communicate directly without the need for routing at the Network layer. The term is somewhat obsolete because many LAN-sized networks implement routing for various reasons since the advent of the Internet.

terminal
A remote display and keyboard/mouse console that can be used to access a computer.

Secure Shell (SSH)
A remote logon protocol that uses strong cryptography to authenticate hosts and users.

NOTE

Remote Access

remote access
The process of accessing services on a remote server without executing software directly on the remote machine.

Remote access refers to the process of accessing resources on a remote Unix machine without actually logging on and running programs on those machines.

The following are examples of remote access:

- ◆ Storing files
- ◆ Transmitting e-mail
- ◆ Retrieving a web page

shell
An executable program that runs immediately after logon and is used as a springboard to launch subsequent programs.

None of these problems involve remotely controlling a *shell* on the Unix machine; rather, they access a service running on the Unix machine and receive data from it.

daemon
An executable in Unix that runs automatically as a service (i.e., with a unique user context) when the computer is booted.

Any programmer can write a *daemon* that allows remote computers to connect to it and receive data. Because the daemon is accessing files locally using the daemon's own *user context* (either from the account that executed the daemon or the owner of the executable file), all file access is controlled by that user account on the local machine.

user context
The user identity under which a process executes that determines which files and resources the process will have access to.

This means that it's up to each and every network service to provide its own method of authenticating the clients that connect to it. This lack of central authentication authority is the primary cause of security problems in the Unix environment. No matter how strong security is for one service, another poorly secured service can provide a portal for hackers to take control of a machine.

spam
Unsolicited e-mail. Unscrupulous spam transmitters typically exploit unsecured mail servers so they won't have to pay for bandwidth.

Many services perform no authentication whatsoever. Simple Mail Transfer Protocol (SMTP) does not include any form of authentication—it will accept connections from any user and deliver any properly formatted e-mail message transmitted to it. This lack of authentication is why the *spam* problem exists. Various jury-rigged methods to authenticate e-mail have been wrapped around SMTP to attempt to eliminate spam, but there is no standard extension to the SMTP protocol for security even today.

one-time passwords
An authentication method that uses synchronized pseudorandom number generation on both the client and the server to prove that both sides know the same original seed number.

There are no rules about what a daemon must do to perform authentication—some do nothing and allow all attempts to access the service to succeed. Others read the `passwd` file and try to authenticate against the traditional user accounts list. Others maintain their own files with lists of users and passwords. Still others use proprietary authentication mechanisms like *one-time passwords* or *smart cards*. Others authenticate against *Kerberos* or a *Lightweight Directory Access Protocol (LDAP)* server. In many cases, services are distributed as source code and require the end user to compile it in whatever security library they want to use for authentication.

The lack of a standardized authentication protocol for Unix was one of the reasons that it was so frequently hacked. There are numerous problems with implementing proprietary logon mechanisms. The programmers may not be particularly rigorous about security and may make naïve mistakes that hackers could exploit. Even well-meaning programmers may not think through the problem entirely, or they may underestimate the risk and choose a lower level of security than most users will require. Finally, the sheer number of mechanisms means that the same users will need multiple methods to access various services, increasing the odds that users themselves will sabotage security for the sake of convenience.

Pluggable Authentication Module (PAM)

Clearly, a unified method for managing authentication methods is necessary to ensure that service writers don't need to keep reinventing the wheel—and so that end users don't have to compile in support for their favorite authentication mechanism.

The *Pluggable Authentication Module (PAM)* library has recently emerged as the solution for standardizing authentication in Unix. Linux, BSD, and Solaris currently support it. By compiling each daemon to support the PAM library, developers can avoid writing their own (potentially insecure) authentication mechanism and can allow end users a choice in establishing their own authentication mechanism.

PAM is a modular library that allows administrators to configure which authentication mechanisms they want to allow without recompiling daemons: Unix passwords, Kerberos, smart cards, one-time passwords, and even Windows authentication are all options. Administrators can configure the PAM library once and rely on any "PAMed" application to use that configuration for authentication.

Configuring PAM is how you would enable the use of alternative forms of authentication in Unix, such as biometric scanners, one-time passwords, and smart cards.

Configuring PAM is simply a matter of editing the application's PAM configuration file in the /etc/pam.d directory. Each file's PAM configuration file is named the same as the service, such as login or imapd. The service's configuration file allows administrators to control which types of authentication are valid (or invalid), various account restrictions, how to control passwords, and what post-authentication session setup is required for each specific service.

---

smart cards

Physical devices with a small amount of nonvolatile memory that stores a random number available only to the device. Authentication software can push a value on to the card, which will be encrypted using the random number and returned. Smart cards thereby create an unforgeable physical key mechanism.

Pluggable Authentication Module (PAM)

An authentication abstraction layer that provides a central mechanism for connecting various authentication schemes to various network services in Unix. Services trust PAM for authentication, and PAM can be configured to use various authentication schemes.

Kerberos

A distributed logon protocol that uses secret keys to authenticate users and machines in a networked environment.

TIP

Lightweight Directory Access Protocol (LDAP)
A Protocol for accessing service configuration data from a central hierarchical database. LDAP is frequently used to store user account information in Unix and is supported as an access method by Microsoft Active Directory.

distributed logon
Any client/server protocol for verifying user identity. The purpose of distributed logon services is to allow users to log on once and use their credentials on any machine within the security domain. This provides the illusion of logging into the network as a whole rather than logging into a single computer.

single-signon
See *distributed logon*.

credentials
Information used to prove identity. Typically, this is a combination of a user account name and a password.

yellow pages (yp)
The original name for Network Information Service (NIS).

PAM is usually distributed with a standard set of authentication modules configured to authenticate services against Unix passwords and/or Kerberos. If you intend to change these settings, configure a new service to use PAM, or otherwise customize PAM security settings, read up on the latest PAM configuration documentation from your Unix vendor by searching it website on "pluggable authentication modules."

Distributed Logon

Distributed logon (also called *single-signon*) is a simple concept: When attaching to a remote networked service, the user's current *credentials* trusted by the local machine are transmitted automatically to the remote service, which, if it trusts the credentials, will automatically allow access without the user being interrupted for credentials.

Distributed logon is essentially a convenience—with it, users need not remember a plethora of logon names and passwords (or running over and reinserting their smart card on the remote machine and other infeasible measures).

As with everything in Unix, there are innumerable ways to achieve distributed logon, among them these common methods:

- Distributed `passwd` files
- NIS and NIS+
- Kerberos

Each of these methods is discussed in the following sections.

Distributed *passwd*

The first method used for achieving distributed logon was simply to copy the same `passwd` file around the organization. While this didn't actually provide seamless logon, it did allow for the same account name and password to be used on every machine. Achieving this distribution is technically easy but labor intensive.

Administrators have hacked various methods to simplify `passwd` distribution, including cron scripts using FTP, using rdist to automatically move the file, and so forth. These administrative hacks frequently opened up security holes of their own.

NIS and NIS+

Network Information Service, originally called *yellow pages* (or *yp*) was developed by Sun Microsystems to simplify logon distribution and allow for the seamless mounting of NFS volumes. The concept is simple: A single master NIS server maintains a database of account names and passwords (and other information). NIS slave servers periodically refresh their own local password map based on the contents of a master NIS server. Client machines use modified login processes (as well as other services) to attach to the NIS server to retrieve logon credentials. The group of machines configured to trust the master NIS server is called an NIS domain.

NIS also does for groups what it does for user accounts: groups (called netgroups in NIS) on the master are the basis for valid GIDs on all machines in the NIS domain.

NIS for Windows Administrators

The NIS architecture is the same as the original Windows NT domain model, where a primary domain controller maintains an official database of user accounts. The accounts are replicated to back up domain controllers that provide logon services, and clients are attached to the domain to trust the domain controllers for secure logon credentials.

The following terms are congruent in the two environments:

domain = domain

primary domain controller = NIS master

backup domain controller = NIS slave

domain member server = NIS client

domain member workstation = NIS client

A newer version of NIS called NIS+ was developed by Sun to shore up some of the early problems with NIS security. NIS+ is significantly more secure than NIS because it encrypts and authenticates communications between clients and servers, but it suffers from stability problems, a lack of wide support across different versions of Unix, and overly complex server-side administration. NIS+ stores logon information in database files rather than in plaintext files. A number of sites that have attempted to use NIS+ have abandoned the effort in favor of simply shoring up the security of NIS.

NIS itself has numerous security flaws that are well documented—data is not encrypted between the clients and server, password maps can be retrieved and decrypted using popular password crackers, and so forth. As with nearly all pre-Internet protocols, NIS is LAN-grade security that simply isn't strong enough to keep the hacking hordes at bay.

For more information about establishing and managing an NIS infrastructure, read *Managing NIS and NFS (2nd ed.)* by Hal Stern et al. (2001, O'Reilly).

NOTE

Kerberos

Kerberos is an authentication protocol that uses secret key cryptography to provide seamless logon among computers in a *security domain* (called a *realm* in Kerberos). Kerberos was developed by MIT and is basically open source under a BSD-style license. MIT will provide it to anyone who wants it.

Official documentation for Kerberos can be found at web.mit.edu/kerberos/www/.

Kerberos is becoming the standard distributed logon mechanism in both Windows and Unix environments that require higher security, and it is clearly the future of distributed logon in both environments. The two platforms are somewhat compatible; with effort, Windows and Unix can be configured to log on interchangeably using Kerberos.

Kerberos in Unix is analogous to Kerberos in Windows: you have *Key Distribution Centers (KDC)* (called domain controllers in Windows parlance) and you have clients. Kerberos v.5 specifies a master KDC and numerous slave KDCs to which changes are propagated on a regular basis. You can optionally use *Distributed Computing Environment (DCE)* as your KDC database so that you can keep a single database of users at your site. (Windows uses Active Directory, a modified Exchange engine, to maintain the database of users and makes it available via LDAP.)

A discussion of the Kerberos security mechanisms can be found in Chapter 10 because Kerberos is a "here now" security solution for Windows. This section concentrates on the current Unix security issues associated with Kerberos.

The road to Kerberos on Unix is a long one. Because Windows is controlled by a single vendor, Microsoft was able to "kerberize" its server services and its clients in a single release. Unix doesn't have a central point of control, and as of this writing, there's no pre-built "Pure Kerberos" distribution available. Installing Kerberos currently in Unix is like making a patchwork quilt of services and being rigorous about which services must be chosen. Kerberos also lacks a "Kerberos wrapper" that can be used to shore up security on any client service (although Cornell University is working on a project called "Sidecar" that will do exactly this).

Configuring Kerberos is complex and well beyond the scope of this book, but a pretty good step-by-step procedure can be found at www.ornl.gov/~jar/HowToKerb.html.

Using Kerberos

Kerberos works by either replacing the standard login mechanism on a host with a kerberized logon or running the kinit program after logging in (if Kerberos is not being used to provide local security). When you log on (or kinit), your credentials are sent to the KDC, which uses them (and the current time) to encrypt a *Ticket Granting Ticket (TGT)* that is transmitted back to your machine. Your host then decrypts the ticket using your stored credentials. TGTs have an expiration period (8 hours by default; 10 hours in Windows) and are encrypted using the current time each time they're used. Think of a TGT as your "all day pass" at an amusement park: Once you've paid for it, it's valid all day.

Whenever you attempt to subsequently access a Kerberos service, your TGT is again encrypted and transmitted to the KDC, which responds with an encrypted service-specific *ticket* that can be provided to a *kerberized* service to gain access to it. Tickets usually have a very short expiration time and must be used within five minutes of their grant. This is analogous to using your "all day pass" to get free "ride tickets" for a specific attraction at the fair from the central ticket booth (the KDC's Ticket Granting service). You can then take the ride tickets to the specific attraction to be admitted.

Kerberos is extremely sensitive to time synchronization among hosts in the domain. You must make sure that all of your hosts are correctly synchronized to the same Network Time Protocol (NTP) server for Kerberos to work correctly.

Ticket Granting Ticket (TGT)
An encrypted value that is stored by a client after a successful logon and used to quickly prove identity in a Kerberos environment.

ticket
In Kerberos, an encrypted value appended with the time to prove identity to a network service.

kerberized
A service or services that have been modified for compatibility with Kerberos.

Kerberos Security

Theoretically, Kerberos security is very strong. By authenticating with a KDC, you get a ticket that can be used to prove your identity to any service in your organization. Keys are automatically managed by your system, so login to various services is seamless. It sounds wonderful, and in Windows, it really works. But Kerberos just isn't completely integrated into any Unix distribution, and without complete integration, it loses much of its appeal and security.

The major problem with Kerberos is its "all or nothing" nature—you can't just add Kerberos to the mix and secure a few protocols, because users will use the same account names and passwords with the as-yet-unsecured services, thus compromising them. You have to convert your entire network services infrastructure to use services that are compatible with Kerberos for authentication or the whole thing isn't really secure. Every service you provide that you want to provide seamless logon for has to be replaced with a kerberized version that knows how to trust the Kerberos authentication mechanism.

Don't use the same user accounts and passwords on your Kerberos systems as you use on non-kerberized services. Non-kerberized services can't protect the passwords, so they will be revealed to sniffers if users are in the habit of using the same passwords on all systems. The best thing to do is to kerberize all of your services or none of them.

This is why deploying Kerberos is so complex. It is possible to use *PAMed* applications that are configured to check Kerberos for applications that haven't been kerberized, but this is problematic because the user's credentials may have to run from the client to the service host in whatever form the service uses before PAM can use Kerberos to validate the password.

PAMed
Describes an application that has been modified to allow for Pluggable Authentication Modules.

WARNING

Don't use PAM to kerberize every service on your machine, because many services transmit passwords in the clear. Depending upon its configuration, PAM may not check the password until it's received on the server, meaning that it has traveled through the network in whatever form the PAMed protocol uses. PAM then receives the password and checks it against a Kerberos KDC. For protocols that transmit passwords in the clear, like Telnet and FTP, using PAM to check Kerberos passwords would reveal the passwords to a sniffer.

Despite the promise of Kerberos to eliminate the vast majority of simple attacks against Unix, it is not going to achieve widespread use until a Unix vendor releases a pure Kerberos distribution that any system administrator can deploy. This is a few years away from actually happening, so unless your organization has significant network administration resources available to properly deploy Kerberos, it's likely to drain more resources away from more immediate security solutions than it is to provide better security in the short term.

File Sharing Security

File sharing security describes those measures taken to protect files that are transmitted on the network.

There are two major types of file sharing protocols:

file sharing protocol
A protocol that allows a rich set of semantics for serving files to clients. File sharing protocols are distinguished by their ability to provide small portions of files and provide locking mechanisms so that multiple users can write to the file simultaneously.

File transfer protocols   Allow users to transfer entire files between computers using a specific client program. They are relatively simple programs that are designed to distribute software and documents to consumers in one direction. Examples of file transfer protocols include FTP, TFTP, and HTTP.

File sharing protocols   (Also called network file systems.) Allow programs to request just the small segments of a file that are actually in use, and they allow files to be locked momentarily by users to prevent conflicting write operations where one user's changes overwrite another user's changes. Essentially, these protocols simulate a hard disk drive by using a network—they allow the full set of semantics that the operating system can use with local files. *File sharing protocols* also allow multiple users to access a file in read/write mode so that updates to the file made by one user are available immediately to all users who have the file open. File sharing protocols can be mounted on the current file system and browsed seam-lessly. Examples of file sharing protocols include SMB (Windows) and NFS (Unix).

Microsoft also frequently refers to Server Message Block (SMB) protocol as the Com-mon Internet File System (CIFS). Microsoft changed the name when it submitted the protocol to the IETF as an Internet standard but has been inconsistent in applying the new name. Most outside the Microsoft camp still refer to the protocol as SMB.

These protocols and their implications on security are covered in the next few sections.

File Transfer Protocol (FTP)

The *File Transfer Protocol (FTP)* is the venerable granddaddy of file sharing solutions. FTP is a simple client/server protocol that allows servers to publish a directory in their file systems to the network. FTP users can then use an FPT cli-ent program to authenticate, list files, download files, and upload files. Because FTP is simple and widely supported, it's a very popular mechanism for trans-ferring files across the Internet.

FTP is what is says it is: A file transfer protocol. It is not a true file sharing pro-tocol because it is not really capable of simulating a local file system.

FTP lacks all of these semantic mechanisms and only allows for the uploading and downloading of complete files.

Companies often use anonymous FTP to publish software to the public. Anonymous FTP is the same thing as normal FTP, but a special account called "anonymous" is provided that will accept any text as a valid password. Typi-cally, public FTP servers will ask you to enter your e-mail address as the pass-word so they can record it in a log, but there's no way to validate the address. Some companies attempt to secure their FTP sites by requiring customers to call first for a valid account/password combination and then always provide the same account/password. This doesn't work because hackers keep track of these in databases. Once a single hacker customer has obtained the working account and password, they all know it.

File Transfer Protocol (FTP)
A simple protocol that allows the com-plete transfer of files between servers and clients. File transfer protocols can-not support simultaneous multiple users. File Transfer Protocol is also the name of the oldest and most widely implemented file transfer protocol.

Using FTP

Configuring an FTP server is simple. If your Unix distribution has an FTP server service installed by default, you need only configure the `/etc/ftphosts` file to determine what domains you wish to allow to log into your server. Permissions for uploading and downloading files are determined by the FTP directory's file system permissions, as explained in Chapter 11. You can configure a welcome message that will be displayed to FTP users by creating a file containing the wel-come text and storing it in the FTP root directory as `.message`, for example, `/home/ftp/.message`.

FTP clients are even simpler: Type `ftp hostname.domainname` at any command prompt (Windows or Unix) and you'll get a logon prompt from the FTP server. Use the `ls` command to list files, `get file` to download a file, and `put file` to upload a file to the FTP server.

FTP Security

FTP has three major security problems:

All public services are a security liability. Like any service, FTP is a potential liability because any service that answers connections on the Internet could potentially contain bugs that allow hackers to exploit it. In the specific case of FTP, hackers discovered a major security flaw in the most popular version of WU-FTP (Washington University FTP) in April of 2001 that allowed hackers to gain remote control of any server running the wu-ftp daemon. It took six months for a patch to be made generally available.

Passwords are transmitted in the clear. This means that hackers can potentially intercept valid account names and passwords while they are in transit on the Internet.

Anonymous writeable FTP servers can be exploited. Hackers will exploit FTP servers that allow file uploads from the public. Besides causing the simple problem of stealing your disk space to store (probably) illegal content like pirated software and copyrighted material, allowing write access to an anonymous FTP server allows hackers to test a number of different file system exploits against your machine. For example, buffer overruns can be embedded inside files so that when the file is uploaded, the hacker can gain root access to your server.

FTP has too many security problems to detail completely, and the specific exploits vary from distribution to distribution. No matter what version you have, allowing anonymous write access spells immediate trouble. As a test for this book, I opened anonymous write access to an FTP server inside a virtual machine. Fourteen minutes later, an automated port scanner found the new machine (on an unlisted IP address), ran a test write against it, and automatically began uploading content to it—including a number of files with different buffer overrun exploits embedded in the filenames. It was extremely difficult to remove some of those files because their strange names prevented the normal file system tools from working.

Don't use FTP on public or private servers if you can avoid it—HTTP provides an easily controlled and more robust file transfer methodology for anonymous files and can be easily secured using SSL. Use anonymous FTP for read-only shares if you can't avoid using FTP. Don't use anonymous FTP access to a writeable share if you can't avoid using anonymous FTP. If you think you have to use writeable FTP access for some reason, you'll change your mind after a few minutes.

Network File System (NFS)

Sun Microsystems developed NFS as a "true" networked file system to replace FTP. With FTP, files actually have to be transferred from the server to the local file system, where they can be modified by various processes and then moved back to the server. This makes it impossible for multiple users to use the file simultaneously and, worse, provides no information about whether a file is in use or has been modified since the last time it was downloaded. Clearly, a protocol like FTP does not provide enough file sharing semantics to allow for true *file sharing*.

NFS was designed to allow transparent file sharing on a local area network, and for that purpose, it does a very good job. However, NFS implements no real security on its own.

NFS Security

Sometimes, security is a matter of usage. NFS is less secure than FTP, but because of that, nobody attempts to use it on the public Internet, which means it's subject to far less exploitation. Don't consider using NFS on an Internet-connected network that doesn't have strong Internet firewalling.

The major flaw in NFS is that it trusts the connecting client to accurately present its UID. This means that anyone who has set up their own host and "stolen" the UID from another legitimate user on the network can access their files. Of course, this is a serious architectural problem with NFS that makes it completely inappropriate for use on the public Internet.

TCP Wrappers is a tool commonly used to shore up this security problem in NFS. By wrapping NFS with TCP Wrappers, you can use the `hosts.allow` and `hosts.deny` files to prevent unknown machines from connecting to your NFS server. However, TCP Wrappers only authenticates the machine, not the user, so while this limits the domain of the problem to computers under your control, it doesn't truly secure the service.

Various other patches have been incorporated into NFS to attempt to shore up security:

◆ NFS was modified to automatically map access attempts from root to the nobody user on the local machine. Basically, this means that root users who access NFS will have no rights rather than all rights.

◆ NFS also performs subtree checking to make sure that a user hasn't changed into a directory below the NFS file system share (or that a link hasn't accessed a file outside the share).

◆ By default, NFS will only export to machines that send requests on ports below 1024. This is because services on these ports must be configured by the root user. This security hack is basically ineffective because hackers are always the root users of their own machines and when they gain access to machines inside your LAN, they usually do it through a remote root access that allows them to set services up as they please.

file sharing
A accessing files using a network file system that includes rich enough file locking semantics to allow files to be read and written to in a random access fashion and to allow multiple users to read and write from them simultaneously; mounting a network file system so that it mimics a local disk drive.

TCP Wrappers
A process that inserts itself before a network service in order to authenticate the hosts that are attempting to connect.

These various changes do little to really secure NFS. Any hacker who has gained remote root access on an NFS client inside your network will have no problem accessing files on the NFS server. All of these security fixes can be disabled on an export-by-export basis to speed up NFS as well.

Never allow public access to NFS exports. Never use NFS on publicly available machines because if they get exploited, hackers can subsequently exploit the NFS server easily. If you use NFS in your local network, always use TCP Wrappers to limit the number of machines that can reach your network. Be very frugal with read/write access to NFS shares.

Hypertext Transfer Protocol (HTTP)

Hypertext Transfer Protocol (HTTP) is the protocol of the World Wide Web. Obviously, HTTP is designed for public access so security is of paramount importance—so much so that HTTP security is the subject of its own chapter, Chapter 13, "Web Server Security," in this book. In this chapter, it's presented as a pure file sharing mechanism without discussing its primary context on the Web.

Under the hood, HTTP is much like FTP with a few extensions. Like FTP, HTTP is a file transfer protocol, not a file sharing protocol, so it's not appropriate for multiuser write access. This is not an issue, however, since the Web uses a pure publication mechanism where clients don't normally expect to be able to modify web pages.

NOTE   The HTTP Web Distributed Authoring and Versioning (WebDAV) extensions add semantics to allow for multiuser file locking so that the Web can be used as a true file sharing protocol. WebDAV was developed to allow easier website editing on live servers by multiple authors, but it is now being incorporated into office programs to allow traditional file sharing over the Internet.

The primary extension that makes HTTP different in the minds of users is the concept of the embedded link that browsers can use to automatically request new documents. Links contain the full, globally unique path to the document, and when a user clicks on them, the browser requests the document from the server. The link request is actually determined and negotiated by the browser—a browser could be configured to run using anonymous FTP and work essentially the same way that HTTP works.

Links aren't what makes HTTP special. HTTP's PUSH and GET semantics, which allow form submission and the passing of parameters between pages as well as the extensions that allow server-side session information to be retained between page loads, are what make HTTP different than FTP. With an FTP-based hypertext system, there would be no method to submit a form except to write a file back to the FTP server—and that would come with all the problems that anonymous writeable FTP sites have.

Configuring a Unix web server is easy: Download the Apache web server from www.apache.org, install it according to the instructions provided with it, and edit the /etc/httpd.conf file to create the root of the www service. From that directory, the files within it are available publicly (usually, although TCP Wrappers and most web servers allow you to limit which machines can attach to the server using their own mechanisms). Although other web servers exist, Apache has stood the test of time and stood up to literally billions of hacking attempts, with few real exploits having succeeded against it. Apache is also among the fastest web servers, and it has reasonably good default security mechanisms to keep novice webmasters from making simple security mistakes.

HTTP Security

There is no protocol more public than HTTP. You are inviting the world onto your server when you use HTTP. Because every web server program written has been exploited at one time or another, you should assume that hackers will be able to exploit your web server if they want to. HTTP security is so critical that it is covered in the next chapter.

Samba

Samba is an open-source implementation of Microsoft's Server Message Block protocol, also called the Common Internet File System. SMB is the file sharing protocol used by Windows, originally in local area networks. Despite its LAN origins, SMB works surprisingly well over the public Internet. When properly used, it can be made secure enough to use on the public Internet. Aside from Samba, commercial SMB/CIFS servers and clients are available for most versions of Unix. SMB runs on all versions of Windows, MS-DOS, OS/2, and Macintosh computers natively as well. After FTP, SMB is the closest protocol there is to a universal file sharing protocol.

SMB is a true file sharing protocol, with rich enough semantics to allow multi-user write locking. To attach to an SMB server from Unix, you can use smbclient, which is much like a standard command-line FTP client. If you're using an open-source Unix that has SMB support compiled into the kernel, you can use the much easier smbmount and smbumount commands, which work exactly as mount and umount work for NFS exports.

For Windows machines, SMB is built right in. By simply specifying a path to the server in the form \\sambaserver.mydomain.dom\sharename, a user can provide logon information and begin using the file system. Windows will attempt a "silent logon" behind the scenes using the user's logon credentials, so if the Samba server has a matching username and password, the logon will be seamless. Otherwise, Windows will prompt for a username and password combination to allow access.   *NOTE*

Samba Security

To avoid en masse the problems involved with sending Unix UIDs across the network (as well as to ensure Windows compatibility), SMB transmits usernames and passwords between the client and the server for authentication. You can configure SMB to use cleartext or encrypted passwords; most Unix installations use cleartext passwords because it's easier and because early versions of Samba did not support encrypted passwords; also, each new version of Windows seems to break Samba's password encryption mechanism, and it takes a few months for Samba to catch up.

Samba is configured by making changes to the /etc/smb.conf file. In this file, you establish *shares*, or directories that SMB will expose to SMB clients. You can specify an unusual number of security options for a Unix file sharing protocol, including what access various users will have, what the default permissions for created files will be, and whether writing is allowed.

Interestingly enough, Samba doesn't use local Unix accounts for SMB security; rather, the Samba daemon authenticates users against a separate list of users. This means that Samba users need not have Unix accounts on the Samba server, but it also means that individual file system permissions can't be used to secure files on an individual basis. In practice, this means that Samba user accounts can't be exploited by testing them against other protocols or by trying to log in directly with them using Telnet or SSH, which significantly improves security.

If you set up a public Samba server, use the same caution that you would with an FTP server. Set up a separate host inside your De-Militarized Zone to transfer files rather than making an internal machine available on the Internet. Don't allow connections originating from that machine; rather, connect to it from within your network to move files off it. Be certain to encrypt passwords. Use a dedicated firewall to filter connections to the server, and use IPChains or IPTables to filter all protocols except ports 135, 137, 138, and 139 directly on your Samba server.

share
A portion of a file system that the SMB service (server.exe in Windows, samba in Unix) exports for access by SMB clients. Access to the share can be configured on a per-user or per-group basis.

NOTE

Windows 2000 allows direct SMB over TCP (without NetBIOS) on port 445. Remember this when you're configuring your firewall policy.

Overall, because of its foreign-OS origin and high code quality, Samba is the most secure commonly used file sharing protocol for Unix. Prefer it to NFS for LAN servers, and consider it over FTP for public servers.

Firewalling Unix Machines

IPChains
A stateless packet filtering mechanism for Unix kernels.

The same software used to turn a Unix machine into a firewall to protect an entire domain can also be used just to protect an individual Unix machine; this is similar to personal firewall software discussed for PC home computers in

Chapter 6. While standard Unix doesn't include much in the way of TCP/IP security mechanisms, freely available packages have become so popular that either they are included in most Unix distributions or they can be added to any Unix distribution.

While *IPChains, IPTables,* FWTK, and TCP Wrappers can all be used to block access to local services and provide some flexibility for access, their simple pass/fail mechanisms often are not rich enough to provide complete authentication and security for services. Use a dedicated firewall device to protect your network. Use these Unix security mechanisms to protect public servers individually.

IPTables
A stateful packet filtering mechanism for Unix kernels.

IPTables and IPChains

A relatively recent addition to the open-source versions of Unix operating system is the ability to perform packet filtering and Network Address Translation in the operating system's kernel. Most commercial Unix distributions do not include any form of integral packet filtering, and it cannot be added without modifying the kernel's source code.

IPChains and IPTables provide a packet filtering mechanism that, while traditionally associated with routers, can also be used to protect a host. IPChains implements a stateless packet filter; IPTables is a newer mechanism that implements stateful inspection. For a router, the distinction is important, but to protect an individual machine they are functionally equal.

Packet-filtering rules are applied to every packet as it arrives, as the packet transits the Linux routing stack, and when the packet exits. In the case of local host protection, we're only worried about packet arrival.

IPChains and IPTables only inspect packets at the TCP and IP layers; protocol inspection must be provided by a higher-level service. TIS FWTK (described later in this chapter) is an excellent proxy server package that interoperates well with other security mechanisms on a Unix server.

IPChains/IPTables Security

IPChains and IPTables filter packets before they are delivered to the IP stack for processing, allowing you to protect your computer from malformed packets and other IP-level attacks. They provide the full range of options for packet filtering on source and destination IP addresses, source and destination ports, packet type, and most other TCP/IP header data elements.

Since they do not inspect the data portions of packets, you will need a proxy service to ensure that the traffic traversing a particular port conforms to the protocol for that port. For example, IPChains will allow traffic to flow over port 80; it won't inspect the payload to ensure that the traffic truly conforms to the HTTP protocol. See the section on FWTK for more information on protocol inspection.

IPChains evaluates every packet received by the network adapters in the firewall computer according to a set of rules you established when you installed IPChains. The rules are applied in order one at a time until IPChains finds a rule that matches the packet and specifies a terminal action, such as ACCEPT or DROP. Since the rules are applied in order, it is very important to craft the rules in the right order.

A useful feature of IPChains (and the feature that gives it its name) is the bundling of sets of rules into chains. IPChains starts out with three—INPUT, FORWARD, and OUTPUT. You can establish additional chains and use a rule in INPUT, FORWARD, or OUTPUT to direct packet analysis to the appropriate chain for the specified type of traffic. This structured rule management makes it easier to plan the security of the host and thereby makes it easier to secure the host.

IPChains is administered using the `ipchains` command, which takes as its arguments the rules to be established or modified in the IPChains packet filter.

NOTE

Step-by-step instructions for installing IPChains on the Internet can be found at the following location, or just search on "IPChains" from any search engine: `www.tldp.org/HOWTO/IPCHAINS-HOWTO.html`.

TCP Wrappers

TCP Wrappers is a security package that "wedges" itself into a daemon's connection process and intercepts connections before the actual service gets them.

TCP Wrappers works by replacing the daemon's executable file with a simple TCP daemon called tcpd. The actual service daemon is moved to another location; tcpd hands off the connection to the actual service daemon only after it has authenticated the attaching client.

TCP Wrappers works by searching its access control file for the service requested and checking the requesting client against the `/etc/hosts.allow` and `/etc/hosts.deny` files. Because TCP Wrappers stops at the first match, an allowed host will be allowed even if it appears in the deny file. TCP Wrappers also logs everything it can about the connection in the syslog.

TCP Wrappers also allows the execution of arbitrary scripts upon connections to various services, which can be exploited to create *honey pots* (or seduction servers), whose purpose is to be exploited in order to keep hackers away from production machines. It can also be used to create booby traps, servers who counterattack in response to an attack.

WARNING

Booby traps are technically illegal in the United States (the FBI does not consider self-defense hacking to be anything other than hacking) and are likely to attract the attention of legions of hackers.

Because the functionality provided by TCP Wrappers is so important (and so sorely lacking in Unix prior to its release), it now comes with many distributions of Unix. If your machine respects the `/etc/hosts.allow` and `/etc/hosts.deny` files, then you've got it. Otherwise, get it.

There is a hacked mutation of TCP Wrappers floating around that ignores the
hosts.deny files. Be certain that you contact your Unix distribution vendor directly
to determine where to get TCP Wrappers if it didn't come with your operating system.
There is no "official" download site for TCP Wrappers, and downloading it randomly
from a website could get you the tainted version. Be certain to run a test deny against
your installation in any case.

WARNING

Firewall Toolkit (FWTK)

The FWTK is the strongest and oldest of the freely available proxy firewalls. You
can download versions for Linux, NetBSD, and Solaris as well as just about any
other flavor of Unix. Although FWTK is traditionally used to create firewalls, it
can easily be used to secure firewall services running on a server itself.

FWTK was created for the Defense Advanced Research Projects Agency
(DARPA) by Trusted Information Systems (TIS) when DARPA realized that no
packet filter would be secure enough to filter protocol content. After TIS fulfilled
the terms of its contract with DARPA (which included making the code public
domain), FWTK further extended the firewalling concept into a commercial
suite known as the Gauntlet Firewall.

FWTK is not a packet filter. Instead, it comes with protocol-scrubbing proxies
for Telnet, rlogin, SMTP, FTP, and HTTP. In addition, it comes with a generic
TCP pass-through redirector (a SOCKS proxy). FWTK also extends its security
controls into the Unix LAN environment, providing centralized network login
and resource control using the netacl and authserv utilities.

FWTK does not filter packets before they are delivered to the IP stack for processing. You must use some other package to protect your computer from malformed packets and other IP-level attacks (IPChains or IPTables are good choices
for packet filtering).

FWTK is a proxy server; it examines the data portions of IP packets to ensure
that the traffic traversing a particular port conforms to the protocol for that port
(that only HTTP requests and replies are going over port 80, for example). This
ensures, for example, that a hacker doesn't use port 80 to access a Trojan horse
with its own protocol, because your packet filter allows only packets to port 80
for HTTP services.

FWTK evaluates data received by the network adapters in the firewall
computer according to a set of rules established in its net-perm rule table. The
rules are defined according to the port to which the data was sent, while permissions are defined according to the source and destination of the data.

You enable FWTK by replacing the services to be proxied in the inetd.conf
file with the corresponding FWTK filter for the service. You then configure the
FWTK protocol proxy to locate the real service. This is the same method used by
TCP Wrappers to check hosts.allow and hosts.deny before allowing access
to an executable. FWTK performs considerably more checking than TCP Wrappers for the protocols that it specifically proxies.

The FWTK proxies read their configuration from the net-perm table, which describes for each protocol those hosts (source and destination) that are allowed to use the proxy.

NOTE

You can find step-by-step instructions for installing FWTK on the Internet—go to http://www.fwtk.org.

Terms to Know

credentials	Pluggable Authentication Module (PAM)
daemon	realm
Distributed Computing Environment (DCE)	remote access
distributed logon	remote logon
file sharing	Secure Shell (SSH)
file sharing protocols	security domain
File Transfer Protocol (FTP)	shares
IPChains	shell
IPTables	single signon
kerberized	smart cards
Kerberos	spam
Key Distribution Centers (KDC)	TCP Wrappers
Lightweight Directory Access Protocol (LDAP)	terminals
local area networks (LANs)	ticket
Network File System (NFS)	Ticket Granting Ticket (TGT)
Network Information System (NIS)	user context
one-time passwords	yellow pages (or yp)
PAMed	

Review Questions

1. Why doesn't Unix have a standard file sharing mechanism?

2. What is the most secure protocol for remotely logging on to a Unix computer?

3. What is the primary authentication mechanism used by SMTP?

4. What does PAM do?

5. What type of encryption does NIS use to protect user credentials?

6. What cryptographic mechanism does Kerberos use to protect user credentials?

7. What is the difference between a file transfer protocol and a file sharing protocol?

8. Does SMB provide any mechanism for securing user credentials over the network?

9. How does TCP Wrappers protect a service?

10. What do IPChains and IPTables provide?

11. What functionality does FWTK provide?

Chapter 13

Web Server Security

In This Chapter

♦ Security flaws in web server applications

This chapter discusses the best practices used to keep web servers secure when they are publicly available. Web and e-mail servers are the two most difficult security problems you will encounter because (in most cases) they must be open to the public in order to fulfill their purpose.

With the exception of exploits based on specific bugs, most web server security problems are generic in nature. Most of this chapter deals with practical security measures for any web server. Because 90 percent of the Internet is run on Apache and IIS, those two web servers are covered specifically.

You've probably heard about security problems with cookies, ActiveX controls, Java applets, and multimedia plug-ins like Real Player. These technologies are problematic, but they only affect the client side—they are not a problem for servers that inspect them or provide them. Serving ActiveX or Java applets is not a security problem for servers, and if you can entice users to actually download your controls, they can frequently be used to provide enhanced server-side security by creating a proprietary interface to your web application that would be far more difficult to hack than a typical HTTP-based interface. This chapter doesn't discuss the security ramifications of web browsing—that problem is well covered in the rest of this book.

Web Security Problems

Bugs in the web server application are the most threatening security problem you will run into when securing web servers. Flaws in the operating system and web server applications are routinely exploited by hackers, and no matter how well you've secured your server, there's very little you can do to prevent these sorts of attacks. In closed-source operating systems, only vendors can repair their code, and the level of support varies widely. Microsoft has been very proactive about patching its web server, Internet Information Server (IIS); in fact, a torrent of patches flows from them on almost a weekly basis. Novell, on the other hand, has allowed known flaws in their web server to go for many months without being patched.

In open-source operating systems, theoretically anyone can fix the flaw, but only the writers of the code are familiar enough with it to actually fix the problem in a short period of time. For this reason, you have to stick with open-source solutions that are being actively maintained and developed by their community. Many older or less popular open-source solutions languish in near abandonment, and security flaws in them may take a long time to be repaired.

NOTE   Washington University's wu-ftp daemon, the most popular FTP daemon, contained a flaw that went six months between exposure and repair because the university did not have an active development effort for the software. This flaw was widely exploited. In contrast, the longest IIS has gone between the exposure of a serious flaw and the release of a patch is three weeks.

Administrative and author access to the server is the next major web security problem. If your web server is outside your network and you've included some file transfer service to allow the website to be updated, hackers can attempt to exploit that service to gain access to the server.

Finally, poorly secured web servers will be exploited. Fortunately, securing a web server is relatively easy to do. This chapter will cover the basics and provide direction to more information.

Implementing Web Server Security

Implementing web server security is relatively simple and methodical.

The first security decision you need to make is which web server to choose. Popular web servers are the target of so much hacking effort that they get exploited routinely even though the vendors are aggressive about patching them. Since 1999, a new serious remote exploit in IIS has been found about once per month. Although Microsoft has always quickly released patches, there's inevitably a few days of vulnerability between the appearance of the attack and the availability of a patch.

Apache has fared much better, with an order of magnitude fewer serious problems, but Linux, the host operating system usually used under Apache, has been exploited more than Windows 2000, the host OS under IIS, in that same time period.

Your choice of a web server and operating system platform is a catch-22. Choose a small-market server and operating system and you'll probably be secure for now, but if an exploit comes along, it may never be patched. Choose a large-market operating system and you're almost guaranteed to be exploitable at some point, but not for very long.

There's no correct answer here. My company uses OpenBSD running Apache for external servers, and we put all of our web servers behind a dedicated firewall that blocks access to everything but port 80.

Apache is a bit more secure from a theoretical standpoint than IIS because it uses a separate user account database, so web accounts are not valid machine accounts. It has also suffered far fewer serious exploits than IIS, bespeaking a higher quality of coding and an understanding of Internet security by its developers. The new 2.0 version runs equally well on Unix and Windows, and some reports show it outperforming IIS on Windows. It brings its separate user accounts to that platform as well, making it a solid choice on either platform.

I would consider the following configurations to be reasonable, listed in order of most to least secure:

- OpenBSD running Apache 2
- Windows 2000 or 2003 running Apache 2
- Linux (kernel 2.6 or later) running Apache 2
- Windows 2000 or 2003 running IIS

The World Wide Web Consortium's WWW security FAQ can be found at www.w3.org/Security/Faq/.

TIP

Common Security Solutions

Although Windows and Unix are completely different platforms, and even though IIS and Apache have very little code in common (though both are based on the early NSCA server), there are a number of security principles that all web server platforms share.

The following sections are the best practices for secure websites irrespective of platform.

Install the Minimum

Web server security begins during the installation. When you install the operating system, install the minimum number of services possible, and only choose those you actually need to serve your website and applications and to administer the website. This almost always means choosing a "custom" installation. Default installations usually install the most popular options for a LAN server, not appropriate options for a public web server.

When you install your web server, choose only those options that you need to use. Avoid extras like indexing services that you won't use, service daemons like FTP, and web-based site administration tools that are poorly secured and can be exploited by hackers.

Don't leave file system permissions in their default state. Before you begin loading files, secure the web root directory correctly so that files you move into the directory will be created with correct security.

WARNING

As a rule, avoid moving files (drag and drop in Windows or mv command in Unix) between directories, because their permissions are not changed to match those of a new parent directory. Use copy operations (Copy and Paste in Windows or cp in Unix) to ensure that a new copy is created in the destination directory and will inherit the permissions of its parent directory.

Beware of Features

bugs
Errors in programming code.

Every line of code potentially contains a bug, especially in "dense" languages like C++ (the language that IIS and Apache were both written in). The more code there is, the more *bugs* exist.

Larger, more expansive web servers (like Apache and IIS) have literally thousands of undiscovered bugs. Simpler, single-purpose web servers on smaller-market operating systems like OS/2 and Mac OS 9 are far harder to exploit because they have less code and fewer features and because fewer hackers are familiar with their operation.

The bugs in those portions of an application that are exercised by most users are well debugged. Vendors have found most of the problems in the well-tested areas of a web server. But the esoteric sections of code, where seldom-used features are implemented, are far less tested. It is in these areas where bugs that affect you are most likely to live.

NOTE

A perfect example of this effect cropped up early in 2002. All versions of Internet Explorer are subject to a remote-root exploit due to major flaw in its support for Gopher—a rarely used protocol predating HTTP that supports hypertext but does not support images or multimedia content. Microsoft's solution was to remove support for Gopher.

There is a paradox here: To avoid problems, deploy only well-tested code. But hackers also test popular software and are more likely to find problems in them than in small-market web servers.

Use Only Dedicated Web Servers

For public web servers, dedicate a machine to the purpose of web service. Any other services running on the machine will only increase the likelihood of the server being exploited.

Don't even consider simply throwing a web server application on an existing server and opening it up to the Internet. If you do this, you will certainly be exploited.

Avoid traditional business applications that have been recently *web enabled*. For the most part, these web-enabled applications are packages of poorly tested scripts that connect directly to your accounting or database application. They are thrown out the door as quickly as possible to compete in the market, usually without rigorous testing of user-provided web input. They typically install the web server with its default security settings and do little to modify them—often leaving notoriously insecure "sample websites" in place. Do not consider making them available on the public Internet.

web enabled
Term used to describe an application that has an HTTP interface, allowing its primary functionality to be used over the Internet.

Use SSL for Sensitive Information

Secure Sockets Layer (SSL), also called HTTPS when used with web service, is the standard for encrypting communications between a web browser and a web server. SSL does not perform authentication—it merely encrypts the data between a server and client for authenticated or anonymous users to protect the data from sniffing attacks. SSL also does not secure data stored on the server.

SSL is a great way to improve security in a multivendor environment. Because there is no universal password encryption standard for the Web besides unencrypted basic authentication, SSL is widely used on public websites. It can be used to encrypt the contents flowing between the browser and the server, thus encrypting both the account name and password in a basic authentication session. SSL is supported by all common web browsers and servers, so this is the perfect solution for secure authentication.

SSL can be a tremendous drag on server performance for popular websites because the web server's CPU is relied upon to encrypt and decrypt many simultaneous sessions. Use hardware-based SSL accelerators to solve this problem or limit SSL encryption to just the information that requires security—like the logon page.

Use workstation grade computers with fast processors but small disks as SSL accelerators for your website. Balance any number of these computers running Linux and Apache 2 in reverse proxy mode on your public facing circuit (also functioning as security proxies to protect the interior web server from worms) to receive and decrypt SSL from web browsers, and have them reverse-proxy your regular website. This is a great way to secure proprietary web servers and web-enabled application servers that aren't compatible with SSL.

TIP

Put Servers behind a Security Proxy

Reverse proxies can be used to inspect URLs before delivering them to a public web server. Many security proxies can also be used to load-balance a single website across a number of actual web servers.

By simply inspecting URLs, you can eliminate most of the buffer overruns and security problems that a web server might be subject to. For example, you're used to seeing a URL in the following form:

```
http://www.google.com
```

But hackers know that most web browsers will do their best to try to deliver a document, and will also interpret URLs as follows:

```
http://www.google.com@63.241.3.69
```

Type this URL into Internet Explorer 5.0 or below and see what happens. Scary, isn't it? This also works in Mozilla and Apple Safari, but Internet Explorer has been patched to fail when this syntax is used. To the uninitiated, it would seem that Google would come up and deliver some sort of specific content or directory. The @ changes everything. In a URL, the content before an @ sign is interpreted as a username, so in this URL, the actual website being delivered is indicated by the 63.241.3.69 IP address.

But this trick is frequently used by hackers to confuse people into clicking on links that will actually take them to a hacker's website, where security flaws in their web browser can be exploited.

Try this URL:

```
http://63%2E241%2E3%2E69
```

This is another simple example of URL obfuscation. This is actually an IP address with the periods replaced by the sequence %2E. The percent sign tells the web browser to interpret the next two characters as the hexadecimal value for the ASCII representation of a character. 2E is the ASCII value for period, which is why this works.

TIP

You can decode encoded URLs using the tables at www.asciitable.com.

Using URL encoding allows hackers to push buffer overruns because they can send any sequence of codes to the URL input buffer on the web server.

The upshot of all of this is that by using a security proxy in front of your web server, you can search every inbound URL for characters like %, which are almost always signs of attempted hacking, and drop them.

NOTE

Some naïve webmasters serve files that have spaces in their filenames, which must be represented by the %20 hexadecimal code. While rare, it is a legitimate use of hexadecimal encoding that may cause problems if you strip URLs for the % character.

You can configure a security proxy to allow you to inspect a URL and drop the connection if it contains characters that are likely to be used by hackers. You can also configure a security proxy to perform more complex connection checking than the server or host operating system provides.

Use a VPN for Intranet Servers

Do not connect intranet servers to the Internet and think that the web server's logon authentication mechanisms will keep you secure. Buffer overruns, the most common type of exploit against a web server, can be perpetrated without logging in. Logon authentication is private network security and is not appropriate for securing servers connected to the public Internet.

To connect remote users to a private website, put your website behind a firewall with a dedicated VPN server. Connect to remote users using a VPN and allow individual users to connect by using a PC-based VPN client. Chapter 6 details ways that home users can connect to company assets securely over the Internet.

Use IP Address and Domain Restrictions for Extranet Servers

If you implement an extranet, use public web-server-grade security and implement SSL to encrypt communications.

Use the operating system's IP filtering to allow only your client's expected addresses. Use TCP Wrappers or your web server's domain restrictions to drop connections from unknown sources. While a dedicated hacker who tries to exploit your site won't be stopped by this sort of protection, it will absolutely eliminate casual hacking attempts.

Use IP Address and Domain Restrictions for Public Servers

Domain restrictions on a public server? Why would you limit your audience on a public server? Because you run a business that doesn't service France, or Russia, or Israel, or China, or India, or 130 other foreign countries. The biggest current threat of hacking activity comes from foreign nations, yet 99 percent of websites don't service more than one language or country. Why allow hackers from anywhere when you don't allow customers from anywhere? You can significantly shore up the security of your website by performing domain restrictions against foreign country code *top level domain names (TLDs)*.

This can provide a significant legal advantage—many hackers don't hack inside the boundaries of their own nation because they can be held legally accountable there, but they have no fear of prosecution in foreign countries. Limiting access to your website to countries that will prosecute hackers is a good way to dramatically reduce the amount of hacking activity you will see against your site.

top level domain names (TLDs)
The first specific level of the domain name hierarchy, TLDs are used to apportion the domain name system into sections that can be administered by different Internet naming authorities. Each country has its own country code TLD (ccTLD), like .us, .ca, .uk, .sp, .fr, .de, and so on. There are also six common general-purpose (non-country specific) TLDs (gTLDs): .com, .net, .org, .edu, .gov, and .mil. Some new gTLDs such as .biz, .info, .pro, and .aero have been released, but there has been no significant interest in them. The Internet Corporation for Assigned Names and Numbers (ICANN) administers the TLD hierarchy.

NOTE Performing reverse DNS lookup for each client will create extra load. Be sure to test performance to make sure you have adequate hardware.

You will want to redirect to a website that explains to legitimate customers what's going on if they can't access your website and give them a phone number or e-mail address to contact so you can explicitly allow them if they run into a problem accessing your site. This should be rare, but some people do come from IP addresses that don't have valid reverse DNS lookups and so won't resolve to a domain name. If you're going to restrict domain names, you have to restrict addresses that don't have reverse DNS names as well or hackers can get around the domain restrictions by using an unregistered address.

Even if you don't bulk-block foreign TLDs, you should comb through your access logs looking for numerous attempts from strange domains or IP addresses. Block these specifically when you find them to prevent hackers who have already knocked on the door from coming back.

Force User Logon for Sensitive Data

As an additional measure to otherwise strong security, you can protect sensitive information using file system permissions. This will cause the web server to prompt the user for logon information and will apply the operating system's security measures to the problem of securing content.

In both IIS and Apache, you can configure a single user account to be used by anonymous browsers, and you can also force users to log on using a local user account. This requires them to have a local or domain user account (IIS) or a web service account (Apache) on the web server.

When you do this, you can subsequently use file system permissions to secure documents on IIS. Apache does not pass authentication through to the operating system, however, so document security remains in the context of the Apache user.

Aside from file system permissions, you can also configure security differently in the various virtual directories within your website. It can be configured using Apache's virtual HTTP user accounts, which (like Samba accounts) are not true Unix user accounts. IIS does not have a facility to manage user accounts that are not real Windows user accounts, which can be a security disadvantage because any account valid on the website is also valid on the server.

Be aware that this logon information is usually sent in the clear, so it can be sniffed. Use only unique account names and passwords on public sites, and use SSL whenever possible to encrypt the communications.

Although both Apache and IIS can be configured to allow encrypted pass-words, the mechanisms for implementing them are by no means universal. Apache (80 percent of the web server market) supports only MD5 authentication, which is only compatible with Internet Explorer 5.0 (and later) and Opera. Netscape Navigator, Mozilla, Konquerer, and most other popular web browsers are not compatible with encrypted passwords in any form. IIS uses only Windows authentication for encryption and its encrypted authentication is only compatible with Internet Explorer.

This basically means that non-Windows clients are out of luck when it comes to encrypted passwords and that if you intend to implement encrypted passwords, you're limited to clients who use Internet Explorer 5.0 and later (which comes with Windows 2000, Me, and XP) and Opera. This is usually not acceptable for public websites, so encrypted passwords is not an option for public websites.

The only universal solution to this problem is to first use SSL to encrypt all data between the browser and server and then use basic authentication. When you do this, the account name and password (as well as the authentication semantics) are encrypted.

Centralize Risky Content

Put your scripts and executables in a single directory, where file system permissions can be maintained correctly. If you distribute scripts and applications all over the place, you have to be especially vigilant to ensure that the permissions are not accidentally changed during a copy or move operation or because permissions are broadly changed in the directory for some other reason. Centralizing this content in a single location makes it easy to determine what the permissions should be.

Place Your Web Servers in a DMZ

Don't place web servers directly on the public Internet if you can avoid it. Place them on your firewall's demilitarized zone (DMZ) interface or use two firewalls (one between the web server and the Internet and one between your private network and the web server) to secure your web servers.

Running a general-purpose operating system like Windows or Unix on the Internet is a bad idea. Operating systems and their TCP/IP stacks are optimized for performance, not security, and there are a number of low-level vulnerabilities that both platforms have been susceptible to in the past. Even with good OS filtering in place, you're better off protecting your web servers with a dedicated firewall.

Don't Allow Connections to the Private Network

Don't allow web servers in the DMZ to establish connections to the interior of your network. Setting up an IP address filter on your website to allow only your web server to connect means nothing because when hackers exploit your web server, they will use the legitimate vector through the firewall to reach the interior of your network.

Place a firewall between your internal network and your web servers as if they were public computers.

Don't Store Sensitive Data on Web Servers

Don't store any data on your web server that isn't stored elsewhere. And don't store sensitive information on your web server.

Always treat public web servers as though hackers will eventually get in and exploit them. Make backups when you update your site content so that you can quickly restore a server to operation if it gets defaced. Never store confidential or sensitive information on a web server because hackers can steal it when they break in.

The purpose of many web servers is to collect data from the public, like account and credit card information. If you can't store the data locally and you can't connect from the DMZ to the internal network to store the data safely, what can you do? There's a catch-22 for sites that must retrieve important data from clients: If it shouldn't be stored on the web server and the server should be shielded from the rest of your network, then how should you retrieve it?

The answer to this question is to set up a secure directory (or table, if you're talking about a database) and set it up on a separate virtual directory with custom security settings. Program your web application to store data retrieved from clients in this more secure area. Then access this private section of your web server from your interior servers to retrieve the data provided by users on a regularly scheduled and frequent basis and remove it from the web server. Because interior servers are connecting out to the DMZ, there's no need for a hole through your firewall; the server in the DMZ can't reach machines in the interior, but machines in the interior can reach the server in the DMZ. This avoids creating connections from the web server that could be exploited by hackers who may have gained control of the machine.

Minimize Services

Don't use the default installation of your operating system on a web server. Both Windows and Unix install a large number of extraneous services that hackers can exploit to hack the machine. Disable all services that aren't required for your website.

In particular, Windows machines should disable the Server service to prevent the machine from allowing Windows file sharing logons. This is the second most important vector for hackers, after pushing buffer overruns, because Windows will always allow the Administrator account to log in without the normal account lockouts. Hackers can run automated tools to try thousands of passwords if your web server is running the Server service. Aside from stopping the service, you should unbind TCP/IP from both the file sharing and the Microsoft networking client in the Network Control Panel and block ports 135, 137, 138, 139, and 445 from entering or leaving the web server.

Most administrators know that port 139, the NetBIOS session port, should be blocked on a public server to prevent attempts at blocking passwords. Most don't know that the new SMB over TCP port introduced in Windows 2000, which provides the same functionality, is on port 445 (the NetLogon port). Hackers can map drives directly using this port as well. Furthermore, a bug in Windows 2000's login time-out security feature allows over 1,200 password attempts per second to be thrown at this port. The entire English language could be cracked in under a minute and every first and last name registered by the IRS in another two.

Windows users should also disable FTP, NNTP, and SMTP if they're not going to be used. These protocols are installed by default with the IIS web server, but you can uncheck them in the installation details panel when you install IIS or disable the services after they are installed.

On Unix machines, disable Telnet, rlogin, and all the other remote logon protocols besides SSH. Run SSH on a non-standard port (other than 22) so that automated attack tools can't find it, and use TCP Wrappers to prevent all hosts but your own from attaching to the server.

It's common to map FTP to the WWW root on your web servers if you provide hosting services for those outside your organization. This allows clients to update their own web pages via FTP logons. Be aware of the security problems with FTP (unencrypted passwords, numerous security flaws in FTP server executables, etc.) before you do this. Consider using WebDAV instead of FTP to reduce the number of services your server requires.

Delete unnecessary executables on dedicated web servers. Windows does not need cmd.exe to operate. Don't use Perl on your Unix machine? Remove it. This is a "last stand" against hackers who have already compromised your machine, but it's remarkably effective—breaking into an empty store doesn't do any good, and the vast majority of hacking exploits are "chain reactions," where a hacker finds a small hole and uses other executables on the web server to make the hole wide enough to squeeze completely through.

Unfortunately, Microsoft built the Server service into the Service Control Manager (along with a few other services like the event log) so it cannot be removed from a web server.

Run Vendor-Provided "Lockdown" Tools

Many vendors provide automated *lockdown programs* that check for common security problems. These applications are sometimes able to remove more unnecessary services than you could remove on your own, because of their tight integration with the operating system and because the vendor knows more about its operating system than most end users know.

lockdown programs
Software designed to automatically configure the security options of an operating system or other application to be optimal for a specific purpose.

Check out `www.bastille-linux.org` for Linux servers, `www.openbsd.org` for BSD Unix, and Microsoft's IIS lockdown tool at `www.microsoft.com/windows2000/downloads/recommended/iislockdown`.

Stay Patched Up-to-Date

Right now, if you install Windows 2000 Server and Internet Information Server 5 from the CD-ROM that came with your server and place it on the public Internet to serve web pages, your server will be exploited by a variant of the Nimda worm within 30 minutes. Guaranteed. When we tested an unpatched version of IIS on the Internet for this book, the Nimda worm found it within 15 minutes of its first boot, pushed its buffer overrun, and began uploading its code to further exploit other servers. Windows Server 2003 with IIS 6 is invulnerable to Nimda, but newer worms have exploited it.

You absolutely cannot deploy a web server without the complete set of security patches from the vendor and expect it to stay secure. You can't even connect it to the Internet just for the time it takes to download the requisite patches and remain secure—you'll be exploited during the patch download process.

To safely deploy a web server these days, you need to install and configure the server inside a firewall that blocks port 80 (HTTP). Once you've got the server completely configured and patched up-to-date (and only then), you can move it out onto the public Internet. You could try disabling the web service to do the patching, but the operating system itself is vulnerable to numerous exploits. Besides, you can only disable the services once the installation has been completed and you've logged in. There's a reasonable chance that your server will be exploited before you can log in for the first time. Don't try it.

Once your server is deployed, subscribe to every security mailing list you can find in order to get an early warning about new threats. Vendors only mention a threat once they've got a patch ready, which can be days or weeks after an exploit has appeared. Independent advisories have no such conflict of interest and often break the news about exploits before vendors do.

If an exploit appears that you may be vulnerable to and the vendor hasn't released a patch yet, you're in no-man's land. You can shut your web server down and wait for a patch, get a good backup and prepare for frequent restorations, implement a proxy server, or purchase a third-party proxy filtering application (like FWTK for Unix machines) that may be invulnerable.

TIP   eEye security produces a TCP Wrapper–like service called SecureIIS that looks for buffer overruns and other URL malformations and blocks them before they get to IIS. It's a good thing. Check it out at `www.eeye.com`.

Analyze CGI and Script Security

Besides delivering files, HTTP also allows programs to be remotely executed on the web server through the Computer Gateway Interface (CGI) mechanism. If you specify the path to an executable in a web browser (and the user account has execute permissions), the server will launch the executable and deliver its text output to the web browser rather than delivering the file itself. It's a simple and powerful mechanism that allows HTTP to act as the user interface to incredibly complex programs. It's also the means by which innumerable hacking exploits can be perpetrated. Poorly written CGI applications are likely to contain unchecked buffers that can be overrun and flaws like taking a filename as a parameter without checking whether the file is in an appropriate directory. These same problems have existed in web servers, so there's no reason to think that custom software would be any more secure.

Modern web browsers also allow the execution of text files instead of delivering them; these text files are called scripts, and the browser determines whether to deliver the text or execute it by examining the file's extension. If the extension is registered as a scripting language extension on the server, then the server will run the script through a scripting language module or executable program and deliver the output of that process to the web browser. This is referred to as server-side scripting.

Scripting allows simpler, less-sophisticated programs to be run on the server. They are easier to write, simpler to debug, and able to take advantage of the (hopefully) secure environment provided by the scripting module. Unfortunately, simpler programs lower the bar for programming talent, and it's common for scriptwriters to accidentally circumvent security without understanding the ramifications of their actions. Fortunately, exploiting individual programming mistakes on a single website takes time and dedication; poorly written scripts will not be subject to the automated hacking attempts that widely deployed problems like buggy web servers will be.

The solution to server-side scripting and CGI is simple: Don't use custom CGI programs or scripts without serious security testing. Here are a few simple things to look for in scripts or programs you write or evaluate.

Never take filenames or database path information directly as a parameter even if you're certain that your own pages are generating the filenames. Rather, create your own aliases for files that need to be accessed and pass those semantic aliases to refer to filenames and database paths by looking them up on the server side. This prevents access to files that you don't intend to serve.

Parse every input from a user for characters outside the legitimate range before inspecting its value. If you find any illegitimate characters, discard the entire input value.

Avoid creating files to the extent possible. If it's not avoidable, be certain to set the file's permissions so that only the web server has access to the file or the file is readable to web users only if the it needs to be subsequently delivered to the web browser.

Never call another executable from a script or CGI program on the server if you can possibly avoid it. This is usually done through the exec or eval calls in scripts. Most unintentional security problems occur because programmers execute software that they didn't write (and can't secure) from within their own relatively secure programs. Write your own code instead.

Never use command shells as the execution environment for a script. Use a scripting language specifically designed for web scripting or text processing, like Perl, PHP, or Python. These languages, while not perfect, have built-in security measures to prevent many of the simple problems that running scripts from a shell environment can allow.

<table>
<tr><td>*WARNING*</td><td>Downloading freely available scripts for common purposes like form mailing or cookie-based logon mechanisms is exceptionally dangerous. Most of the popular scripts have known exploits, and adding them to your site will make your site vulnerable to those exploits. Even if you're doing the same thing as a freely available script, writing a custom script at least requires hackers to specifically exploit your script.</td></tr>
</table>

Avoid Web-Based Server Managers

Web-based server managers are popular on both Windows and Unix machines—IIS comes with one installed out of the box, and Webmin is a popular open-source administrative website for Unix machines.

Don't use either one. Both have significant security problems, not the least of which is the fact that by default, they're open to public hacking attempts.

On Windows servers, use the far less exploitable Terminal Services in administrative mode. It's free and gives you complete access to the host operating system. Password exchanges are secure, and you can configure the server to encrypt the entire session if you want. Remove the Administrative Site, the default site, and the sample sites before you make the server public.

On Unix machines, learn to configure the system from the command shell and use SSH as your remote administrative tool.

Apache Security

The Apache HTTP server project is the second most successful open-source development effort, after Linux. Apache is based on the public domain NCSA HTTP daemon developed by the National Center for Supercomputing Applications at the University of Illinois. After the original author left the university in 1994, development of NCSA stalled and various webmasters began writing their own extensions, and a small group of them began coordinating their changes and distributing them to one another. Within a short period of time, this core group began releasing complete compiled versions of their servers and coordinating the implementation of new features: Apache was born.

<table>
<tr><td>*NOTE*</td><td>Apache's name is derived from "A Patchy Server." It was originally the NCSA web server with a bunch of patches applied to fix various problems and add features.</td></tr>
</table>

About a year after the first public release of Apache, it became the most popular web server on the Internet and remains so today. Versions of Apache are available for all operating systems. Apache 2.0 was released in 2002 as a complete redevelopment, designed to be efficient on all supported platforms rather than being developed primarily for Unix and running through POSIX emulation on other platforms.

TIP

Apache is actually faster and more secure than IIS when running on a Windows 2000 server. Windows webmasters should seriously consider replacing IIS with Apache 2.0 to avoid the constant barrage of hacking attempts that are IIS specific.

Apache configuration is performed by editing the `/etc/httpd/conf/httpd.conf` file and modifying the directives contained therein. The following graphic shows some of the virtual directory configuration options for an Apache web server.

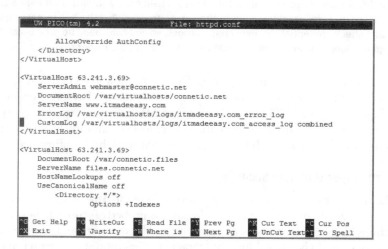

The Apache HTTP daemon process runs as root but spawns a new user context for every web session served. This means that users who browse web pages are served by a process using the user account defined by the user directive.

There are three major levels of directives in Apache:

♦ Global directives determine the configuration of the server as a whole.

♦ ServerRoot directives determine the configuration of the default website.

♦ VirtualHost directives determine the configuration of individual *virtual hosts*.

virtual host
A web server administration feature that allows a single web server to serve numerous websites as if each were hosted by its own server. The web server inspects the URL header, IP address, or port number from the client connection to determine which virtual host should deliver a specific page request.

The official source for Apache configuration settings is `httpd.apache.org/docs-2.0/`**.**

TIP

Use User-Based Security

Apache user-based security, like most secure network services in Unix, uses its own user/password file, so web accounts are not the same as operating system user accounts. This is a very important security feature because it does not provide an open door to the operating system for someone who has intercepted web credentials.

Apache can be configured to use different user password files for each virtual server, which means that if you host multiple websites on a single server, you should configure Apache to use a different list of users for each website. Information on how to do this is included with the official documentation.

Because Apache user security is not passed through to the operating system, you can't rely on file system permissions to secure documents against specific web users. File permissions can only be set for the standard Apache user.

TIP

Unlike IIS, Apache does not spin off the session using the authenticated user's credentials, so security checking is up to the server process. Apache has to parse user files and check credentials for every page access, so you can speed up processing for a large number of users by using DBM formatted user files rather than text files.

Apache supports MD5 message digest authentication to securely exchange passwords. Most popular web browsers, including Internet Explorer versions 5 and higher, support MD5 authentication. Use MD5 authentication to encrypt credentials when you use user authentication unless you absolutely have to support users with obsolete web browsers, or use SSL with basic authentication.

Ensure Proper Directory Security

taint

In Perl, a flag indicating that the information contained in the flagged variable was directly entered by a web user and should not be trusted. Taint is copied with the variable contents and can only be removed by interpreting the variable's contents rather than simply passing them through to a function or another application.

Make sure that your ServerRoot directory (where the Apache executable is stored, as defined by the ServerRoot directive) is properly secured against modifications by the anonymous web user account. This directory and all of its subdirectories should be owned by root (chown 0), the group should be set to the root (wheel) group (chgrp 0), and permission should be set to disallow writes by group and everyone (chmod 0755). If anonymous web users can modify this directory, you open up the possibility of a remote-root exploit.

Scripting Security

Use Perl as your scripting language, and enable taint checks. *Taint* is a flag on a variable that indicates that the data that it contains came directly from a web user. As the data in a variable is copied around from one variable to another, the taint flag is copied with it. If taint checks are enabled, Perl will not allow data from a tainted variable to be used to open or execute files. Taint basically forces you to use proper data checking procedures on user input. No other web scripting language provides this security feature.

If you download a script that says you must turn off taint checks to use it, it's a sure sign that the script is not secure. If you can't get your own scripts working with taint checks enabled, keep working until you can. Disabling taint checks is an admission of security failure.

Internet Information Services Security

Internet Information Services is Microsoft's web server for the Windows platform. Like Apache, IIS is based on the public domain NCSA web server developed by Rob McCool at the University of Illinois. IIS 1.0 was little more than NCSA with a Windows interface and was available for download from Microsoft. NT Server 4 shipped with IIS 2, but it was quickly supplanted by the considerably superior IIS 3. During the life cycle of NT 4, IIS 4 became the standard, introducing numerous new features like name-based virtual hosting and numerous security fixes. IIS 4 also introduced an entirely new tree-based management console. IIS 5 is a security fix version of IIS 4 that shipped with Windows 2000. IIS 5 includes WebDAV support and numerous other esoteric features; otherwise, IIS 5 is basically the same as IIS 4 and they're difficult to tell apart. IIS 6 comes with Windows Server 2003 and includes performance improvements and security fixes over IIS 5 as well as support for .NET scripting.

Microsoft changed the name from Internet Information Server 4 to Internet Information Services 5 for the version included with Windows 2000. So now you have to search on both terms to find information on the Web.

Microsoft includes IIS for free with the operating system when you buy Windows NT/2000 Server. However, there's a serious "gotcha" embedded in Microsoft's licensing terms when it comes to web service:

◆ Anonymous users are free.

◆ Users who authenticate with the server require a client access license per user or an Internet Connector License for unlimited logons.

Microsoft has concocted this convoluted licensing scheme to extract money from those who use IIS to create intranets and extranets while remaining competitive for its use for public websites. The folks at Microsoft know that most companies deploy Windows-based websites, not because they've performed a competitive analysis of server technologies, but because their programmers only know Visual Basic—and once a site is developed on Visual Basic, the users are locked into Windows and IIS.

Microsoft's position is basically that it charges per authenticated user for server services. Since anonymous users don't authenticate, there is no additional cost to support them. It's blatantly obvious that anonymous users are only free because Apache and Linux exist.

Microsoft packages the Internet Connector license as an operating system license, not an IIS license. This means that the same licensing applies whether you use Apache or IIS to serve "authenticated" pages—quite clever, since this way you're required to pay for an Internet Connector License for authenticated users even if you run Apache to serve your pages. However, since Apache uses its own user authentication accounts, users are not logged into actual Windows accounts, thus technically nullifying Microsoft's licensing argument—no Windows-based authentication is being used.

TIP

If you're worried about licensing issues (such as trying to figure out how much you're supposed to pay Microsoft for various modes of access), use Linux or BSD with Apache for your public website.

A "workstation" version of IIS called Peer Web Services exists; it's the same software, but it is subject to the limitation that Windows NT 4 Workstation, Windows 2000 Professional, and Windows XP will only serve 10 simultaneous IP-based logons. However, there is no per-client charge for authenticated users when Peer Web Services is running on these operating systems.

Windows Server 2003 Web Edition is a version of Windows streamlined specifically for web service. If you know you are going to use a server only to provide Web service, consider this version. In addition to being cheaper, is doesn't contain many of the services in standard Windows that hackers may attempt to exploit.

IIS is simple to install and configure. The management console shown here is from a default installation. It can take a moment to figure out what's going on, but like all Microsoft Management Console apps, the configuration is easy to figure out once you're used to the paradigm.

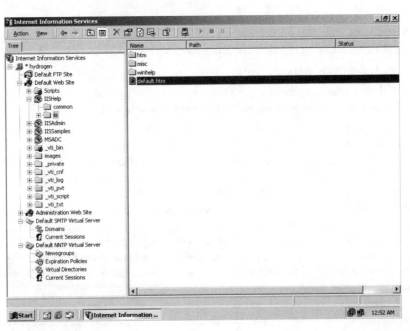

IIS can serve numerous virtual hosts, which are distinguished by either IP address, TCP port number, or host header domain name. The default website runs on port 80 and is served in the absence of any more specific information about which website the user wants. IIS allows you to create as many virtual hosts as you want.

There are many properties in IIS that can be configured globally for all sites, for both performance and security. These properties are basically the same as the properties that can be configured for individual hosts; the global configuration merely creates the default template that all sites inherit. Setting the master configuration before you begin adding websites is a good way to start off with better security. The master properties section for the IIS server shown here is the gateway for global configuration.

Under the default website, the IISHelp, IISAdmin, IISSamples, and MSADC nodes are *virtual directories* that are linked into the default website as subdirectories, so that `http://hostname.dom/IISHelp` will deliver the content pointed to by the IISHelp virtual directory even though it's not stored in a folder that is actually contained in the www root directory where the default site is stored. Virtual directories can also be redirects to a different website.

virtual directory
A portion of a website with its own specific configuration and security settings. A virtual directory appears as a directory inside the website but may be located anywhere on the Internet.

Use Virtual Directories to Customize Security

Virtual directories have their own IIS security settings and can be used to modify security settings within a website. The following graphic shows the properties panel of a virtual directory.

With virtual directories, you can change the following on a directory-by-directory basis:

- Access to scripts
- Directory browsing
- Read and write access
- Logging of access
- Indexing of files
- Execution permissions (none, scripts, executables)
- Partitioning of CGI, ISAPI, and script applications
- Enabling sessions
- Associating document types with scripting engines

You can manage snippets (small applications or scripts with an associated user interface that are intended to be included in other web pages) by using virtual directories. Place a specific snippet in its own directory and use virtual directories to include it in the rest of your websites. This way, you can control its security settings globally and store only a single copy of it.

Avoid IIS User Authentication

The IIS host process (the World Wide Web Server service) runs under the account credentials configured in the Services Control Panel—by default, the LocalSystem account. But every user session connected starts under the context of the IUSR_COMPUTERNAME user account, which is created when IIS is installed. This can be changed to any other user account if desired. If users authenticate with the server, then a new session is started using the credentials supplied. The three authentication methods shown here are available in IIS.

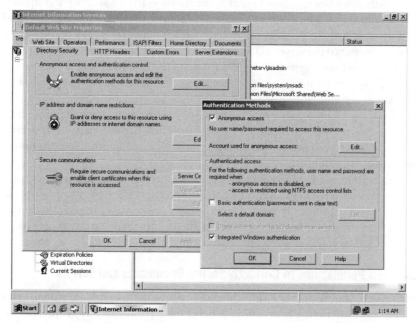

You can configure IIS to use three types of user authentication for any website:

Anonymous Access　The default mechanism. When a session is connected, the connection process is spun off using the IUSR_COMPUTERNAME user account context by default or whatever other user the administrator configures. If you use the NTFS file system, all public web directories and their contents need to be configured to allow read access for the anonymous web user. They should not be configured to allow write access.

Basic Authentication　The traditional method of user logon supported by all web browsers and servers. User accounts and passwords are transmitted in unencrypted form, and because they are valid Windows accounts, they can be used to exploit the server directly using other services if those services are running and open to the Web. If you choose to use basic authentication, use SSL to encrypt the web session and protect user credentials from sniffing attacks.

Windows Authentication　Also called NTLM authentication or pass-through authentication. A proprietary mechanism supported only by IIS and Internet Explorer. NTLM transmits the password in encrypted form using the standard Windows hash algorithm.

If the web server attempts to load a page that the default web user does not have permission to access, the web browser will prompt for different credentials. Assuming the logon is successful, the web server will open a new process using the supplied user credentials and again attempt to load the page.

IIS falls flat when it comes to user authentication from a security standpoint. IIS does not support web-service-only user accounts, which means that any valid web account is also a valid logon account, which of course means that it can be used to connect to the server via any other configured network service. Although IIS also doesn't use a separate list of user accounts for virtual hosts, you can use NTFS file system permissions to restrict access to different virtual hosts based on groups.

IIS does not support encrypted passwords for browsers other than Internet Explorer, so it is not widely used for public websites. Because passwords cannot be reliably encrypted unless you intend to limit access to Internet Explorer users only, its utility is limited.

Finally, Internet Explorer will automatically provide the credentials of the user logged onto the client machine before it prompts for separate credentials. While this isn't specifically a server-side security problem, it can provide a mechanism whereby the credentials of your legitimate intranet or extranet users could be suborned by hackers on the Internet.

Use NTFS Permissions to Correctly Secure Documents and Scripts

When you install IIS, the `Scripts` directory (where most scripts are stored) is set to "full control" for the Everyone group. Set these permissions to Read and Execute for only those accounts that will be used by web users. Windows Server 2003 improves the default security settings, but you should still tighten them up for your specific circumstance.

Use a Security Proxy

IIS is subject to a phenomenal number of buffer overruns, and because its root process runs by default as the LocalSystem account, exploits provide even wider access to the machine than the Administrator account allows. If you serve a public website using IIS, use a security proxy to shore up security.

Microsoft's Internet Security and Acceleration Server is a good and relatively inexpensive choice that provides an astounding array of security services. It can be run directly on the web server or as a firewall in front of an array of web servers, where it can assist in load-balancing across the pool of servers. Check out ISA Server at www.Microsoft.com.

eEye's SecureIIS security filter is another good (and inexpensive) way to eliminate most of the egregious security problems in IIS. eEye's filter runs on each web server and checks inbound URLs and user input for suspicious characters and invalid length. Check it out at www.eeye.com.

Apache in reverse proxy mode is also pretty good choice to create a low-cost proxy for IIS—because it's a different application running on a different operating system, it's not subject to the same buffer overruns and won't pass them through to IIS. You can use Apache's very expressive mod-rewrite utility to scan URLs for invalid characters and URL sequences and drop them.

Terms to Know

bugs	virtual directory
lockdown programs	virtual host
taint	web enabled
top level domain (TLD)	

Review Questions

1. Over 90 percent of the public Internet is served from which two web server applications?

2. What is the most threatening security problem facing public web servers?

3. Which is more secure, closed-source or open-source operating systems?

4. Which is more secure, IIS or Apache?

5. Why should websites only be deployed on dedicated web servers?

6. Where are bugs most likely to be found in a program?

7. What service does SSL perform?

8. What's the best way to secure intranet servers?

9. What is the universal encrypted authentication mechanism?

10. How do you configure Apache?

11. What is taint?

Chapter 14

E-mail Security

All modern businesses require Internet e-mail of one form or another. E-mail is the first truly new method of communication to come along since the invention of the telephone, and its effect on business efficiency has been just as dramatic as its vocal predecessor.

As with all public services, running an SMTP service entails risking that the service itself could be exploited to run arbitrary code on the mail server. In fact, this has occurred with every major e-mail server system, including sendmail, Exchange, and Lotus Notes. The only solution to this problem is to keep e-mail servers in your demilitarized zone (DMZ) or outside your firewall so that if they're exploited, they don't allow further access to the interior of your network. E-mail servers must be kept up-to-date on server software and security patches to prevent exploits related to bugs.

This chapter will teach you how to mitigate e-mail security risks.

E-mail Encryption and Authentication

The only way to make *e-mail* truly secure is to encrypt it. Encryption protects against sniffing, accidental misdirection, loss of attached document security, and even forgery.

E-mail encryption foils all attempts to strip attachments or scan for viruses because the e-mail server cannot decrypt the mail to check it. Be certain that you receive encrypted mail only from trusted sources—those whose own e-mail systems cannot be suborned to transmit viruses.

All e-mail encryption methods use public key encryption to secure messages. To establish secure e-mail, your e-mail encryption package will create a private key for you and a public key that you can send to those who need to receive secure e-mail from you.

This chapter discusses public e-mail security methods. Numerous methods exist to secure private e-mail services within a single organization, but these proprietary systems cannot be effectively used on the public Internet because they only work with e-mail servers of the exact same type. Private mail system security is rarely important since purely private e-mail systems cannot be attacked from the Internet, so server-to-server encryption systems have little real value.

electronic mail (e-mail)
A queued message delivery system that allows users to transmit relatively short text messages to other users over the Internet. The messages wait in a mail queue until they are downloaded and read by the ultimate recipient.

Secure Multipurpose Internet Mail Extensions (S/MIME)
MIME with extensions that provide encryption.

Pretty Good Privacy (PGP)
A freely available encryption package that supports file and e-mail encryption for nearly all computing platforms.

Forgery can be prevented through public key encryption. The ability to decrypt a message with a specific public key proves that it was encrypted with the corresponding private key, which in turn proves that the message is from whoever sent you the public key. However, unless both parties know that all e-mail should always be encrypted and that unencrypted e-mail should not be trusted, forgery can still occur by the transmission of an unencrypted message.

In the early days of encrypted e-mail, you had to manually encrypt messages by piping the message through an external encryption program. More modern e-mail encryption packages automate the encryption process by keeping track of those to whom you've sent a public key and subsequently encrypt mail to those recipients.

Every encryption system is different, and both recipients must be using the same system in order to exchange encrypted e-mail. Fortunately, two systems have emerged as the market leaders: *Secure Multipurpose Internet Mail Extensions (S/MIME)* and *Pretty Good Privacy (PGP)*. PGP is proprietary but free. S/MIME is an open standard supported by multiple vendors, but requires rooted certificates that you will have to pay for. Both systems are somewhat free to use, but S/MIME requires you to have an X.509 digital certificate installed that gives the root certificate authorities something to charge you for if you want to have transitive trusts between organizations.

Encrypted e-mail hasn't caught on because it's an extra layer of hassle. End users have a hard time obtaining *rooted* digital certificates; businesses are hesitant to pay for or administer rooted certificate services. Finally, if an end user has problems with their e-mail system and loses their ring of public keys, they won't be able to open mail from their associates until they bother them for a new key.

rooted
Describes a transitive trust system that relies upon a hierarchy that culminates in a single entity that all participants implicitly trust.

S/MIME

S/MIME is the future of encrypted e-mail. Developed by RSA Security (originators of the first commercial public key encryption implementation), it's an open standard that has wide industry support, except from the open-source community, which doesn't like the fact that S/MIME is based on rooted X.509 certificates that come only from commercial entities. There's no reason why the open-source community couldn't make their own root CA, but without the resources to verify subscriber's true identities, it would become a hornet's nest of fraudulent certifications. Organizations can create their own non-rooted certificates as well, using the Windows Certificate Server service or Open SSL, but it's a fairly complex process and they must be traded manually among organizations that want to be able exchange secure mail.

S/MIME encryption is built into the e-mail client or is an add-on package for the e-mail client once the encryption certificate is installed. To use S/MIME encryption, obtain a digital certificate from some certificate authority and install it into your e-mail client.

S/MIME doesn't specify an encryption algorithm or standard. The original S/MIME implementations used RC2 40-bit encryption (the same as early SSL encryption), which is extremely weak and can be cracked in a trivial amount of time using brute force methods. This algorithm was originally used because it was the strongest grade of security that the U.S. would allow to be exported.

Thawte provides free, uncertified personal certificates at `www.thawte.com`.

TIP

Another popular algorithm is 56-bit DES, which is also now considered weak. The minimum secure standard for S/MIME today is Triple-DES, which provides 168-bit security. Unfortunately, the stronger the algorithm is, the less likely any specific implementation is to support it.

To use encrypted e-mail on the client side, you simply download your certificate from a trusted provider and import it into your mail client. Once done, you have the option to encrypt e-mail that you send to anyone. You must first send them an e-mail containing your public key, which will be installed in their *key ring* when they open the attachment.

key ring
A database of public keys that have been received by a user.

PGP

PGP (and the newer OpenPGP) e-mail encryption works essentially the same way, but instead of using S/MIME, it uses a proprietary protocol to encrypt mail. PGP is also not supported natively by most e-mail applications, but it can be added as a module or extension to most of them.

PGP is a little less transparent than S/MIME, but it's easier to administer for small sites or individuals because you can easily generate your own key pairs rather than obtaining them from a certificate authority.

Although PGP lacks any concept of rooted transitive trust, it does use a *grass-rooted* methodology called a *web of trust,* where individuals who use the system sign the posted public keys of those individuals that they know personally to certify that they know the person has honestly posted the key—in other words, they vouch for their identity. The more users that have vouched for an individual, the more likely it is that you will know one of them.

The idea is that when everyone has vouched for everyone they know, the result will be a "six degrees of Kevin Bacon" effect where you know someone who knows someone who knows someone who signed the key of the person you're authenticating, and so transitive trust exists without a central certifying authority. It's a nice idea, but it takes massive participation for it to actually be of any real value. It is perfectly fine for business partners, however, because they can simply certify each other and be assured that they're talking to real individuals. Thawte is building a web of trust system for its S/MIME-based, free personal certificates as well.

grass-rooted
Describes a trust system that has no hierarchy; instead it relies upon massive participation to provide a transitive trust mechanism that requires no supporting commercial organization.

web of trust
The PGP grass-rooted transitive-trust mechanism for encrypted e-mail.

Mail Forgery

Outside of automated spam and virus propagation, mail forgery is about as uncommon as standard document forgery, but it's much easier to perpetrate. It is rare only because it takes truly criminal intent to forge e-mail.

There is no *SMTP* authentication mechanism. This lack of inherent security allows mail forgery to occur. But despite this, there are a few things you can do to make mail forgery difficult.

It's pointless to forge e-mail unless you can get a human to do something based on the contents of the message. Given that this is the case, you can mitigate the effectiveness of an e-mail forgery attempt by making a few acceptable-use policies concerning the e-mailing of highly sensitive information. For example, you should never mail passwords, but many users may not know this. If everyone knows that passwords are never e-mailed, then a forged e-mail from an administrator asking a user for a password will immediately be exposed as a forgery. You should also make policies concerning the request for e-mail attachments (at the very least attachments containing sensitive information). If everyone within your organization knows that only links to documents should be e-mailed, then requests for attachments will also be foiled. With just these two policies, the majority of mail forgery exploits can be prevented.

Simple Mail Transfer Protocol (SMTP)
The Internet protocol that controls the transmission of e-mail between servers. SMTP is also used to transmit e-mail from clients to servers, but it's usually not used to receive it because SMTP requires recipient machines to be online at all times.

You can configure your e-mail server to reject SMTP connections from any e-mail server that doesn't have a valid registered domain name. People you do business with have a mail server with a registered domain name, so you aren't going to lose mail from them. You can take this a step further by rejecting mail from domains that you don't do business with. For example, if you work at a small business, it's likely that you don't do business internationally, so there's no point in receiving mail from most foreign countries. By dropping connection attempts from countries that you have no business interest in, you can eliminate the source of numerous mail forgery attempts, a tremendous amount of spam, and the origin point of numerous automated e-mail–based Internet worms and viruses.

If an e-mail message is important, use encrypted e-mail even if you don't need privacy. E-mail encryption not only secures the contents of e-mail, it proves that the message came from the same person who sent you the public key.

None of these measures eliminate the possibility of mail forgery, but they do reduce the risk substantially.

E-mail Viruses

E-mail is the new favorite vector of virus writers. Personal information managers that store contact information are also used as e-mail clients, putting the information that an e-mail virus needs to propagate in the same execution environment as the virus itself. More than 99 percent of all virus strikes now enter via e-mail—in fact, non–e-mail virus strikes are now exceptionally rare because e-mail has all but eliminated the use of removable media such as floppy or Zip disks to transfer documents among computers.

The fact that most viruses propagate via e-mail is actually a serious advantage for network administrators.

For computers inside a corporation, an e-mail gateway virus scanner can eliminate the need to deploy virus scanners on every workstation. You need only run a virus scanner on your e-mail server to detect viruses as they come through the gateway, and you can be almost certain that your individual workstations will be protected; that is, as long as your virus definitions are up-to-date and your virus scanner vendor releases updates fast enough to make sure that even new viruses are caught. If a virus does slip through your e-mail gateway, workstation scanners won't catch it either. But to remove the virus once you do update your virus definitions, you will need scanners on your workstations.

Beware of e-mail virus hoaxes. Hoaxes are just as common as actual viruses, and they can be just as destructive. Recently, a friend called me saying he'd gotten a virus warning that urged him to "check for the virus" by looking up certain files, and if they existed, to delete them. Of course, the files were critical system files, and we had to reinstall the operating system to restore them.

WARNING

A side effect of e-mail viruses is the plague of misdirected virus response notifications. Newer viruses forge the From address in the mail they send out. When the recipient's virus scanner cleans the mail and responds to the sender with a "You have a virus" automated notice, a third-party recipient (the one whose address was forged into the From field) receives the "You have a virus" notification from the recipient's mail server. This inevitably spooks users into thinking they have a virus, and explaining why they got the notification is difficult. Turn off virus response notifications from your antivirus software—the original recipient won't get them anyway, and at this point they're just wasting bandwidth.

Outlook Viruses

Outlook
Microsoft's extremely popular, but poorly secured, e-mail client and personal information manager.

Outlook and *Outlook Express* have special security problems related to their incorporation of Windows scripting directly into e-mail. These two e-mail clients will automatically execute scripts that are contained in an e-mail message.

Most outlook viruses operate by rifling through your Outlook contacts and then e-mailing themselves to either all of your contacts or randomly selected contacts. The authentication problem is that they look like they've come from you, so your colleagues will be off guard when they open the e-mail and may even be induced to open an attachment. Note that if you have S/MIME public keys for a recipient who receives only encrypted mail, the virus will be able to encrypt itself since it's running within your outlook context and logon, and transmit itself securely. E-mail encryption cannot stop automated e-mail viruses.

Outlook Express
A stripped-down version of Outlook that handles only the minimum set of features necessary to propagate e-mail viruses.

The scripts are included in e-mail as a special type of attachment and can be easily stripped at the e-mail server, so the solution to this problem is the same as the solution to stripping attachments.

NOTE   Outlook 2003 is more secure by default than previous versions because it disables some scripting by default and blocks the downloading of executable attachments. Upgrade to it if you use Outlook.

Commercial Gateway Virus Scanners

There are numerous virus-scanning packages to choose from. They all use the same type of technology to search for the signature characteristics of viruses. They operate like a spell checker searching through a document for misspelled words. Code quality varies a bit, but most of them do the job. Other technologies that attempted to predict "virus-like" behavior had too many false positives and didn't always catch new types of viruses, so they did not gain widespread acceptance. This effect is much like the attempts now being made to detect "hacker-like activity" in intrusion detection systems, which are being bested by simple signature-based intrusion detectors. Most gateway virus scanners also include spam filters as well.

Where the scanners vary is mostly in the speed at which the vendors find and post new virus definitions, the ease with which you can update your definitions, the cost of their software, and the automation of deployment.

I could go on at length about the merits of various commercial virus scanners, but there's a simple bottom line: Symantec AntiVirus is better in every category (except spam filtering) than any of its competitors, and it's priced at about the mid-range of virus solutions. It's simple to install, it automatically deploys clients, and it automatically receives updates. Symantec is very fast in deploying new virus definitions, and it costs less than $25 per workstation. Every time I've walked into a client site where they use another enterprise virus scanner, I wind up replacing it because either the code quality is low and causes problems for users or the update mechanism is prone to failure or the vendor isn't fast enough to catch new viruses and deploy updates so new viruses slip through.

When you buy Symantec AntiVirus Enterprise Edition, you get the scanning software for servers and e-mail servers along with the package. If you buy retail versions of their desktop scanner, you don't.

Unfortunately, none of the major vendors really provide decent support for Unix- or Linux-based machines, but viruses don't usually attack those platforms, so virus-scanning software is usually not necessary for them. Unix avoids viruses by remaining incompatible with Microsoft Office, the engine behind 99 percent of all current virus activity.

AMaViS

Unix isn't all that susceptible to viruses, so virus scanners are uncommon in the Unix world. But there is a place for them: when Unix e-mail servers host e-mail for Windows clients. In this situation, you need to scan for Windows viruses, but you need to do it on a Unix machine.

Many commercial vendors (such as Kaspersky) provide solutions for this problem by selling special Unix e-mail gateway scanning software. Unfortunately, they charge for their software per mailbox, which means that if you host thousands of e-mail boxes on a mail server, you'll pay tens of thousands of dollars for the same software that someone else paid just hundreds for.

AMaViS, an open-source solution for scanning e-mail, is my favorite solution to this problem. It does an end run around silly licensing practices by allowing you to use a single workstation license virus scanner for Unix to check all the e-mail that flows through it. Furthermore, it decompresses attachments to make sure that viruses aren't hiding inside ZIP files, and it's reasonably efficient. You do have to use it in conjunction with a commercial Unix virus scanner, so make sure that the vendor's *EULA* doesn't expressly forbid this type of use. You can check it out at www.amavis.org.

end user license agreement (EULA)
A contract between the developer of software and the users of software. The contract limits the user's right to use and distribute the software as specified by the developer.

Attachment Security

attachment

A file encoded in text form for transmission in an e-mail message, such as a `word.doc` or `picture.jpg` file.

Every mail client suffers from one problem: Hackers can send a Trojan horse or virus to users as an executable *attachment* and, if the user is induced to open the attachment, the content may execute automatically. This is a fundamentally different problem than Outlook viruses because these viruses or Trojan horses don't rely upon the execution environment of the e-mail client; they rely upon being extracted from the e-mail message and executed by the user in the execution environment of the host operating system.

Multipurpose Internet Mail Extension (MIME)

An IETF protocol for encoding and transmitting files along with metadata that determines how the files should be decoded and what applications should be used to interpret them.

Attachments, a relatively new feature of e-mail, are files that are encoded in a format that can be transmitted as text. *Multipurpose Internet Mail Extension (MIME)* is the protocol that describes how e-mail attachments should be handled. MIME is also used on the Web to transfer multimedia content in web pages.

Some e-mail clients are better than others at helping to mitigate this problem by requiring you to actually download the file before it can be executed, but this won't stop a user who has been fooled by the body text. The latest mail clients will automatically quarantine attachments that are considered too dangerous to e-mail as well.

There are four ways to deal with attachments (in order from most to least secure):

- Strip all attachments.
- Allow only the specific attachment types you commonly use.
- Strip only known dangerous attachments.
- Don't strip attachments.

These methodologies are discussed in the following sections, except for the last one because it's not a security measure.

Exchange

Microsoft's e-mail and messaging server. Exchange was originally designed for private interoffice messaging, with Internet functionality provided as an add-on. It uses the proprietary Microsoft MAPI protocol for exchanging mail between Exchange servers and clients and SMTP for transmitting e-mail on the public Internet, and it can be configured to allow POP3, IMAP, and WebMail access as well.

Strip All Attachments

Configuring your e-mail server to strip all attachments is usually relatively simple, but somewhat draconian. It limits e-mail to a communication mechanism only, but it prevents e-mail hacking (except e-mail forgery) and virus activity.

Exchange and most open-source e-mail servers can be easily configured to strip attachments. Consult your e-mail server's documentation for information on how to configure it for e-mail security.

TIP

Many attachment strippers work only during the transfer to individual mailboxes and can't be used to strip attachments on a relay mail server. MIMEDefang can act as a mail relay to strip attachments, as well as perform a number of other utility functions on e-mail passing through the server (such as blocking spam). Check it out at `www.roaringpenguin.com/mimedefang`.

Even if your e-mail server doesn't support the functionality required to strip attachments, you can add the functionality to any network by putting a Unix-based *relay server* between the Internet and your mail server. Configure your *MX records* to send e-mail to the relay server and configure the relay server to forward to your interior proprietary mail server. You can then use one of many methods available to the open-source community to strip attachments on the open-source e-mail server before they are forwarded to your proprietary server, guaranteeing that it never even sees the attachments. This same method can be used to add e-mail virus scanning to any e-mail server.

Attachment stripping needn't be completely draconian. You can configure the e-mail server to decode and move attachments to an FTP directory on the mail server where administrators could forward the files to end users if they actually needed them for a legitimate purpose. Don't go too far to make the process convenient, however. The attachment could be automatically replaced by a link to the attachment, making the whole process so seamless that you might as well have done nothing.

relay server
An intermediate e-mail server configured to route e-mail between e-mail servers.

mail exchange (MX) records
DNS entries that identify the hostnames of e-mail servers for a specific domain.

Allow Only Specific Attachments

The next best security measure for attachments is to allow only the document types you actually use to be transmitted as attachments. This would include office documents, Acrobat files, Visio diagrams, CAD drawings, and so on. By stripping superfluous attachments at your border e-mail server, you can eliminate most of the problem while still allowing the business use of e-mail attachments.

This is significant security degradation from complete stripping because most of the office documents that people use can contain macro viruses, but it's far better than nothing and is practical for every organization.

Administrators won't always know the *extensions* for the document types people legitimately use, but you shouldn't let that discourage you. If a person can't get an attachment through, they'll let you know and you can reconfigure the server to allow that type, as necessary. Using this methodology, you'll always have the minimum set of attachment types that you actually know you need.

extensions
Filename suffixes that identify a document type so that the operating system (and users) can determine which program should be used to interpret the contents of the document.

Strip Only Dangerous Attachments

At a bare minimum, you should at least strip the attachment types that represent an extreme risk and have almost no legitimate reason to be e-mailed. These attachment types are usually directly interpreted by the base operating system and have the potential to allow widespread intrusion if they are opened.

You can eliminate this problem by configuring your mail server to strip attachments that have executable extensions. You should always strip, without exception, the following attachment extensions on your mail server:

Executable (.exe)   The standard extension for programs in systems descended from MS-DOS. Originally, files with the .exe extension were programs larger than 64Kb that required paging memory extensions and 16-bit processors to execute.

Command (.com)   The standard extension for MS-DOS command programs. These programs were less than 64Kb in size and could be directly executed on all Intel 8-bit processors.

Command (.cmd)   Windows NT command scripts (batch files that use NT-specific command-line programs).

Batch file (.bat)   A text file executed by COMMAND.COM (MS-DOS through Windows ME) or CMD.EXE (NT, 2000, XP, .NET) that contains shell commands to be executed.

Program Information File (.pif)   An accessory file for Windows 3.1 systems that specified icons and program associations for DOS executables. While these files were replaced in Windows 95 and later, modern versions of Windows still respect the files and will launch the executables they specify.

Screensaver (.scr)   A binary file that acts as a screensaver. This extension is frequently used by hackers, because the system will launch it as an executable automatically, and most systems that strip attachments aren't configured to stop it because many administrators don't know about it.

JavaScript (.js or .jse)   A Windows Scripting Host file written in JavaScript. These files are automatically executed by the Windows Scripting Host built into Explorer.exe and can call any system objects available in Visual Basic and perform any function on your computer. The language and capabilities are essentially the same as an Office macro or an IIS server-side web script.

Visual Basic script (.vb, .vbe, .vbs)   A Windows Scripting Host file written in Visual Basic. This is the same thing as a JS script, but Visual Basic syntax rather than JavaScript syntax is used.

HTML application (.hta)   A web page that runs in the Microsoft HTML Host, a simple browser without the security restrictions of Internet Explorer. This is an executable file type that can perform any function Internet Explorer can perform without the security sandbox that makes web pages somewhat safe. HTAs are just as dangerous as JS or VBS scripting host files. Very few administrators or users know what HTA files are, so they are a new threat that most people do not expect. HTA support is automatically included in Internet Explorer 5 and later.

Microsoft Installer package (.msi, .mst, .msp)   An automated program installer package (.msi) or transform (.mst) or patch (.msp). Clicking on an MSI file will automatically install a program that can perform any action on your computer, including installing services that will execute automatically and automatically launch the file that it installs. MSI files are extremely dangerous attachments. Installer packages were developed for Windows 2000 and Windows XP.

Registry files (.reg)   Text files that update values in the Registry and can be used to disable systems, reconfigure services, or perform other limited mischievous acts. Registry files don't actually execute code, but they can reconfigure a computer to launch programs the next time they are started, connect to remote servers on the Internet, or carry out an array of other attacks.

Program links (.lnk)   Shortcuts to executable files, which can contain parameters to control how the program executes. Hackers could use LNK files to send shortcuts to CMD.EXE that include command-line parameters to perform nearly any action.

Executable extensions aren't the only problem. They represent extensions that will run on any Windows system, but Windows automatically runs the program associated with any registered extension. So by choosing a common program that has an execution environment associated with it, hackers can get right through attachment stripping programs.

Microsoft considers the following attachment types so dangerous that Outlook 2002 automatically quarantines them, as well as the extremely dangerous extensions in the preceding list. You should also strip these attachments on your mail server irrespective of who sends them:

Extension	File Type
.ade	Microsoft Access project extension
.adp	Microsoft Access project
.bas	Microsoft Visual Basic class module
.chm	Compiled HTML help file
.cpl	Control Panel extension
.crt	Security certificate
.hlp	Help file
.inf	Setup information
.ins	Internet Naming Service

Extension	File Type
.isp	Internet communication settings
.mda	Microsoft Access add-in program
.mdb	Microsoft Access program
.mde	Microsoft Access MDE database
.mdz	Microsoft Access wizard program
.msc	Microsoft Common Console document
.mst	Visual Test source files
.pcd	Microsoft Visual Test compiled script (also used by PhotoCD)
.sct	Windows script component
.shs	Shell scrap object
.url	Internet shortcut
.wsc	Windows script component
.wsf	Windows Script file
.wsh	Windows Script Host settings file

Practical Extraction and Reporting Language (Perl)
A popular scripting language used in websites and the administration of Unix machines. Windows versions are available.

Beyond this list, there are certainly many types of applications that can be used to gain control of a system. For example, many administrators of cross-platform networks install *Perl* as an administration scripting language, so the .pl and .pls extensions it uses will be just as dangerous as any other scripting language's extensions. Because these applications are rarer, hackers are less likely to target them unless they know you're using these applications.

Post Office Protocol, version 3 (POP3)
An e-mail client protocol used to download e-mail from mail servers into mail client programs.

As you can see, the list of known dangerous attachments just for Office and Windows is large, and this isn't a complete set. To be safest, you should configure your e-mail server to strip all attachments except the types you actually use.

Foreign E-mail Servers

Internet Message Access Protocol (IMAP)
A client e-mail access protocol typically used in situations in which it's appropriate to allow users to leave e-mail on the mail server rather than downloading it to their client computer.

You can solve nearly all e-mail security problems without regard to the type of mail client used in your organization by turning your e-mail server into an e-mail firewall. An e-mail firewall strips e-mail attachments, cleans scripts out of e-mail files, and drops connections from hosts that don't have legitimate DNS names, come from parts of the world that you don't do business with, or come from open relays.

But as with all firewalls, beware the unchecked border crossing: All your server-side security is for naught if you allow users to set up their e-mail clients to also check their own personal e-mail accounts at work. By allowing *POP3* to transit through your firewall, you will be allowing users to circumvent every e-mail security measure you enforce on your corporate e-mail servers. You'll find that users will actually tell business associates to send files to their personal accounts because you strip attachments on the server. To enforce e-mail security, you have to block POP3 and *IMAP* access going out from your network to the Internet at your firewall, and you may have to block access to Web-based e-mail providers like Hotmail and proprietary e-mail protocols like *AOL*.

America Online (AOL)
A popular graphical BBS system that has transformed into the largest consumer Internet service provider. Due to its non-Internet origins, AOL uses a proprietary e-mail mechanism that (among other things) does not support true MIME attachments or use standard ports for transmitting e-mail.

Spam

In the context of the Internet, *spam* is unwanted, unsolicited e-mail. The name comes from an early newsgroup poster who referred to unsolicited e-mailers as those who would throw a brick of Spam at a fan to distribute it as widely as possible—spam was probably being used as a euphemism, but the term stuck.

spam
Unsolicited, unwanted e-mail.

The posting user may have already been familiar with the term from its original connotation in early Internet chatrooms, which referred to pasting the word *spam* repeatedly into the chat sessions to interrupt the conversation. *Spam* was chosen for this usage in tribute to the Monty Python sketch, "Spam," where the waiter keeps listing menu items that contain various amounts of Spam. Hormel has been gracious about the co-opting of its trademark by the Internet community.

———— **NOTE** ————

Rather than making any attempt to determine who might want their product, spam marketers simply send an advertisement to every e-mail address they can find. Originally, receiving spam wasn't that big of a deal for most people. But since 2003, the amount of spam being sent has increased by many orders of magnitude—to the point that 90 percent or more of many e-mail user's mail is spam.

Posting your e-mail address on any website will guarantee an unlimited supply of spam. Most spammers cull valid e-mail addresses using web crawling software.

Consistently using a "spam account" on a public free e-mail provider like Hotmail whenever you have to enter your e-mail address on a website can easily defeat spam. Reserve your "real" e-mail address for sending to people whom you actually know personally.

There are two types of *spammers*. The first type includes large, legitimate marketing companies who don't care about annoying people and who use their own resources and bandwidth to transmit e-mail. Like any other infrastructure costs, bandwidth and e-mail servers cost money, so these marketers have at least some cost to send e-mail, small as it is. The real plague issues forth from the second type of spammers, the legion of smaller illegitimate marketers who steal the greater resources of others like parasites to transmit e-mail. Many

spammers
Those who send spam. Usually, the term is applied to those who steal bandwidth to send spam, as opposed to legitimate e-mail marketers who send spam.

unscrupulous e-marketers don't have the equipment or bandwidth required to transmit the massive volumes of e-mail that they want to transmit, so they steal the bandwidth of others. By scanning for mail servers and then testing to see if they can send e-mail back to themselves through the server, spammers identify and target *open relay servers.* Open relays are mail servers that will relay e-mail for anyone, not just those on the local domain, because they haven't been properly secured or because they use obsolete versions of the SMTP service software.

When they find open relays, they send a single message with hundreds or thousands of recipients at a time. They pay only for the bandwidth to transmit a single message with thousands of names, whereas the sender (the exploited relay) pays for the bandwidth to transmit every message. By exploiting open relays, spammers can transmit a few orders of magnitude more spam then their own pipes could handle—at no cost to themselves.

Because open relays have become rare lately, illegitimate spammers have taken to a new tactic: Taking over broadband home computers that have been exploited by worms and using them to send spam. There is actually now a black market in hackers selling the access codes to large blocks of exploited "zombie" computers to spammers using Internet auction sites like eBay and coded auctions.

Spam is a common plague on the Internet that occurs because SMTP does not have an authentication mechanism built into the protocol and because most early implementations of mail servers did not validate the source of e-mail transmissions.

Sending spam is now illegal in the U.S., thanks to the CAN-SPAM Act. However, like individual hackers, these marketers are difficult to find and even more difficult to prosecute. Because they almost always cross state lines, you have to get the federal government to prosecute them. But because it's difficult to quantify the value of bandwidth or determine how much was stolen, it's difficult to prove that the $5,000 threshold has been crossed in order to get FBI attention. So by spreading their crime across many thousands of victims rather than concentrating on a few, relay spammers can avoid prosecution. Most victims never find out, unless they pay for metered bandwidth or have congestion problems so severe that they call in a network analyst to determine what's happening.

Authenticating SMTP

Stopping relay spammers is simple: Close your open relay. A closed relay only sends e-mail that originates from machines that either have authenticated with it by providing credentials or are assumed to be allowed based on some property like their IP address.

There are numerous effective ways to close relays:

◆ Only relay mail for computers in the same domain or an allowed domain list.

◆ Only relay mail based on some authentication mechanism.

◆ Use a separate service like the Web to receive mail content and generate the actual e-mail directly on the mail server.

open relay servers
E-mail servers that perform no authentication whatsoever on transmitted e-mail.

There's no standard way to authenticate with an SMTP server. Most e-mail servers support a range of authentication methods, and various clients support their own range of methods. Not all clients are compatible with all server methods.

Fortunately, Outlook (the most popular client) is compatible with *sendmail*, *qmail*, Exchange, and *Postfix*—the four most popular e-mail servers—using its default AUTH mechanism. The various standard authentication mechanisms are described in the next section.

Host- and Network-Based Authentication

An e-mail server with network-based authentication only relays mail from recipients inside the local IP domain and only receives mail for recipients in the hosted domain list. So, for example, a mail server with an IP address of 10.4.7.3/16 named mail.connetic.net will only send e-mail for hosts with an IP address in the 10.4.0.0/16 network and will only receive e-mail for addresses that end in connetic.net.

Setting up SMTP to reject mail from unknown hosts is relatively easy. In most e-mail systems, you can simply reject relaying for hosts outside your local domain and be done with the problem. Your e-mail server will not relay mail if you set this up.

But you will quickly find that roaming users with laptops or users who work from home won't be able to send mail through your server if you do this. This may not be a big problem: Home users can simply set their SMTP server to be their own ISP's mail server, and roaming users can set their SMTP host to be that of their dial-up ISP. You don't have to use your company's SMTP server to send e-mail.

Specifications for closing open relays vary for every individual mail server, and some older mail servers cannot be closed and, therefore, must be replaced to avoid exploitation by relay spammers. An exhaustive list of instructions for closing open relays can be found at `http://mail-abuse.org/tsi/ar-fix.html`**.**

The remaining users who will have problems are those who travel frequently amongst ISPs. These users may not know the name of their temporary ISP's SMTP server, how to configure their mail client settings, or even which ISP is servicing them. This happens most frequently to traveling executives and salespeople, who are least equipped to deal with it and most likely to rely on e-mail. To solve this problem, you need to use authenticated SMTP or perhaps a web mail interface.

Web E-mail Interfaces

Web e-mail interfaces are websites that are integrated with mail servers to provide a site from which users can send and receive e-mail. Web e-mail interfaces are typified by Hotmail, the first really popular public web e-mail site, but they don't have to be public.

sendmail
The most popular e-mail service, sendmail is open source and was originally part of the BSD. Many commercial e-mail services are based on sendmail.

qmail
A popular e-mail service for Unix systems.

Postfix
A popular and highly secure e-mail service for Unix systems.

TIP

TIP
Check www.freshmeat.net for current versions of open-source web e-mail interfaces (and pretty much everything else) for most platforms.

You can run one on your own e-mail server to easily provide a web interface for your users. Using a web e-mail interface can provide a reasonably secure mechanism for traveling users to check their mail from their own laptops, the computers of business partners, Internet cafes, handheld web-enabled devices, and anything else that can access the Web. They eliminate the need for e-mail client software and custom configurations. They aren't as easy to use as a true client, but they are reasonably secure and can be used from any computer without requiring the user to know anything more than a website URL and their account credentials.

WARNING
Be sure to use SSL rather than unencrypted HTTP for all web e-mail interfaces because passwords are unencrypted. Also, stay up-to-date on security mailing lists and patches for your web e-mail interface because these services (like most popular website scripts) have been exploited.

Exchange comes with Outlook Web Access, which is a website that has the look and feel of Outlook. Web Mail and the more popular Squirrel Mail are open-source alternatives that can be freely downloaded and run on any Unix mail server. These applications solve the SMTP problem by generating mail locally on the e-mail server.

WARNING
Outlook Web Access has been subject to numerous different exploits. Be sure to check Microsoft's security site for Outlook Web Access security problems, solutions, and recommendations before you consider setting it up in your environment.

POP before SMTP Authentication

The most compatible method used is POP before SMTP authentication (also called SMTP after POP authentication, of course). POP before SMTP is a simple and effective trick that opens up e-mail relaying to any computer IP address that has previously authenticated with the POP service. Basically, it's a simple transitive trust mechanism that assumes that a computer from which a valid POP authentication originated must have a legitimate user operating it. While this isn't always true, it's more than satisfactory for SMTP relay purposes.

Sadly, this simple method doesn't work well with Outlook (the most popular e-mail client), Outlook Express, or Netscape Messenger because these clients always check SMTP first. This means that users will get an initial error message when Outlook tries to send e-mail because the server won't relay for them, but they will receive their e-mail. They can subsequently press the Send/Receive button again to send e-mail.

You can automate POP before SMTP authentication for these clients by creating two e-mail accounts. The second account uses the same settings as the first, but because the check of the first account provided POP authentication, the SMTP service is open for the second account to transmit. Be sure to set the second account as the default SMTP account. You can't avoid the error indication, but you can teach users to ignore it.

TIP

Many other e-mail clients can be configured to check SMTP first or natively check POP before transmitting with SMTP and work seamlessly with POP before SMTP authentication.

Systemic Spam Prevention

Systemic spam prevention measures attempt to stop spammers using broad methods that aren't specific to any single server; they attempt to prevent spammers from sending mail in the first place or delete spam that has been sent. Some of these measures attempt to stop spammers from sending mail, others attempt to block mail from open relays assuming that the open relay must have been exploited, and others analyze e-mail to find individual spam that they then block on a message-by-message basis.

Mail Abuse Prevention System

MAPS is a service that scans the Web looking for mail servers that are open relays by attempting to transmit an e-mail message back to itself through the mail server. If MAPS receives the e-mail it attempted to send, it adds the mail server's hostname and IP address to its list of open relays.

Mail administrators can subscribe to the MAPS service to receive a copy of their database of open relays (the Realtime Blackhole List) and thereby block e-mail coming from open relays in an attempt to block e-mail that originates from spammers.

In theory, this makes sense. In practice, it's a huge waste of effort. While the idea is noble, the implementation is fundamentally flawed. Simply put, it just doesn't actually work that well.

First, it can take months for the MAPS server to find a mail server that is an open relay. New, unsecured mail servers appear on the Internet by the thousands every day. In those months, you've been getting spam from all these new open relays because MAPS hasn't found them yet. Spammers exploit different mail servers every day. They jump from mail server to mail server like mosquitoes, and they know to avoid mail servers that have been blacklisted by MAPS. The large spam organizations subscribe to MAPS, so they know which servers to remove from their open relay lists!

Second, MAPS won't find legitimate spammers that don't exploit open relays; they use their own secured e-mail servers. While MAPS has blacklisted notorious spammers, they can't list everyone, and sending spam is still not a crime unless you exploit open relays. So, because MAPS doesn't stop legitimate spammers, it doesn't stop spam. MAPS has been successfully sued by legitimate spammers who have used the courts to force MAPS to remove them from their spammer's blacklist.

Third, if you subscribe to MAPS, you'll also find that about once per quarter an executive in your company will come to you claiming that some crucial business partner can't send e-mail to him because your e-mail server is blocking mail from them. Why? Because that crucial business partner's e-mail server is (or was) an open relay. Whether or not they are being exploited by relaying spam, they can't send you e-mail because they are on the MAPS list.

It also takes months of hassle and effort for MAPS to de-list a formerly open relay from their service and distribute that de-listing to their clients, so having that crucial business partner secure their e-mail server won't mean that you can immediately receive mail from them.

Finally, hosting an open relay isn't a crime, and there are legitimate reasons to do it, especially if you have a lot of traveling users whose e-mail configurations cannot be controlled easily because they use a myriad of different e-mail programs. Clever administrators can prevent spammers from abusing an open rely by detecting "spam-like" bulk mailing activities and then denying the originating host access to the mail server, but they can't stay off the MAPS list because the MAPS open relay probe is a single message that wouldn't be detected.

Ultimately, open relay blocking lists are not effective in preventing spam, and they cause administrative problems. The hard line "we don't need e-mail from anyone who can't secure their mail server" attitude might strike a chord with technicians, but is your business really willing to lose clients or customers because their mail is hosted on an open relay? Eliminating 50 percent of the spam and 1 percent of your clients is an easy business decision to make. Spam isn't that important—clients are.

There are a number of other blocking lists: Open Relay Blocking System (ORBS), Spam Prevention Early Warning System (SPEWS), and so forth. These services vary in their listing techniques, but they all ultimately suffer from the same set of problems as open relay blocking: They can't block all spammers, and they will block those who are legitimate mailers, sometimes simply for using the same ISP as a known spammer.

Other predictive blockers use reverse DNS lookup and reject mail from mail servers that don't have names, mail servers from foreign nations that the business isn't commercially involved with, or the client networks of consumer ISPs like dial-up providers and cable-modem systems. Reverse DNS blocking is actually a pretty good way to go if you implement it conservatively: Create your own list, and block only those servers that you've received spam from. While this doesn't eliminate spam, it blocks the majority of it and it doesn't block legitimate businesses.

While they undoubtedly reduce the amount of spam on the Internet, MAPS and similar services are not completely effective, cannot be completely effective, and can cause serious administrative problems for those who have been blacklisted and their business partners. Don't use blacklisting services unless e-mail isn't a critical tool for your business.

Spam Filters

Spam filters are applications that block spam by recognizing bulk mailings across a list of subscribers to a service or by recognizing spam by using statistical filters. They don't prevent your servers from being exploited to relay spam; they just protect your users from seeing most of it.

Spam filters work by intercepting e-mail. The spam filter scans inbound e-mail messages for spam and relays the non-spam messages to your internal e-mail server.

Spam filters that work by detecting signature words and scoring them statistically suffer from an inability to discern legitimate mail that seems like spam, which means that some spam gets through, and worse, that some legitimate mail is scored as spam. This means that users must check their "spam inbox" regularly to make sure that no legitimate mail shows up there. So, since you have to check the spam anyway, there's little point in using this type of filtering. This type of filtering is typified by SpamAssassin, an open-source spam filter that is incorporated into McAffee's spam filter as well.

A new type of spam filtering has recently emerged that uses peer-to-peer methods to detect spam. When users see spam in their inboxes, they "vote it out" by clicking a spam button. The vote is sent to a central server, and once enough users have voted that a particular message is spam, a notice is sent to all subscribers and that particular message is removed from all subscribers' inboxes. This type of spam filtering is highly effective and has no possible false positives; it is typified by the Cloudmark spam filter.

While spam filters don't reduce the amount of spam congesting the Internet at large, they do keep it from clogging your user's inbox. Spam filters are probably the best way to eliminate spam without causing ancillary blocking of mail from open relays.

SMTP Port Blocking by ISPs

Many ISPs that cater to the end-user market have begun firewalling outbound SMTP traffic, blocking it at the firewall and forcing users within their networks to use the ISP's own SMTP servers if they want to send mail. This prevents their clients from being spammers because they can't reach servers outside the ISPs network, so they can't send spam. This tactic is now used by every major national dial-up ISP (even by EarthLink, who claims to give you the unfiltered Internet), nearly all cable-modem providers, satellite broadband providers, and many consumer DSL providers. Business-grade providers never implement SMTP port blocking because most businesses use their own SMTP servers.

SMTP port blocking is not implemented by ISPs out of some sense of concern for the Internet community; it's implemented to reduce the amount of traffic that the ISP has to carry. While it's effective in preventing the least-sophisticated tier of spammers from operating, it only takes a slightly more sophisticated spammer to purchase business-grade DSL for about twice as much as residential cable-modem service, and business-grade DSL won't have SMTP blocking. Spammers trade information about which ISPs do and don't block SMTP, so anyone who cares about spamming will just move to a different ISP.

For you, SMTP port blocking will be an annoyance. Traveling users will be unable to connect to your mail server and unable to transmit mail unless they configure their SMTP server to match the ISP. The easiest way around this problem is to implement a web e-mail interface and teach users how to use it. Or you can set up an SMTP server to listen on a port other than 25 (such as 2525) and configure mail clients to use that higher-numbered port, which won't be blocked by their ISP.

Terms to Know

America Online (AOL)	Post Office Protocol, version 3 (POP3)
attachment	Postfix
electronic mail (e-mail)	Practical Extractions and Reporting Language (Perl)
end user license agreement (EULA)	Pretty Good Privacy (PGP)
Exchange	qmail
extensions	relay server
grass-rooted	rooted
Internet Mail Access Protocol (IMAP)	Secure Multipurpose Internet Mail Extensions (S/MIME)
key ring	sendmail
mail exchange (MX) records	Simple Mail Transfer Protocol (SMTP)
Multipurpose Internet Mail Extension (MIME)	spam
open relay servers	spammers
Outlook	web of trust
Outlook Express	

Review Questions

1. What problems can e-mail encryption cause?

2. What feature of e-mail causes the majority of security risks?

3. What is the most commonly implemented form of e-mail encryption?

4. Besides privacy, what other important security function does e-mail encryption provide?

5. Why is it possible to forge e-mail?

6. How common are e-mail viruses?

7. Can your e-mail server solve all possible e-mail security problems?

8. What is the most secure method of dealing with attachments?

9. What is the most practical method of stripping e-mail attachments for most users?

10. What can be done to provide attachment security for proprietary e-mail servers that cannot be configured to strip attachments?

11. What's the most practical method of attachment security for most organizations?

12. What e-mail clients are more susceptible to e-mail viruses?

13. What is spam?

14. What mechanism do illegal spammers exploit to send spam?

15. How do you close an open relay?

16. What is the problem with spam blocking lists?

17. How do ISPs prevent their clients from sending spam?

Chapter 15

Intrusion Detection

If someone broke into your network, how would you know? There wouldn't be any muddy footprints. There wouldn't be any broken glass. If you had a strong firewall that has good logging capabilities, you might find evidence of an attack in your logs, but a smart hacker can even get around that.

To see what's really going on, you need an intrusion detection system. These systems watch for the telltale signs of hacking and alert you immediately when they occur. They are a necessary component of any truly secure network.

In This Chapter

- Securing your network against attacks your firewall can't prevent
- Determining when you've been attacked
- Assessing the scope of the damage of a successful attack
- Saving money by using intrusion detection techniques that don't require costly specialized software

Intrusion Detection Systems

intrusion detection system (IDS)
Systems that detect unauthorized access to other systems.

Intrusion detection systems (IDSs) are software systems that detect intrusions to your network based on a number of telltale signs. *Active IDSs* attempt to block attacks, respond with countermeasures, or at least alert administrators while the attack progresses. *Passive IDSs* merely log the intrusion or create *audit trails* that are apparent after the attack has succeeded.

active IDS
An intrusion detection system that can create responses, such as blocking network traffic or alerting on intrusion attempts.

While passive systems may seem lackluster and somewhat useless for preventing attacks, there are a number of intrusion indicators that are only apparent after an intrusion has taken place. For example, if a disgruntled network administrator for your network decided to attack, he'd have all the keys and passwords necessary to log right in. No active response system would alert you to anything. Passive IDSs can still detect the changes that an administrator makes to system files, deletions, or whatever mischief has been caused.

passive IDS
IDS that records information about intrusions but does not have the capability of acting on that information.

Widespread hacking and the deployment of automated worms like Code Red and Nimda into the wild have created a sort of *background radiation* of hacking attempts on the Internet—there's a constant knocking on the door, and teeming millions of script kiddies looking to try their warez out on some unsuspecting default Windows or aging Red Hat installation.

audit trail
A log of intrusion detection events that can be analyzed for patterns or to create a body of evidence.

My company's intrusion detection system routinely logs hundreds of automated hacking attempts every day and at least 10 or so perpetrated by humans.

This means that any intrusion detection system is going to log numerous attempts all the time. You will need to tune your filters to ignore threats that you know you aren't vulnerable to so that you aren't overwhelmed searching through your logs for events that mean that you're being targeted. You might as well not bother with an intrusion detection system if it cries wolf all the time and you learn to ignore it.

Inspectors

background radiation
The normal, mostly futile, hacking activity caused by automated worms and script kiddies.

Inspectors are the most common type of IDS. These intrusion detectors observe the activity on a host or network and make judgments about whether an intrusion is occurring or has occurred based either on programmed rules or on historical indications of normal use. The intrusion detectors built into firewalls and operating systems as well as most commercially available independent intrusion detectors are inspection based.

inspectors
IDSs that detect intrusions by searching all incoming data for the known signature patterns of hacking attempts.

Intrusion detectors rely upon indications of inappropriate use. These indicators include the following:

◆ Network traffic, like ICMP scans, port scans, or connections to unauthorized ports.

◆ Signatures of known common attacks like worms or buffer overruns.

◆ Resource utilization, such as CPU, RAM, or network I/O surges at unexpected times. This can indicate an automated attack against the network.

♦ File activity, including newly created files, modifications to system files, changes to user files, or the modification of user accounts or security permissions.

Inspectors monitor various combinations of those telltale signs and create log entries. The body of these log entries is called an audit trail, which consists of the sum of observed parameters for a given accessed object like a user account or a source IP address. *Auditors* can monitor the audit trails to determine when intrusions occur.

IDSs always require system resources to operate. Network IDSs usually run on firewalls, public hosts, or dedicated computers; resource utilization usually isn't a problem because resources are available on these machines. Host-based IDSs designed to protect interior servers can be a serious impediment, however.

Inspectors can detect only known intrusion vectors, so new types of intrusions cannot be detected. Auditors stand a better chance of detecting unknown intrusion vectors, but they cannot detect them until after the fact, and there's no guarantee that unknown attacks will be detected.

Inspectors suffer from the same set of problems as virus scanners—you can't detect attacks until their patterns are known. You can think of them as virus scanners for network streams.

However, unlike viruses, useful hacks are somewhat limited in their scope and far more predictable in nature. Contests have emerged among ethical hackers to find new unique hacks and immediately publish their signatures. This sort of preemptive hacking is becoming quite popular as a pastime among those who practice hacking as an art rather than a crime, and their product helps to secure networks before they can be hacked.

Because of their limitations, IDSs generally require monitoring by human security administrators to be effective. So much hacking activity occurs as a normal course of business these days that security administrators are really only looking for things they've never seen before or indications that they are being specifically attacked. Countermeasure technology and response systems that temporarily increase the host's security posture during attacks are all in the theoretical research stage. Current IDSs rely upon alerting human administrators to the presence of an attack, which makes human administrators an active part of the intrusion detection system.

auditors
IDSs that simply record changes made to a system.

Decoys

Decoy IDSs (also called *honey pots*) operate by mimicking the expressive behavior of a target system, except instead of providing an intrusion vector for the attacker, they alarm on any use at all. Decoys look just like a real target that hasn't been properly secured.

decoys
IDSs that detect intrusions by mimicking actual systems and alerting on any use.

honey pots
Decoy IDSs, especially those that are sanitized installations of actual operating systems as opposed to software that mimics actual systems.

When a hacker attacks a network, they perform a fairly methodical series of well-known attacks like address range scans and port scans to determine which hosts are available and which services those hosts provide. By providing decoy hosts or services, you can seduce the hacker into attacking a host or service that isn't important to you and is designed to alert on any use at all.

Decoys may operate as a single decoy service on an operative host, a range of decoy services on an operative host, a decoy host, or an entire decoy network.

TIP

Rather than spending effort on decoy services, you should simply establish an entire decoy host. It's much easier and far more effective at catching actual intrusion attempts.

You can establish an effective decoy host by installing a real running copy of the operating system of your choice on a computer with all normal services active. Using your firewall's NAT port forwarding service, send all access to your public domain name to the decoy machine by default. Then add rules to move specific ports to your other service computers; for example, translate only port 80 to your actual web server.

When a hacker scans your site, they'll see all the services provided by your decoy host plus the services you actually provide on your Internet servers as if they all came from the same machine. Because the services running on the decoy host include services that are easy to attack, like the NetBIOS or NFS ports, the hacker will be immediately attracted to them. You can then set up alarms to alert on any access to those services using the operating system's built-in tools. You'll be secure in the knowledge that if the hacker intrudes into the system, they'll be on a system that contains no proprietary information. You can then let the attack progress to identify the methods the attacker uses to intrude into your system. I suggest installing an inspector-based IDS on the decoy host so you can keep logs of specific packet-based attacks as well.

Decoy hosts are highly secure because they shunt actual attacks away from your service hosts and to hosts that will satisfy the hacker's thirst for conquest, giving you plenty of time to respond to the attack. The hacker will be thrilled that they were able to break into a system and will be completely unaware of the fact that they're not on your real Internet server until they browse around for a while. You might even consider creating a bogus "cleaned" copy of your website on the decoy server to maintain the illusion in the hacker's mind that the actual site has been penetrated. Any desecration performed on the decoy site won't show up on your actual site.

Best of all, decoy intrusion detection costs only as much as a copy of the operating system (Linux can mimic any professional Unix server for free), target hardware, and your existing firewall. You won't have to pay for esoteric software.

Don't have spare computers lying around? Use VMware (www.vmware.com) to create a virtual intrusion detection host system that runs on your actual host but absorbs attacks into a virtual sanitized environment that won't affect your main machine. You won't even need a second OS license because operating systems are licensed per processor and your virtual host will be running on the same processor. Use the host's own NAT service to forward all ports to the virtual machine except those used specifically for servicing legitimate clients. Configure the virtual machine to use non-persistent disk mode so that any changes made by a successful hacker or virus can be eliminated by rebooting the virtual machine—all while your host machine remains online.

TIP

Auditors

Audit-based intrusion detectors simply keep track of everything that normal users do (at least those things that concern security) in order to create an audit trail. This audit trail can be examined whenever hacking activity is suspected.

Audit-based intrusion detectors take a number of forms, from built-in operating system audit policies that can be configured to record password changes to software that records changes in critical system files that should never be changed to systems that record every packet that flows over a network.

Sophisticated audit-based systems attempt to increase the value of the audit trail by automatically examining it for the telltale signs of intrusion. These vary from system to system, but they typically involve looking for *red flag* activities like changing an administrative account password and then examining the activities that surround that event. If, for example, a password change were followed quickly by a system file change, the intrusion detector would raise the alert.

red flag
A simple detected event that has a very high probability of being a real hacking attempt with serious consequences, as opposed to a normal administrative event or background radiation.

Available IDSs

Only a few reliable intrusion detection systems really exist, and that number has only been dwindling in recent years as IDS vendors fail to convince clients that intrusion detection is worth spending money on. The nail in the coffin for commercial vendors is the success of free systems like Tripwire and Snort, which work far better than commercial offerings and are open source. But what's bad for the industry is good for you because you can now deploy a robust intrusion detection system for free.

Firewalls with logging and alerting mechanisms are by far the most widely deployed, and the majority of those have no way to respond to an attack in any automated fashion.

Both Windows and Unix have strong logging and auditing features embedded in their file systems. Windows also has an exceptionally strong performance monitoring subsystem that can be used to generate real-time alerts to sudden increases in various activities. This allows you to create simple IDSs for your servers without adding much in the way of hardware.

Windows System

Windows has strong operating system support for reporting object use. This support manifests in the performance monitoring and auditing capabilities of the operating system and in the fact that the file system can be updated with date-time stamps each time certain types of access occur. These capabilities make strong inherent security measures easy to perform.

File System and Security Auditing

auditing
The process of recording the use of resources in an automated system for the purpose of subsequent inspection.

Windows has exceptionally strong support for file system and security *auditing*. You can configure Windows using the group policies to create log entries in the security log each time any one of the following events succeeds or fails:

♦ Logon attempts

♦ File or object access, such as copying or opening a file

♦ Use of special rights, such as backing up the system

♦ User or group management activities, such as adding a user account

♦ Changes to the security policy

♦ System restart or shutdown

♦ Process tracking, such as each time a certain program is run

What all this means is that you can create your own intrusion detection software simply by configuring Windows to audit any sort of behavior that could indicate an intrusion attempt.

Pervasive audit policies can slow down a Windows server dramatically, so you have to be careful of how wide ranging your audits are in systems that are already under load. Audit unusual events, such as the use of user rights, user logon and logoff, security policy changes, and restarts.

File and object access is a special case in auditing. You have to enable file and object auditing and then use the security tab of each file or folder's property sheet to enable auditing for specific files. This allows you to limit the files that you audit. For system files, you should audit for writes, changes, and deletes. For proprietary or secret information you store, you should audit read access.

File and object access occurs constantly, so if you audit a large number of commonly used files, you'll increase the amount of chaff (useless information) in your log files and slow down your computer. Audit only those files that are real intrusion targets, like the system files and your proprietary information.

There is a problem with Windows's audit policy: If a hacker actually gains administrative control of your system, the hacker is free to erase your audit trail after it has been changed.

Tripwire

Tripwire scans files and directories on Unix systems to create a snapshot record of their size, date, and signature hash. If you suspect an intrusion in the future, Tripwire will rescan your server and report any changed files by comparing the file signatures to the stored records. Tripwire was an open-source project of Purdue University, but it continues development as a licensed package of Tripwire Security Systems (www.tripwiresecurity.com). The maintained open-source version is at www.tripwire.org.

Snort

Snort (www.snort.org) is an open-source intrusion detection system that relies upon raw packet capture (sniffing) and attack signature scanning to detect an extremely wide array of attacks. Snort is widely considered to be the best available intrusion detection system because of the enormous body of attack signatures that the open source community has created for it. The fact that it's free and cross platform pretty much ensures that the commercial IDSs won't develop much beyond where they are now. Snort was originally developed for Unix and has been ported to Windows.

Snort relies upon an open-source packet capture driver that does not currently support multiprocessor machines. If your public hosts are multiprocessor machines, you'll have to use a dedicated single-processor Snort host for intrusion detection.

WARNING

Configuring Snort and writing attack-sensing scripts is no trivial task, but the website provides a wealth of information for the intrepid administrator to plow through. And a Snort community has arisen that allows you to simply download detection scripts for every known hacking methodology there is, much like you would download updates for a virus scanner.

The most important thing to consider when deploying Snort is where to place your *sensors* (Snort installations) to determine when attacks are occurring. You could place them outside your firewall, in your DMZ, on your public hosts, and on the interior of your network. In practice, that's more than you need.

sensor
Intrusion detection software that is designed to run directly on public hosts and report to a central management station.

Placing a sensor outside your network is a waste of time unless you just want to see what's out there for the sake of curiosity. You'll pick up a lot of background radiation that's meaningless because it didn't penetrate your firewall anyway. Avoid looking through a lot of meaningless scripts by not bothering to sense attacks on the public Internet.

You definitely want to place a Snort sensor in your DMZ. The best way is to use a hub and attach a dedicated machine running Snort alongside your public sites. This way, the public machines don't have to run Snort and your dedicated machine can handle everything. If you can't use a hub because of bandwidth constraints, you'll have to run Snort on each of your public properties in order to detect intrusions. This is because switches direct traffic to the specific host that is addressed, so a Snort sensor on the switch won't see that traffic. It's easier to place a small hub on the firewall's DMZ port and connect only your switch and the Snort machine to the hub, which won't affect your switching and will allow Snort to detect intrusions across your entire DMZ.

Finally, you should place at least one Snort sensor on a hub inside your network so you can trap any events that make it through your firewall. Even if you used a switched environment, I recommend placing a small high-performance hub between your firewall's private interface and your interior switches so that you can attach a Snort sensor in stealth mode. It won't affect your bandwidth since the Snort sensor won't be transmitting on the network, and you'll be able to sense everything that makes it through the firewall.

Don't bother placing Snort sensors on all of your internal servers. You only need to sense traffic coming in through your firewalls, unless you seriously believe there are hackers active on the interior of your network (as there would be at a university or on an ISP's network, for example).

So, to recap, you only need a Snort sensor in your DMZ and in your private network. If you can't use a Snort sensor in your DMZ due to switching constraints or because you don't have a DMZ, put a sensor on every public host.

TIP   Snort can be configured as a "stealth" IDS by simply setting it up on an interface that doesn't have an IP address. This interface will receive traffic that can be sniffed, but it won't respond to any IP traffic.

Demarc PureSecure

Demarc PureSecure (www.demarc.com) is a best-of-breed network monitoring and intrusion detection system descended from Snort. PureSecure is a commercial product that uses Snort as its intrusion detector, but it adds typical network monitoring functions like CPU, network, memory, disk load, ping testing, and service monitoring to the sensors that run on every host.

Demarc creates a web-based client/server architecture where the sensor clients report back to the central Demarc server, which runs the reporting website. By pointing your web browser at the Demarc server, you get an overview of the health of your network in one shot.

Demarc can be configured to alert on all types of events, so keeping track of your network becomes quite easy. This is why Demarc's summary page is cool.

It's quite clever, and well worth its price: $1,500 for the monitoring software, plus $100 per sensor.

NFR Network Intrusion Detector

Network Flight Recorder (NFR, www.nfr.com) was one of the first inspector-based intrusion detection systems on the market and was originally offered as a network appliance. Now available as both software and network appliances, NFR has evolved into a commercial product very similar to Snort in its capabilities.

What sets NFR apart from Snort is not the software—it's the company behind it. NFR can consult with you directly to analyze intrusion attempts, to train your staff, and to provide product support for its products. You lose these services when you go with open-source software because there's no company backing the product.

Terms to Know

active IDS	honey pots
audit trail	inspectors
auditing	intrusion detection system (IDS)
auditors	passive IDS
background radiation	red flag
decoys	sensor

Review Questions

1. How many automated hacking attempts would be normal against a public site in a 24-hour period?

2. What are the three common types of intrusion detection systems?

3. What common network software are inspectors related to?

4. What software would you use to implement a decoy?

5. What is the common file system auditor for Unix called?

6. What is the most popular intrusion detection system?

7. How many sensors do you need, at a minimum, in an inspector-based intrusion detection system?

Appendix A

Answers to Review Questions

Chapter 1

1. What is security?

    Answer: Security is the sum of all measures taken to prevent loss of any kind.

2. What is the most common reason security measures fail?

    Answer: Security measures fail most often because strong security is an annoyance to users and administrators.

3. Why would vendors release a product even when they suspected that there could be security problems with the software?

    Answer: Vendors release products they suspect have security flaws because if they spent time to fix them, they would be eclipsed by their nonsecure competition, who could deliver feature-rich applications faster.

4. How many operating systems make up 90 percent of the operating system market?

    Answer: Two operating systems make up 90 per cent of the market, Windows and Unix.

5. Factoring in the growth of the Internet, at what rate is the number of computer security incidents increasing?

    Answer: The number of computer security incidents is increasing at 50 percent per year.

6. Why weren't computers designed with security in mind from the beginning?

    Answer: Computers weren't originally designed with security in mind because security requires computing power, which was precious in the early days of computing.

7. During what era did "hacking" begin to occur en masse?

    Answer: Hacking began to occur in earnest between 1975 and 1985.

8. In what year was public key encryption developed?

    Answer: Public key encryption was invented in 1975.

9. Prior to the Internet, how did most hackers share information?

    Answer: Before the Internet, hackers shared information primarily via bulletin-board systems (BBSs).

10. Why is it likely that applications (other than those designed to implement security) that concentrate on security will fail in the marketplace?

    Answer: Applications whose creators stop to consider security will come to market more slowly and therefore fail to gain the requisite market share for widespread adoption as a standard.

11. What is the process of determining the identity of a user called?

    Answer: The process of determining the identity of a user is called authentication.

12. When a new computer is first set up, how does the system know that the person setting up the computer is authorized to do so?

    Answer: The first user is implicitly trusted to be the owner.

13. What is the most secure form of authentication?

    Answer: Biometric authentication is the most secure form of authentication so long as it is implemented correctly and cannot be replayed or spoofed.

14. How can a hacker circumvent permissions-based access control?

    Answer: Permissions-based access control can be circumvented by shutting down the section of the operating system that interprets permissions.

15. How can a hacker circumvent correctly implemented encryption-based access control?

    Answer: Strong encryption-based access control cannot be exploited using computational methods.

Chapter 2

1. What is the most common type of hacker?

    Answer: The most common type of hackers are script kiddies.

2. Which type of hacker represents the most likely risk to your network?

    Answer: The type of hackers most likely to affect a business are disgruntled employees.

3. What is the most damaging type of hacker?

    Answer: The most damaging type of hackers are disgruntled employees.

4. What four methods can hackers use to connect to a network?

    Answer: Hackers can use direct intrusion, dial-up, Internet, or wireless methods to connect to a network.

5. What is the most common vector used by hackers to connect to networks?

    Answer: The Internet is the most common vector used by hackers.

6. What are the three phases of a hacking session?

    Answer: The phases of a hacking section are target selection, information gathering, and attack.

7.   What method would a hacker use to find random targets?

    Answer: Scanning enables a hacker to find random targets.

8.   What type of target selection indicates that a hacker has specifically targeted your systems for attack?

    Answer: A port scan indicates that a hacker has specifically targeted your systems for attack.

9.   Which method of target selection attack is employed by worms to find targets?

    Answer: Worms use service scanning to find targets.

10.   What activity does sniffing refer to?

    Answer: Sniffing refers to the activity of examining the uninterpreted contents of packets directly.

11.   What is the simplest type of attack a hacker can perpetrate?

    Answer: The simplest type of attack is a denial-of-service attack.

12.   What security mechanisms are implemented by e-mail to prevent forgery?

    Answer: There are no security mechanisms employed by e-mail to prevent forgery.

13.   What would a hacker use a Trojan horse for?

    Answer: A hacker would use a Trojan horse to install a back door program that would allow further access.

14.   Currently, what is the most serious hacking threat?

    Answer: Currently, the most serious hacking threat is the use of buffer overruns in service applications.

Chapter 3

1.   What is the primary purpose of encryption?

    Answer: Encryption is used to keep secrets.

2.   Secret key encryption is said to be symmetrical. Why?

    Answer: Secret key encryption is considered symmetrical because the same key is used on both ends of the communication.

3.   What is a hash?

    Answer: A hash is the result of a one-way function that is used to validate the contents of a larger plaintext message or verify knowledge of a secret without transmitting the secret itself.

4.   What is the most common use for hashing algorithms?

    Answer: Hashing algorithms are most commonly used to encrypt passwords.

5.   What is the difference between public key encryption and secret key encryption?

    Answer: Public key encryption is asymmetrical; it uses two different keys to encode and decode plaintext. Secret key encryption uses the same key to encode and decode.

6. What long-standing security problem does public key encryption solve?

   Answer: Public key encryption solves the dilemma of secure key exchange.

7. What is the major problem with public key encryption when compared to secret key encryption?

   Answer: The major problem with public key encryption is that it is much slower than secret key encryption.

8. What is a hybrid cryptosystem?

   Answer: A hybrid cryptosystem uses public key encryption to securely exchange secret keys and then uses secret key encryption for subsequent encryption.

9. What is authentication used for?

   Answer: Authentication is used to determine the identity of a user.

10. What hacking attack is challenge/response authentication used to prevent?

    Answer: Challenge/response authentication is used to prevent replay attacks.

11. How are sessions kept secure against hijacking?

    Answer: Using unpredictable sequence numbers secures sessions against hijacking.

12. What is the difference between a random number and a pseudorandom number?

    Answer: Pseudorandom numbers appear to be random but occur in a predefined sequence.

13. What is a digital signature?

    Answer: A digital signature is identity information that can be decoded by anyone but encoded only by the holder of a specific key.

14. What is the difference between a certificate and a digital signature?

    Answer: A certificate is a digital signature that has been digitally signed by a trusted authority.

15. What sort of characteristics are typically used for biometric authentication?

    Answer: Biometric authentication includes the use of fingerprints, speech patterns, facial features, retinal patterns, and DNA.

Chapter 4

1. What is the purpose of a security policy?

   Answer: A security policy describes security rules for your computer systems and defends against all known threats.

2. What is the first step in developing a security policy?

   Answer: The first step in establishing a security policy is to establish functional requirements, features, and security requirements.

3. Why is it important to automate security policies as much as possible?

   Answer: Automated security policies avoid the weakness of having to be enforced by humans.

4. Why is an appropriate use policy important?

   Answer: An appropriate use policy allows users to understand their security responsibilities.

5. How often should users be required to change their passwords?

   Answer: Users should not be required to change passwords often; rather, they should select extremely strong passwords that can be relied upon for much longer periods of time than simple passwords.

6. What is the minimum length of a password that could be considered to be "strong" in the context of today's computing power?

   Answer: Eight characters should be the minimum length of a password in today's environment.

7. Why is the inconvenient policy of enforcing a password lockout after a few incorrect attempts important?

   Answer: Enforcing password lockout after failed attempts prevents automated password guessing.

8. Why are execution environments dangerous?

   Answer: Execution environments are dangerous because they can be exploited to propagate viruses and Trojan horses.

9. Which is more secure: ActiveX or Java?

   Answer: Java is limited to a sandbox environment, which, although not perfect, is far more secure than the unlimited ActiveX execution environment.

10. Why doesn't a digital signature mean that an ActiveX control is secure?

    Answer: Digital signatures are only a means of verification. They do not perform any security function beyond attesting that content has not been modified and that it originates from a known source.

Chapter 5

1. Firewalls are derived from what type of network component?

   Answer: Firewalls are derived from routers.

2. What is the most important border security measure?

   Answer: The most important border security measure is to control every crossing.

3. Why is it important that every firewall on your network have the same security policy applied?

   Answer: Your effective border security is the lowest common denominator among the policies enforced by your various firewalls.

4. What is a demilitarized zone?

   Answer: A DMZ is a network segment with a relaxed security policy where public servers are partitioned away from the interior of the network.

5. Why is it important to deny by default rather than simply block dangerous protocols?

    Answer: It's better to deny by default because a new protocol (used by a Trojan horse) that you aren't aware of may crop up and would then have free access to your network if you only blocked known threats.

6. What fundamental firewall function was developed first?

    Answer: Packet filtering was the original firewall function.

7. Why was Network Address Translation originally developed?

    Answer: NAT was originally developed to conserve public IP addresses.

8. Why can't hackers attack computers inside a network address translator directly?

    Answer: There's no way to address computers directly since the public address connection has to use the IP address of the network address translator itself.

9. How do proxies block malformed TCP/IP packet attacks?

    Answer: Malformed TCP/IP packet attacks are blocked by terminating and regenerating the TCP/IP connection for all protocols that flow through them.

Chapter 6

1. What are the three fundamental methods implemented by VPNs to securely transport data?

    Answer: The three fundamental methods implemented by VPNs are encapsulation, authentication, and encryption.

2. What is encapsulation?

    Answer: Encapsulation is embedding a complete packet within another packet at the same networking layer.

3. Why are VPNs easier to establish than WANs?

    Answer: VPNs can be established wherever an IP connection to the Internet exists, without the necessity of coordinating with outside organizations.

4. What is the difference between IPSec transport mode and IPSec tunnel mode?

    Answer: Transport mode does not provide encapsulation, whereas tunnel mode does.

5. What functions does IKE perform?

    Answer: IKE enables cryptographic key exchange with encryption and authentication protocol negotiation between VPN endpoints.

6. What common sense measure can you take to ensure the reliability and speed of a VPN?

    Answer: Use the same (or the fewest possible) ISP for all VPN endpoints.

7. What is the most common protocol used among VPN vendors?

    Answer: The most common VPN protocol is IPSec with IKE.

8. What's the primary difference between L2TP and PPP?

    Answer: L2TP separates the physical device used to answer a connection from the device that re-creates the original stream.

9. What encryption algorithm is specified for L2TP?

    Answer: No algorithm is specified for L2TP. Microsoft's implementation uses IPSec to perform the encryption.

Chapter 7

1. Why are VPN connections potentially dangerous?

    Answer: VPN connections are potentially dangerous because the VPN endpoint could be exploited, allowing the attacker to use the VPN to penetrate the firewall.

2. What threats are presented to network security by laptop users?

    Answer: Laptops are easy to steal and may contain all the information necessary to connect to the company's network.

3. Why are laptops the most likely source of virus infection in a protected network?

    Answer: Laptops are the most likely source of virus infection in a protected network because they are frequently connected to other networks that may not be well protected.

4. What percentage of corporate crimes has the FBI traced back to stolen laptops?

    Answer: The FBI has traced 57 percent of corporate crimes back to stolen laptops.

5. What software should be used to protect laptops from hackers?

    Answer: Personal firewall application software should be used to protect laptops from hackers.

6. What is the best way to protect home computers from hackers?

    Answer: Using NAT devices or light firewall devices is the best way to protect home computers from hackers.

7. How should you reduce the risk posed by lost information when a laptop is stolen?

    Answer: Encrypting documents stored on the laptop reduces the risk posed by lost information when the laptop is stolen.

8. What is the best way to prevent the loss of data from a damaged or stolen laptop?

    Answer: Storing data on removable flash media in encrypted form that is not stored with the laptop is the best way to prevent the loss of data from a damaged or stolen laptop.

9. Are VPNs always the most secure way to provide remote access to secure networks?

    Answer: No. Opening a single secure protocol to direct access is usually more secure than allowing open access to VPN clients.

Chapter 8

1. Where do viruses come from?

   Answer: Hackers write viruses.

2. Can data contain a virus?

   Answer: No. Pure data can be corrupted by a virus, but only executable code can contain a virus.

3. Do all viruses cause problems?

   Answer: No. All viruses waste computer resources, but many have no other effect than to propagate.

4. What is a worm?

   Answer: A worm is a virus that propagates without human action.

5. Are all applications susceptible to macro viruses?

   Answer: No. Only applications that allow you to write macros and contain a scripting host powerful enough to allow self-replication are susceptible to viruses.

6. What is the only family of e-mail clients that are susceptible to e-mail viruses?

   Answer: Microsoft Outlook and Outlook Express are susceptible to e-mail viruses.

7. If you run NT kernel–based operating systems, do you still need antivirus protection?

   Answer: Yes. NT kernel–based operating systems are only immune to executable viruses when run under non-administrative privilege and do not prevent the spread of macro viruses.

8. What two types of antivirus methods are required for total virus defense?

   Answer: Inoculators to block an infection and scanners to eliminate dormant viruses are required for total virus defense.

9. How often should you update your virus definitions?

   Answer: You should update virus definitions daily.

10. Where is antivirus software typically installed?

    Answer: Antivirus software is typically installed on clients, servers, and e-mail gateways.

Chapter 9

1. What are the four major causes for loss, in order of likelihood?

   Answer: The four major causes for data loss are human error, routine failure, crimes, and environmental events.

2. What is the best way to recover from the effects of human error?

Answer: Having a good archiving policy is the best way to recover from the effects of human error.

3. What is the most likely component to fail in a computer?

Answer: The hard disk is the most likely component to fail in a computer.

4. What is the most difficult component to replace in a computer?

Answer: The hard disk is the most difficult component to replace in a computer.

5. What is the easiest way to avoid software bugs and compatibility problems?

Answer: Deployment testing is the easiest way to avoid software bugs and compatibility problems.

6. How can you recover from a circuit failure when you have no control over the ISP's repair actions?

Answer: Using multiple circuits from different ISPs will help you recover from a circuit failure.

7. What are the best ways to mitigate the effects of hacking?

Answer: Strong border security, permissions security, and offline backup are the best ways to minimize the damage caused by hackers.

8. What is the most common form of fault tolerance?

Answer: Tape backups are the most common form of fault tolerance.

9. What is the difference between an incremental backup and a differential backup?

Answer: An incremental backup contains all the files changed since the last incremental backup, while a differential backup contains the files changed since the last full system backup.

10. What causes the majority of failures in a tape backup solution?

Answer: Humans cause the majority of failures in a tape backup system.

11. Why is RAID-0 not appropriate as a form of fault tolerance?

Answer: RAID-0 actually makes failure more likely rather than less likely.

12. RAID-10 is a combination of which two technologies?

Answer: RAID-1 and RAID-0 are combined in RAID-10.

13. If you create a RAID-5 pack out of five 36GB disks, how much storage will be available?

Answer: Since you have to leave one disk for parity information, the storage available would be $(5 - 1) \times 36GB = 144GB$.

14. What are the two methods used to perform offsite storage?

Answer: Physically moving offline backup media to another location and transmitting data to another facility via a network are the two methods used to perform offsite storage.

15. What is the difference between backup and archiving?

    Answer: Backup is the process of making a copy of every file for the purpose of restoration. Archiving is the process of retaining a copy of every version of all files created by users for the purpose of restoring individual files in case of human error.

16. What are the two common types of clustering?

    Answer: The two common types of clustering are fail-over clustering and load balancing.

Chapter 10

1. Upon what foundation is Windows security built?

    Answer: Mandatory user logon is the foundation of security in Windows.

2. Where is the list of local computer accounts stored?

    Answer: The local computer accounts are stored in the Registry.

3. What represents user accounts in Windows security?

    Answer: Security identifiers (SIDs) represent user accounts.

4. What process manages logging in?

    Answer: The WinLogon process manages the login process.

5. What protocol is used to authenticate a user account in a Windows 2000 domain?

    Answer: Kerberos is used to authenticate user accounts in Windows 2000 domains.

6. How is the user's identity passed on to running programs?

    Answer: The user's identity is passed to running programs by the inheritance of the access token from the launching program.

7. When you attempt to access a file, what does the LSA compare your access token to in order to determine whether or not you should have access?

    Answer: The LSA compares your access token to the object's security descriptor (access control list) in order to determine whether or not you should have access.

8. What special right does an object's owner possess?

    Answer: An object's owner has the right to change the object's permissions irrespective of a user's permissions to the object.

9. For what purpose is the System Access Control List used?

    Answer: The System Access Control List is used to audit various types of access to an object.

10. What is the difference between a right and a permission?

    Answer: Rights affect many or all objects, whereas permissions are specific to each object.

11. What does the term *inheritance* mean in the context of file system permissions?

    Answer: *Inheritance* refers to objects receiving a copy of the containing folder's ACL when they are created.

12. Where are user accounts stored in a domain?

    Answer: User accounts are stored in the Active Directory.

13. In a Kerberos authentication, can a user in Domain A log on to a computer in Domain C if Domain C trusts Domain B and Domain B trusts Domain A?

    Answer: Yes. In Kerberos, trusts transit domain relationships.

14. What is the primary mechanism for controlling the configuration of client computers in Windows?

    Answer: Group Policy is the primary mechanism for controlling the configuration of client computers in Windows.

15. Can more than one Group Policy be applied to a single machine?

    Answer: Yes. Early policy changes are overwritten by later policy changes when multiple policies are applied.

16. Does share security work on FAT file system shares?

    Answer: Yes. Share security works on FAT file system shares.

Chapter 11

1. Why is Unix security so simple?

   Answer: Unix was originally designed to not include rigorous security in order to solve problems that didn't require high-level security.

2. Why did AT&T originally give UNIX away to anyone who wanted a copy?

   Answer: AT&T gave UNIX away in the beginning because its monopoly agreement with the U.S. government prevented it from selling software.

3. Why are there so many variations of Unix?

   Answer: AT&T essentially lost control of its development of Unix when it gave it away to universities in the 1970s. It also licensed it to numerous hardware developers who modified it as they saw fit. Finally, hackers created their own version using the Internet, and the result is a variety of variations.

4. In Unix, every system object is represented and controlled by what primary structure?

   Answer: The file system represents and controls every system object in Unix.

5. What is the primary security mechanism in Unix?

   Answer: File system permissions are the primary security mechanism in Unix.

6. Which component stores permissions?

   Answer: File inodes store permissions in Unix.

7. Where is user account information stored on a Unix system?

    Answer: Unix user account information is stored in the `/etc/passwd` file.

8. How are permissions handled for the root user in Unix?

    Answer: Permissions are not checked for the root user in Unix.

9. What is the GID of the wheel or superuser group?

    Answer: The GID of the wheel or superuser group is 0.

10. What are the basic permissions that can be set for owners, group members, and everyone else in an inode?

    Answer: Read, Write, and Execute are the basic permissions that can be set in an inode.

11. Which two commands are typically used to modify ownership and permissions on an inode?

    Answer: Typically, the `chmod` and `chown` commands are used to modify ownership and permissions on an inode.

12. What does it mean when an executable has its `setuid` flag enabled?

    Answer: Having an executable's `setuid` flag enabled means that it runs under the user account context of the file's owner rather than the logged-on user who executes it.

13. What makes a daemon different than a normal executable in Unix?

    Answer: Nothing. Daemons are standard executables that run using SetUID permissions.

Chapter 12

1. Why doesn't Unix have a standard file sharing mechanism?

    Answer: There is no standard file sharing mechanism for Unix because Unix was developed before local area networks made file sharing popular.

2. What is the most secure protocol for remotely logging on to a Unix computer?

    Answer: Secure Shell (SSH) is the most secure protocol for remotely logging on to a Unix computer.

3. What is the primary authentication mechanism used by SMTP?

    Answer: SMTP has no authentication mechanisms.

4. What does PAM do?

    Answer: PAM provides a standardized method for services to authenticate users against a wide array of authentication mechanisms.

5. What type of encryption does NIS use to protect user credentials?

    Answer: NIS provides no encryption.

6. What cryptographic mechanism does Kerberos use to protect user credentials?

    Answer: Kerberos uses secret key encryption.

7. What is the difference between a file transfer protocol and a file sharing protocol?

    Answer: File sharing protocols are capable of transmitting segments of files and allowing multiple users to access files simultaneously. File transfer protocols do not have these capabilities.

8. Does SMB provide any mechanism for securing user credentials over the network?

    Answer: Yes, Samba passwords are encrypted by default in Windows, and encryption can be enabled in Samba and most other SMB implementations.

9. How does TCP Wrappers protect a service?

    Answer: TCP Wrappers provides protection by replacing the service executable with a service that first authenticates the source of the connection and then allows access to the service.

10. What do IPChains and IPTables provide?

    Answer: IPChains and IPTables provide TCP/IP packet filtering.

11. What functionality does FWTK provide?

    Answer: FWTK provides protocol level filtering and a proxy service.

Chapter 13

1. Over 90 percent of the public Internet is served from which two web server applications?

    Answer: Microsoft Internet Information Services and Apache serve over 90 percent of the public Internet.

2. What is the most threatening security problem facing public web servers?

    Answer: The bugs in the operating system or web server software are the most threatening security problems for public web servers.

3. Which is more secure, closed-source or open-source operating systems?

    Answer: Closed-source and open-source operating systems are about equally secure.

4. Which is more secure, IIS or Apache?

    Answer: Apache is both theoretically and operationally more secure than IIS.

5. Why should websites only be deployed on dedicated web servers?

    Answer: Websites should only be deployed on dedicated web servers because general-purpose servers are more likely to be exploited and you could lose valuable information stored by other services if you run public websites on them.

6. Where are bugs most likely to be found in a program?

    Answer: Bugs are most likely found in sections of programs that implement rarely used or esoteric features.

7. What service does SSL perform?

    Answer: SSL encrypts web data flowing between the browser and the server.

8. What's the best way to secure intranet servers?

    Answer: You can secure intranet servers by placing them inside a VPN and not making them public.

9. What is the universal encrypted authentication mechanism?

    Answer: The universal encrypted authentication mechanism is using SSL to secure basic authentication.

10. How do you configure Apache?

    Answer: Configure Apache by editing the /etc/httpd/conf/httpd.conf file.

11. What is taint?

    Answer: In Perl, taint is a marker that indicates that data has been typed in by a user and should not be trusted.

Chapter 14

1. What problems can e-mail encryption cause?

    Answer: Encrypted e-mail cannot be stripped of attachments or scanned for viruses by mail servers.

2. What feature of e-mail causes the majority of security risks?

    Answer: Attachments causes the majority of security risks for e-mail systems.

3. What is the most commonly implemented form of e-mail encryption?

    Answer: Secure Multipurpose Internet Mail Extensions (S/MIME) is the most common implementation of e-mail encryption.

4. Besides privacy, what other important security function does e-mail encryption provide?

    Answer: E-mail encryption provides authentication in addition to privacy.

5. Why is it possible to forge e-mail?

    Answer: It is possible to forge e-mail because there is no standard SMTP authentication mechanism.

6. How common are e-mail viruses?

    Answer: E-mail viruses are very common. E-mail is the most common propagation mechanism for viruses.

7. Can your e-mail server solve all possible e-mail security problems?

    Answer: Private e-mail servers cannot solve all possible e-mail security problems. Clients that check outside e-mail servers are still a threat.

8. What is the most secure method of dealing with attachments?

    Answer: The most secure method of dealing with attachments is to strip them and discard them at the e-mail server.

9. What is the most practical method of stripping e-mail attachments for most users?

    Answer: The most practical method of stripping e-mail attachments is to allow only approved types of attachments to be passed through the mail server.

10. What can be done to provide attachment security for proprietary e-mail servers that cannot be configured to strip attachments?

    Answer: By relaying the e-mail through an open-source e-mail server that can be configured to strip attachments, you can provide attachment security for proprietary e-mail servers.

11. What's the most practical method of attachment security for most organizations?

    Answer: Allowing only approved attachment types is the most practical method of attachment security for most organizations.

12. What e-mail clients are more susceptible to e-mail viruses?

    Answer: Outlook and Outlook Express are more susceptible to e-mail viruses than other e-mail clients.

13. What is spam?

    Answer: Spam is unwanted, unsolicited e-mail.

14. What mechanism do illegal spammers exploit to send spam?

    Answer: Illegal spammers use open relays, relays that will relay mail from any host rather than just hosts within their own domain, to send spam.

15. How do you close an open relay?

    Answer: To close an open relay, require some form of authentication from those who want to send e-mail to a domain other than your own and who originate from outside your network.

16. What is the problem with spam blocking lists?

    Answer: Spam blocking lists can't block all spam, and they do block a small percentage of legitimate e-mail.

17. How do ISPs prevent their clients from sending spam?

    Answer: ISPs prevent their clients from sending spam by blocking SMTP access to all mail servers except their own.

Chapter 15

1. How many automated hacking attempts would be normal against a public site in a 24-hour period?
   Answer: Hundreds of hacking attempts a day are normal for a public site.

2. What are the three common types of intrusion detection systems?
   Answer: Inspectors, decoys, and auditors are common intrusion detection systems.

3. What common network software are inspectors related to?
   Answer: Virus scanners are similar to inspectors.

4. What software would you use to implement a decoy?
   Answer: A standard operating system and service software are all you need to implement a decoy.

5. What is the common file system auditor for Unix called?

   Answer: Tripwire is the common file system auditor for Unix.

6. What is the most popular intrusion detection system?

   Answer: Snort is the most popular IDS.

7. How many sensors do you need, at a minimum, in an inspector-based intrusion detection system?

   Answer: You need at least two sensors in an inspector-based IDS; one in your DMZ and one in your private network.

Glossary

802.11b The most common wireless networking protocol, 802.11b is used in many businesses and homes to provide convenient Internet access and is available free in public areas around the world. 802.11b is plagued by a poorly designed security protocol (WEP) that is trivially easy to hack.

access control entry (ACE) In an access control list, an entry that joins a security identifier to a type of allowed or denied access.

access token A combination of security identifiers that represents the user account and the security groups that it belongs to. Access tokens are passed from the initial logon to all user-mode programs executed subsequently.

Active Directory A database that is distributed among the domain controllers in a domain or tree that contains user accounts, machine accounts, and other administrative information concerning the network.

active IDS An intrusion detection system that can create responses, such as blocking network traffic or alerting on intrusion attempts.

ActiveX An execution environment for the Microsoft Internet Explorer web browser and Windows applications that allow code to be delivered over the Internet and executed on the local machine.

algorithm A method expressed in a mathematical form (such as computer code) for performing a specific function or operation.

America Online (AOL) A popular graphical BBS system that has transformed into the largest consumer Internet service provider.

Due to its non-Internet origins, AOL uses a proprietary e-mail mechanism that (among other things) does not support true MIME attachments or use standard ports for transmitting e-mail.

AppleTalk The protocol over which the AppleShare proprietary file and resource sharing mechanism for Apple Macintosh computers ran before Apple adopted TCP/IP. Recent versions of the MacOS are also compatible with the Windows (SMB) file sharing protocol.

application Software that allows users to perform their work, as opposed to software used to manage systems, entertain, or perform other utility functions. Applications are the reason that systems are implemented.

application-layer proxy A proxy server that provides a different proxy service tailored to each protocol that it forwards, allowing it to inspect the details of that service for maximum security.

appropriate use policy A policy that explains how humans are allowed to use a system.

archive marking A method used by operating systems to indicate when a file has been changed and should thus be included in an incremental backup.

archiving The process of retaining a copy of every version of files created by users for the purpose of restoring individual files in case of human error.

asymmetric algorithm A mathematical function that has no reciprocal function.

Asynchronous Transfer Mode (ATM) A packet-switched Data-Link layer framing protocol used for high-speed digital circuits that is compatible across a wide range of physical circuit speeds. ATM is typically used for intercity and metropolitan area circuits.

attachment A file encoded in text form for transmission/insertion in an e-mail message, such as a word.doc or picture.jpg file.

audit trail A log of intrusion detection events that can be analyzed for patterns or to create a body of evidence.

auditing The process of recording the use of resources in an automated system for the purpose of subsequent inspection.

auditors Intrusion detection systems that simply record changes made to a system.

authentication The process of determining a user's identity in order to allow access.

background radiation The normal, mostly futile, hacking activity caused by automated worms and script kiddies.

benign viruses Viruses that do not destroy data. Benign viruses simply propagate without performing any other function.

Berkeley Software Distribution (BSD) A highly customized version of Unix, originally distributed by the University of California, Berkeley.

biometric authentication Authentication by means of invariant and unique biological characteristics such as fingerprints or DNA.

BIOS (Basic Input/Output System) The low-level program built into the computer's motherboard that is used to configure hardware and load the operating system.

block devices Peripherals that transfer mass quantities of information in large units (i.e., processing occurs for each large block of information received rather than for every byte). Block devices are typically high-speed devices like hard disk drives or local area network adapters.

boot sector The first executable code stored on a disk. Used to load the operating system.

border gateway See *firewall*.

brute-force attack An attack in which every possible combination of values is tried in sequence against a password system. Given an infinite amount of time, these attacks will always succeed, but they are impractical against long passwords.

buffer overrun A common type of hacking attack that exploits flaws in programming code. Specifically, when an input buffer for a public service (such as the URL field of a web browser) is provided with more data than the buffer is programmed to accept, the extra data can overwrite programming code and will be executed in the context of the application that received the data. By determining exactly how the overwritten code will be executed, hackers can craft input to take over control of the executing program on the remote computer.

bugs Errors in programming code.

bulletin-board system (BBS) Use of a single central computer to which many computers have intermittent access to shared information.

call-back security Dial-up networking security that is implemented by having the main system call the remote user back, thus ensuring that the user attempting to gain access is an authorized one (so long as the phone system remains secure).

certificate A digital identity that has been digitally signed by one or more trusted authorities.

challenge/response A method used to prove that a party knows a password without transmitting the password in any recoverable form over a network.

character devices A class of peripherals that transmit or receive information one byte at a time (i.e., processing occurs for each byte received). Typically, character devices are lower-speed devices like keyboards, mice, and serial ports.

cipher   A mathematical function used to transform a plain message into a form that cannot be read without decoding it. Ciphers can encode any message.

circuit   In the context of information technology, a circuit is a data network connection between two points, usually different facilities. The term *circuit* traditionally applies to high-capacity telephone trunk lines.

circuit-layer switch   A proxy server for the TCP protocol. Circuit layer switches operate like application layer proxies except that they proxy TCP and can therefore be used to proxy any protocol that runs over TCP.

code   An agreed-upon set of symbols that represent concepts. Both parties must be using the same code in order to communicate, and only predetermined concepts can be communicated.

combination   A numeric code used to open a physical lock.

commercial Internet exchange (CIX)   One of an increasing number of regional datacenters where the various tier-1 ISPs interconnect their private networks via TCP/IP to form the nexus of the Internet.

computer accounts   Security identifiers that uniquely identify computers in a domain and authenticate their participation in the domain.

computer policy   The portion of a Group Policy that is applied irrespective of which user account logs on.

content blocking   A security measure that blocks access to websites based on keywords contained in the content.

content signing   The process of embedding a hash in a document or executable code to prove that the content has not been modified and to identify with certainty the author of the content.

credentials   Information used to prove identity. Typically, this is a combination of a user account name and a password.

cryptography   The study of codes, ciphers, and encryption.

cryptosystem   A computing system that implements one or more specific encryption algorithms.

daemon   An executable in Unix that runs automatically as a service (i.e., with a unique user context) when the computer is booted. Similar to a *service* in Windows.

data   Information that represents some real-world information, like a novel, a picture, a sound, or a bank account. Data is processed by code to create answers that are themselves represented by data and can be further processed.

Data Encryption Standard (DES)   A secret key encryption algorithm developed by IBM, under contract to the U.S. government, for public use.

decoys   Intrusion detection systems that detect intrusions by mimicking actual systems and alerting on any use.

dedicated leased lines   Digital telephone trunk lines leased from a telephone company and used to transmit digitized voice or data. With a true dedicated leased line, circuits are leased and connected together permanently between two points to form a permanent physical circuit.

demilitarized zone (DMZ)   A security zone with a separate, more relaxed security policy that is used to partition public servers like e-mail and web servers away from the internal network while providing them with firewall protection.

denial of service (DoS) attacks   Hacking attacks that attempt to stop a server from providing its service rather than gain access to it. DoS attacks can be as simple as generating a flood of legitimate requests that the server does not have the capacity to respond to, or may exploit a flaw in the service to cause it to crash.

deny ACE An access control entry that specifically denies permissions in order to override other permissions that might allow access to the account.

dial-up modem bank A collection of modems that are connected to a high-speed network and are dedicated to the task of answering calls from the modems of end users, thereby connecting them to the network.

digital signature Any identity information encrypted with a private key and therefore decryptable using a public key. Digital signatures are used to prove the validity of publicly available documents by proving that they were encrypted with a specific secretly held private key.

directory A file that contains the names of other files or directories.

Directory Services Agent (DSA) The service that communicates between the Local Security Authority (LSA) and the Active Directory in order to authenticate domain users.

Discretionary Access Control List (DACL) The access control list that is used to allow or deny access to an object.

disk packs Multiple identical hard disk drives configured to store a single volume in a RAID set.

Distributed Computing Environment (DCE) An early initiative by the Open Software Foundation to provide distributed a login mechanism for Unix and Windows. DCE is supported by many commercial Unix distributions and by Windows.

distributed logon Any client/server protocol for verifying user identity. The purpose of distributed logon services is to allow users to log on once and use their credentials on any machine within the security domain. This provides the illusion of logging into the network as a whole rather than logging onto a single computer.

distributions A specific packaging of a Unix operating system and associated utility files and applications.

document A work product created by an application that is intended for human interpretation.

domain A collection of computers that trust the same set of user accounts. Domain accounts are stored in the Active Directory.

Domain Name Service (DNS) The Internet directory service used to convert a human readable domain name into an IP address.

electronic mail (e-mail) A queued message delivery system that allows users to transmit relatively short text messages to other users over the Internet. The messages wait in a mail queue until they are downloaded and read by the ultimate recipient.

encapsulation The insertion of a complete Network layer packet within another packet of the same layer. The encapsulated protocol may or may not be the same as the encapsulating protocol and may or may not be encrypted.

encryption The process of encoding a plaintext message using a cipher so that it cannot be understood by intermediate parties who do not know the key to decrypt it.

end user license agreement (EULA) A contract between the developer of software and the users of software. The contract limits a user's right to use and distribute the software as specified by the developer.

Exchange Microsoft's e-mail and messaging server. Exchange was originally designed for private interoffice messaging, with Internet functionality provided as an add-on. It uses the proprietary Microsoft MAPI protocol for exchanging mail between Exchange servers and clients and SMTP for transmitting e-mail on the public Internet, and it can be configured to allow POP3, IMAP, and WebMail access as well.

executable code Information that represents computer instructions. Lists of code (called programs) are executed by a microprocessor in order to perform a function.

execution environments   Any environment that interprets data as actions and performs those actions. An execution environment might be a microprocessor, a virtual machine, or an application that interprets a script or macro.

export   A directory tree that is published by NFS for remote mounting by NFS clients. Analogous to an SMB share.

extensions   Filename suffixes that identify a document type so that the operating system (and users) can determine which program should be used to interpret the contents of the document.

fail-over clustering   A fault tolerance method where a server can assume the services of a failed server.

fault tolerance   The ability of a system to withstand failure and remain operational.

file   A sequence of data that is permanently stored on a mass-storage device, such as a hard disk, and referenced by a name.

file shares   A directory tree that is published by SMB for remote attachment by SMB clients. Analogous to an NFS export.

file sharing protocol   A protocol that allows a rich set of semantics for serving files to clients. File sharing protocols are distinguished by their ability to provide small portions of files and provide locking mechanisms so that multiple users can write to a file simultaneously.

file synchronization   The process of comparing files in different locations and transmitting the differences between them to ensure that both copies remain the same. Synchronization is only easy if you can guarantee that the two files won't change on both ends at the same time. If they can, then decisions must be made about which version to keep, and depending upon the nature of the information, it may not be possible to automate the decision-making process.

file transfer protocol (FTP)   A simple protocol that allows the complete transfer of files between servers and clients. File transfer protocols cannot support simultaneous multiple users. File Transfer Protocol is also the name of the oldest and most widely implemented file transfer protocol.

firewall   A gateway device that filters communications between a private network and a public network, allowing only those that respect the company's security policy.

flash memory   A trade name for electronically erasable programmable read-only memory (EEPROM) that can be erased using the same voltage levels with which it can be programmed. Flash memory is nonvolatile permanent storage that is exceptionally reliable and is now used in almost every computing device on the market to store upgradeable boot loaders or operating systems. Flash memory is also used to make a wide variety of convenient memory storage for cameras, PDAs, and laptops in various forms.

flood   A massive amount of network traffic generated with the specific purpose of overwhelming a service computer to perpetrate a denial of service attack.

Frame Relay   A Data-Link layer packet-switching protocol that emulates a traditional point-to-point leased line. Frame Relay allows the telephone companies to create a permanent virtual circuit between any two points on their digital networks by programming routes into their Frame Relay routers. This way, "frames" can be "relayed" between two endpoints without requiring a dedicated leased line between them.

grass-rooted   Describes a trust system that has no hierarchy but instead relies upon massive participation to provide a transitive trust mechanism that requires no supporting commercial organization.

Group Policy   A collection of computer and user configuration policies that are applied to computers based upon their association within an Active Directory container like a domain or organizational unit.

hacker   One who engages in hacking.

hacking   The act of attempting to gain access to computers without authorization.

hard links   Multiple filenames for a single inode. Hard links allow a single file to exist in multiple places in the directory hierarchy.

hash   The result of applying a one-way function to a value.

hijack   A specific type of hacking attack where a hacker watches the establishment of an authenticated session and then inserts specially crafted packets that seem to come from the legitimate user in order to take over the session. This type of attack is exceptionally difficult to accomplish because it requires the hacker to be able to successfully predict in real time the pseudorandom sequence numbers of upcoming packets.

honey pots   Decoy IDSs, especially those that are sanitized installations of actual operating systems as opposed to software that mimics actual systems.

hybrid cryptosystem   A cryptosystem that exchanges secret keys using public key encryption to secure the key exchange and then uses the higher speed allowed by secret key encryption to transmit subsequent data.

I/O port   An interface to peripherals, like serial devices, printers, and so on.

inherit   To receive a copy of security information from the launching program, containing folder, or other such precursor.

inoculator   Antivirus software that scans data files and executables at the moment they are invoked and block them from being loaded if they contain a virus. Inoculators can prevent viruses from spreading.

inode (index node)   A file descriptor in Unix systems that describes ownership, permissions, and other metadata about a file.

inspectors   Intrusion detection systems that detect intrusions by searching all incoming data for the known signature patterns of hacking attempts.

Internet Key Exchange (IKE)   A protocol that allows the exchange of IPSec security associations based on trust established by knowledge of a private key.

Internet Message Access Protocol (IMAP)   A client e-mail access protocol typically used in situations where it's appropriate to allow users to leave e-mail on the mail server rather than downloading it to their client computer.

Internetwork Packet Exchange (IPX)   The routable LAN protocol developed by Novell for its NetWare server operating system. IPX is very similar to TCP/IP, but it uses the Data-Link layer Media Access Control (MAC) address for unique addressing rather than a user-configured address and is therefore easier to configure. IPX routes broadcasts around the entire network and is therefore unsuitable in larger networks.

interpreter   A programming language application that loads scripts as data and then interprets commands step-by-step rather than by compiling them to machine language.

intrusion detection system (IDS)   System that detects unauthorized access to other systems.

IPChains   A stateless packet filtering mechanism for Unix kernels.

IPTables   A stateful packet filtering mechanism for Unix kernels.

Java   A cross-platform execution environment developed by Sun Microsystems that allows the same program to be executed across many different operating systems. Java applets can be delivered automatically from web servers to browsers and executed within the web browser's security context.

kerberized   Describes a service that has been modified for compatibility with Kerberos.

Kerberos   An authentication protocol that uses secret keys to authenticate users and machines in a networked environment. Kerberos allows for a transitive trust between widely diverse domains and is the primary authentication protocol for Windows 2000 and many Unix distributions.

key   A secret value used to encrypt information.

Key Distribution Center (KDC)   In Kerberos, the authentication server that manages user accounts; a domain controller.

key ring   A database of public keys that have been received by a user.

Layer 2 Tunneling Protocol (L2TP)   An industry standard protocol for separating the Data-Link layer transmission of packets from the flow control, session, authentication, compression, and encryption protocols. L2TP is typically used for remote access applications and is the successor to PPP.

lessons learned   A documented failure analysis that is disseminated to system users in order to prevent the same failure from recurring.

Lightweight Directory Access Protocol (LDAP)   A protocol for accessing service configuration data from a central hierarchical database. LDAP is frequently used to store user account information in Unix and is supported as an access method by Microsoft Active Directory.

load balancing   A clustering mechanism whereby individual client sessions are connected to any one of a number of identically configured servers so that the entire load of client sessions is spread evenly among the pool of servers.

local area networks (LAN)   High-speed short distance networks existing usually within a single building. Computers on the same local area network can directly address one another using Data Link layer protocols like Ethernet or Token Ring and do not require routing in order to reach other computers on the same LAN. The term is becoming somewhat obsolete as routing within networks becomes more common and long distance technologies become faster than LAN technologies.

Local Security Authority (LSA)   The process that controls access to secured objects in Windows.

locally unique identifier (LUID)   An identifier that is created for each logged-on instance of a user account to differentiate it from other logon sessions.

lockdown programs   Software designed to automatically configure the security options of an operating system or other application to be optimal for a specific purpose.

logon prompt   The interface through which users identify themselves to the computer.

macro   A list of instructions embedded within a document and stored as data that is interpreted by a scripting host.

macro virus   Viruses that exist in the interpreted code embedded in Office documents. These viruses are not capable of escaping the confines of their interpreted environment, so they cannot infect executables.

mail exchange (MX) records   DNS entries that identify the hostnames of e-mail servers for a specific domain.

mainframe   A large and powerful computer that many users share via terminal displays.

malignant viruses   Viruses that contain attack code that performs some malicious act.

man-in-the-middle   An attack where a hacker appears to be the server to a client and the client to a server. These attacks are typically initiated by inducing the user to connect to the hacker's computer and then proxying the legitimate server service so that the hackers computer looks and acts exactly like the legitimate server.

mean time between failures (MTBF)   The average life expectancy of electronic equipment. Most hard disks have an MTBF of about five years.

mount   To connect a file system on a block device to the operating system. The term comes from the act of mounting a reel of tape on a tape reader.

Multics   A complex operating system developed in the 1960s with many innovative concepts, such as multitasking. Multics was the precursor to the simpler and more portable Unix.

Multipurpose Internet Mail Extension (MIME)   An IETF protocol for encoding and transmitting files along with metadata that determines how the files should be decoded and what applications should be used to interpret them.

NAT routers   Small routers that provide (typically) just the network address translation function of a firewall. Originally used to share a single IP connection for home users, they have recently become more important for home computer security since they are natural firewalls. These devices are frequently marketed as "cable-DSL routers."

nearline   Data that is stored on offline media that can be automatically mounted and made available in a reasonably short period of time without human intervention.

NetBEUI   Microsoft's original networking protocol that allows for file and resource sharing but is not routable and is therefore limited to operation on a single LAN. As with any protocol, NetBEUI can be encapsulated within a routable protocol to bridge distant networks.

NetBIOS   Network Basic Input Output System. An older network file and print sharing service developed by IBM and adopted by Microsoft for use in Windows.

Network Address Translation (NAT)   The process of rewriting the IP addresses of a packet stream as it flows through a router for the purpose of multiplexing a single IP address across a network of interior computers and for hiding internal hosts.

Network File System (NFS)   A widely supported file sharing protocol developed by Sun Microsystems for use in Unix environments. NFS allows clients to mount portions of a server's file system into their own file systems.

Network Information Service (NIS)   A simple distributed logon mechanism developed by Sun Microsystems for Unix, originally to support single sign-on for NFS.

New Technology File System (NTFS)   The standard file system for Windows that provides secure object access, compression, checkpointing, and other sophisticated file management functions.

New Technology LAN Manager (NTLM)   The network authentication protocol used prior to Kerberos in Windows NT. NTLM is a much simpler authentication protocol that does not support transitive trusts and stores domain user accounts in the SAM of the primary domain controller.

No Access permission   See *deny ACE.*

objects   Data structures in a computer environment, such as files, directories, printers, shares, and so forth.

offline   Describes data that is not immediately available to running systems, such as data stored on tape.

one-time passwords   An authentication method that uses synchronized pseudorandom number generation on both the client and the server to prove that both sides know the same original seed number.

one-way function   An algorithm that has no reciprocal function and cannot therefore be reversed in order to discover the data originally encoded.

online   Describes data that is immediately available to running systems because it is stored on active disks.

open relay servers   E-mail servers that perform no authentication whatsoever on transmitted e-mail.

open source   Software produced by a free association of programmers who have all agreed to make their work available at no cost along with the original source code. Actual licensing terms vary, but generally there are stipulations that prevent the code from being incorporated into otherwise copyrighted software.

operating system   The program that controls the overall operation of a computer.

Outlook   Microsoft's extremely popular, but poorly secured, e-mail client and personal information manager.

Outlook Express   A stripped-down version of Outlook that handles only the minimum set of features necessary to propagate e-mail viruses.

owner   The user account that created an object or was otherwise assigned ownership. The owner of an object has the right to change its permissions irrespective of user accounts permissions.

packet filter   A router that is capable of dropping packets that don't meet security requirements.

PAMed   Describes an application that has been modified to allow for Pluggable Authentication Modules.

parent   The preceding process (for programs) or the containing folder (for objects, directories or files).

partition   A low-level division of a hard disk. A partition contains a file system.

pass phrase   A very long password consisting of multiple words.

passive IDS   Intrusion detection system that record information about intrusions but does not have the capability of acting on that information.

password   A secret key known to both a system and a user that can be used to prove a user's identity to gain access to the system.

permission   An access control entry in an object's Discretionary Access Control List (DACL).

permissions   A security mechanism that controls access to individual resources, like files, based on user identity.

personal firewall applications   Software programs that protect an individual computer from intrusion by filtering all communications that enter through network connections.

pipe   An interprocess communication mechanism that emulates a serial character device.

Pluggable Authentication Module (PAM)   An authentication abstraction layer that provides a central mechanism for connecting various authentication schemes to various network services in Unix. Services trust PAM for authentication, and PAM can be configured to use various authentication schemes.

Point-to-Point Protocol (PPP)   A protocol originally developed to allow modem links to carry different types of Network layer protocols like TCP/IP, IPX, NetBEUI, and AppleTalk. PPP includes authentication and protocol negotiation as well as control signals between the two points, but it does not allow for addressing because only two participants are involved in the communication.

policy   A collection of rules.

port   A parameter of a TCP stream that indicates which process on the remote should receive the data. Public servers listen on "well-known" ports established by convention to monitor specific processes like web or e-mail servers.

Post Office Protocol, version 3 (POP3)   An e-mail client protocol used to download e-mail from mail servers into mail client programs.

Postfix   A popular and highly secure e-mail service for Unix systems.

Practical Extraction and Reporting Language (Perl)   A popular scripting language used in websites and the administration of Unix machines. Windows versions are available.

Pretty Good Privacy (PGP)   A freely available encryption package that supports file and e-mail encryption for nearly all computing platforms.

private key   A secretly held key for an asymmetrical encryption algorithm that can only be used to decode messages or encode digital signatures.

probe   An attempt to elicit a response from a host in order to glean information from the host.

process   A running program.

propagation engine   The code used by a virus to self-replicate.

protocol   An agreed-upon method of communicating between two computers.

proxy server   A server that hosts application proxies.

pseudorandom number   A member of a set of numbers that has all the same properties as a similarly sized set of truly random numbers—like even distribution in a set, no predictable reoccurrences, and incompressibility—but that occur in a predictable order from a given starting point (seed).

pseudorandom number generator (PRNG)   An algorithm that generates pseudorandom numbers.

public key   A publicly distributed key for an asymmetrical encryption algorithm, which can only be used to encode messages or decode digital signatures.

public key authentication   Authentication by means of a digital signature.

public key encryption   Encryption by means of a public key. Public key encryption solves the problem posed by exchanging secret keys by using different but related ciphers for encoding and decoding. Because different keys are used to encode and decode, the public key (encoder) can be widely disseminated without risk.

qmail   A popular e-mail service for Unix systems.

realm   A Kerberos security domain defined by a group of hosts that all trust the same Key Distribution Center.

red flag   A simple detected event that has a very high probability of being a real hacking attempt with serious consequences as opposed to a normal administrative event or background radiation.

Redundant Array of Independent Disks (RAID)   A family of related technologies that allow multiple disks to be combined into a volume. With all RAID versions except 0, the volume can tolerate the failure of at least one hard disk and remain fully functional.

Registry   A hierarchical database local to each Windows computer used for storing configuration information.

relay server   An intermediate e-mail server configured to route e-mail between e-mail servers.

remote access   The process of accessing services on a remote server without executing software directly on the remote machine.

remote logon   The process of logging on to a remote machine in order to execute software on it.

removable media   Computer storage media that can be removed from the drive, such as floppy disks, flash cards, and tape.

replay attack   An attack in which a secret value like a hash is captured and then reused at a later time to gain access to a system without ever decrypting or decoding the hash. Replay attacks only work against systems that don't uniquely encrypt hashes for each session.

requirements   A list of functions that are necessary in a system.

reverse proxy   A web proxy that receives requests for pages from the Internet and passes them through to one member of a pool of identical web servers. Reverse proxies can be used both for load balancing and security checking.

root   The Unix superuser administrative account. Permissions are not checked for the root user.

Root Certifying Authority (Root CA)   An organization that exists simply to be trusted by participants in order to provide transitive trust. Root CAs certify the identities of all members so that members who trust the Root CA can trust anyone that they've certified. A Root CA is analogous to a notary public.

rooted   Describes a transitive trust system that relies upon a hierarchy that culminates in a single entity that all participants implicitly trust.

sandbox   An execution environment that does not allow accesses outside itself and so cannot be exploited to cause problem on the host system.

scan   A methodical search through a numerical space, such as an address or port range.

script kiddie   A novice hacker.

scripting hosts   Execution environments that can be called from applications in order to execute scripts contained in the application's data.

secret key   A key that must be kept secret by all parties because it can be used to both encrypt and decrypt messages.

secret key encryption   Encryption by means of a secret key.

Secure Multipurpose Internet Mail Extensions (S/MIME)   MIME with extensions that provide encryption.

Secure Shell (SSH)   A secure encrypted version of the classic Telnet application. SSH uses public key cryptography to authenticate SSH connections and private key encryption with changing keys to secure data while in transit.

Secure Sockets Layer (SSL)   A public key encryption technology that uses certificates to establish encrypted links without exchanging authentication information. SSL is used to provide encryption for public services or services that otherwise do not require identification of the parties involved but where privacy is important. SSL does not perform encapsulation.

Security Accounts Manager (SAM)   The process that controls access to the user account database in the Registry.

security associations (SA)   A set of cryptographic keys and protocol identifiers programmed into a VPN endpoint to allow communication with a reciprocal VPN endpoint. IKE allows security associations to be negotiated on the fly between two devices if they both know the same secret key.

security descriptor   Information stored with each object that specifies the owner and contains the access control list.

security domain   A collection of machines that all trust the same database of user credentials.

security group   A construct containing a SID that is used to create permissions for an object. User accounts are associated with security groups and inherit their permissions from them.

security identifier (SID)   A globally unique serial number used to identify user, computer, and security group accounts in Windows.

security principle   A user, computer, or security group account.

seed   The starting point for a specific set of pseudo-random numbers for a specific pseudorandom number generator (PRNG).

self-replicating   Describes something that has the ability to create copies of itself.

sendmail   The most popular e-mail service, send-mail is open source and was originally part of the Berkeley Software Distribution (BSD). Many commercial e-mail services are based on sendmail.

sensor   Intrusion detection software that is designed to run directly on public hosts and reports to a central management station.

session   An authenticated stream of related packets.

shadow passwords   A security tactic in Unix that separates password information from user account information while remaining compatible with software written for the earlier combined method.

share A portion of a file system that the SMB service (`server.exe` in Windows, Samba in Unix) exports for access by SMB clients. Access to the share can be configured on a per-user or per-group basis.

shares Constructs used by the Server service to determine how users should be able to access folders across the network.

shell The program that is launched after a successful login and presents the user environment. Typically, shells allow a user to launch subsequent programs.

signature A short sequence of codes known to be unique to a specific virus, which indicates that virus's presence in a system.

Simple Mail Transfer Protocol (SMTP) The Internet protocol that controls the transmission of e-mail between servers. SMTP is also used to transmit e-mail from clients to servers but usually not to receive it because SMTP requires recipient machines to be online at all times.

Simple Network Management Protocol (SNMP) A protocol with no inherent security used to query equipment status and modify the configuration of network devices.

single signon See *distributed logon*.

smart cards Physical devices that have a small amount of nonvolatile memory that stores a random number that is only available to the device. Authentication software can push a value on to the card, which will be encrypted using the random number and returned. Smart cards thereby create an unforgeable physical key mechanism.

sniffing The process of wiretapping and recording information that flows over a network for analytical purposes.

socket A specific TCP or UDP port on a specific IP address; for example, 192.168.0.1:80. Sockets are used to transmit information between two participating computers in a network environment. Sockets are block devices.

source routing A test mechanism that is allowed by the IP protocol and allows the sender to specify the route that a packet should take through a network rather than rely upon the routing tables built into intermediate routers.

spam Unsolicited, unwanted e-mail.

spammers Those who send spam. Usually, the term is applied to those who steal bandwidth to send spam as opposed to legitimate e-mail marketers who send spam.

spyware Any software that hides its true functionality behind claims of benign and useful functionality in order to entice end users to download it. A Trojan horse that uses enticement in order to get end users to install it. Users are enticed to accept a license agreement prior to download which indemnifies the vendor, thus preventing the software from being technically illegal.

stateful inspection A packet filtering methodology that retains the state of a TCP connection and can pass or reject packets based on that state rather than simply on information contained in the packet.

stateless packet filters Packet filters that make pass/reject decisions based only on the information contained in each individual packet.

stateless protocol Protocols that do not maintain any information about the client session on the server side. Stateless protocols can be easily clustered across multiple machines without fear of data loss or side effects because it does not matter which server the client connects to from one instance to the next.

symmetrical algorithm An algorithm that uses the same secret key for encryption and decryption.

system A collection of processing entities, such as computers, firewalls, domain controllers, network devices, e-mail systems, applications, and humans.

System Access Control List (SACL)   An access control list used to determine how to audit objects.

T1 leased lines   The traditional designator for the most common type of digital leased line. T1 lines operate at 1.544Mbps (as a single channel, or 1.536Mbps when multiplexed into 24 channels) over two pairs of category 2 twisted-pair wiring. T1s were originally designed to carry 24 digital voice lines between a private branch exchange (PBX) and the local telephone company for businesses that required numerous voice lines. Most small to medium-sized businesses rely on T1 lines for their primary connections to the Internet. Outside the U.S. and Canada, the 2.048Mbps E1 circuit with 32 voice channels is most commonly used.

taint   In Perl, a flag indicating that the information contained in the flagged variable was directly entered by a web user and should not be trusted. Taint is copied with the variable contents and can only be removed by interpreting the variable's contents rather than simply copying the data to a function or another application.

TCP Wrappers   A process that inserts itself before a network service in order to authenticate the hosts that are attempting to connect.

terminal   A remote display and keyboard/mouse console that can be used to access a computer.

ticket   In Kerberos, an encrypted value appended with the time to prove identity to a network service.

Ticket Granting Ticket (TGT)   An encrypted value stored by a client after a successful logon that is used to quickly prove identity in a Kerberos environment.

top level domain names (TLDs)   The first specific level of the domain name hierarchy, TLDs are used to apportion the domain name system into sections that can be administered by different Internet naming authorities. Each country has its own country-code TLD (ccTLD), like .us, .ca, .uk, .sp, .fr, .de, and so on. There are also six common general-purpose

(non-country-specific) TLDs (gTLDs): .com, .net, .org, .edu, .gov, and .mil. Some new gTLDs such as .biz, .info, .pro, and .aero have been released, but there has been no significant interest in them. The Internet Corporation for Assigned Names and Numbers (ICANN) administers the TLD hierarchy.

transparent   Describes a proxy server that is capable of automatically proxying a protocol without the client's awareness.

Trojan horse   A program that is surreptitiously installed on a computer for the purpose of providing access to a hacker.

trust provider   A trusted third party that certifies the identity of all parties in a secure transaction. Trust providers do this by verifying the identity of each party and generating digital certificates that can be used to determine that identity. A trust provider performs a function analogous to a notary public.

tunneling   The process of encapsulating packets within IP packets for the purpose of transporting the interior packets through many public intermediate systems. When reassembled at the remote end, the interior packets will appear to have transited only one router on the private networks.

Unix   A family of multiuser operating systems that all conform completely to the Portable Operating System Interface for Unix (POSIX) specification and operate in very similar fashion. Unix includes AT&T UNIX, BSD, Linux, and derivatives of these major versions.

user account   The association between a user account name, a password, and a security identifier (Windows) or a user identifier (Unix).

user context   The user identity under which a process executes that determines which files and resources the process will have access to.

User Identifier (UID)   An integer that identifies a user account to the system in Unix.

user policy   The portion of a Group Policy object that applies to the logged-on user.

user rights   Actions that a user account can perform that apply to many or all objects in a system.

virtual directory   A portion of a website with its own specific configuration and security settings. A virtual directory appears as a directory inside the website but may be located anywhere on the Internet.

virtual host   A web server administration feature that allows a single web server to serve numerous websites as if they were hosted by their own server. The web server inspects the URL header, IP address, or port number from the client connection to determine which virtual host should deliver a specific page request.

virtual private network (VPN)   A packet stream that is encrypted, encapsulated, and transmitted over a nonsecure network like the Internet.

virus   Any program that automatically replicates itself.

virus scanner   Software that scans every executable file on a computer searching for virus signatures.

virus scanning   The process of searching a file or communication stream for the identifying signature of a virus. A virus signature is simply a series of bytes that is deemed to be unique to the virus.

VPN software client   A software application for individual computers that creates VPN connections to VPN servers or devices.

web of trust   The PGP grass-rooted transitive-trust mechanism for encrypted e-mail.

web-enabled   Designation for a traditional application that has an HTTP interface, allowing its primary functionality to be used over the Internet.

wide area networks (WAN)   Networks that span long distances using digital telephony trunks like dedicated leased lines, Frame Relay, satellite, or alternative access technologies to link local area networks.

Windows   A family of single-user operating systems developed by Microsoft for small computers. The most recent version has incorporated enhancements to allow multiple users to run programs directly on the same machine.

Windows Explorer   The shell program in Windows from which most user-mode programs are launched.

Windows Terminal Services   A service of Windows that implements the Remote Data Protocol (RDP), which intercepts video calls to the operating system and repackages them for transmission to a remote user (as well as receiving keystrokes and mouse pointer data from the remote user), thus enabling a low-bandwidth remotely controlled desktop environment in which any applications can be run.

Wireless Access Point (WAP)   An 802.11b wireless network hub.

Wired-Equivalent Privacy (WEP)   A flawed encryption protocol used by the 802.11b wireless networking protocol.

worm   Any program that takes active measures to replicate itself onto other machines in a network. A network virus.

yellow pages (yp)   The original name for Network Information Service (NIS).

Index

Note to the reader: Throughout this index **boldfaced** page numbers indicate primary discussions of a topic. *Italicized* page numbers indicate illustrations.

TELL US WHAT YOU THINK!

Your feedback is critical to our efforts to provide you with the best books and software on the market. Tell us what you think about the products you've purchased. It's simple:

1. Go to the Sybex website.
2. Find your book by typing the ISBN or title into the Search field.
3. Click on the book title when it appears.
4. Click **Submit a Review.**
5. Fill out the questionnaire and comments.
6. Click **Submit.**

With your feedback, we can continue to publish the highest quality computer books and software products that today's busy IT professionals deserve.

www.sybex.com

SYBEX Inc. • 1151 Marina Village Parkway, Alameda, CA 94501 • 510-523-8233